Debate about deregulation has focused considerable attention on the pricing policies of public utilities. Much work has been done by economists on this subject, and in this book the results of that research are presented and made accessible to students of economics.

The main subject is the policy to be followed by a regulated monopoly, but the analysis is broadened to take account of a fringe of competitive suppliers. So the analysis is most relevant to electric utilities and local telephone companies in the U.S.A., to P.T.T.s in Europe, to the possible privatization of telecommunications in Australia, and to the telecommunications structure in the U.K. where the dominant supplier has been recently privatized. The authors discuss and give a new perspective on such issues as whether telephone companies should be required to allow resale of services sold under quantity discounts, and what levels should be set on block tariffs for electricity supply.

The theory of public utility pricing gives a unified and simplified exposition of the modern theory of efficient pricing that is not available elsewhere. The theoretical discussion is supplemented by numerical simulations comparing Fully Distributed Cost Pricing, Ramsay Pricing, and Optimal Nonuniform Pricing.

The book will be of interest to policy makers, regulators, economists, and students in graduate and undergraduate courses on Industrialization Organization, Regulation, and Applied Microeconomics.

The theory of public utility pricing

The theory of public utility pricing

STEPHEN J. BROWN

Yale School of Organization and Management
New Haven, Connecticut

DAVID S. SIBLEY

Bell Communications Research Inc.
Morristown, New Jersey

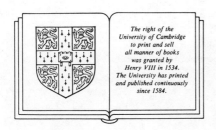

The right of the
University of Cambridge
to print and sell
all manner of books
was granted by
Henry VIII in 1534.
The University has printed
and published continuously
since 1584.

CAMBRIDGE UNIVERSITY PRESS

Cambridge

London   New York   New Rochelle

Melbourne   Sydney

Published by the Press Syndicate of the University of Cambridge
The Pitt Building, Trumpington Street, Cambridge CB2 1RP
32 East 57th Street, New York, NY 10022, USA
10 Stamford Road, Oakleigh, Melbourne 3166, Australia

First published 1986

Printed in the United States of America

Library of Congress Cataloging-in-Publication Data

Brown, Stephen J.

The theory of public utility pricing.

Bibliography: p.
Includes index.
1. Public utilities—Rates.   I. Sibley, David S.
(David Sumner), 1947–   . II. Title.
HD2763.B69   1985   338.4'33636   85-21259

British Library Cataloguing in Publication Data

Brown, Stephen J.

The theory of public utility pricing.
1. Public utilities—Rates
I. Title   II. Sibley, David S.
338.4'33636   HD2763

ISBN 0-521-30626-4 hard covers
ISBN 0-521-31400-3 paperback

Contents

*
Starred chapters and sections are meant for the technical reader.

Preface

In recent years there has been much debate within the United States on the regulation of public utilities. This debate has been coincident with a burgeoning of interest on the part of professional economists in public utility pricing issues and in the theory of regulation. The purpose of this book is to show how some of the recent advances in the theory pertain to the policy discussion. We hope that by making these advances accessible to policy makers we may foster a mutually beneficial interchange between economists, regulators and the public utilities.

Our interest in this area dates back to the mid 70's and was actively supported and encouraged by Elizabeth Bailey, Gerald Faulhaber and Edward Zajac who were responsible for the economics research activity at Bell Laboratories. We owe a debt of gratitude to our present and past colleagues at AT&T Bell Laboratories and Bell Communications Research for stimulating discussions on the subject matter of this book. Our debt to Peter Linhart, Patrick Marfisi, John Panzar, Jeffrey Rohlfs, William Sharkey and Robert Willig is particularly strong. We have benefitted not only from their research results, but from conversations extending back a period of years. Panzar, Sharkey, Leonard Mirman, Peter Grandstaff, David Mandy and Donald Brown also provided us with detailed comments on portions of the book. We would also like to acknowledge helpful conversations and feedback from Stanley Winkler, Roger Noll, and David Sappington. Finally, we acknowledge a particular debt of gratitude to Ms. Geraldine Moore who set the type for this book. The quality of her work is evident on this and succeeding pages. We must also express our deep gratitude to our wives, Catherine and Laurel, and the rest of our families, grandparents and in-laws for their support and encouragement during the lengthy process of writing this book.

It should be noted that the work on this book was completed while Stephen Brown was a Member of Technical Staff at Bell Communications Research.

CHAPTER 1

Introduction and overview

This book aims to make recent developments in public utility pricing theory accessible to the non-technical reader and to show how they can be usefully applied to major policy issues in ratemaking. Several policy issues have arisen within the last fifteen years or so which cannot be analyzed correctly without these developments. The classic treatise of Kahn [1970], although offering a wealth of institutional detail and breadth which we cannot match, summarizes the relevant economic theory at a point in time just short of a series of major advances which began to take place shortly after the appearance of Kahn's book. It is useful to sketch the policy issues and the research advances to which they led.

One policy question has to do with the rationale for declining block tariffs. Traditionally, such tariffs have been justified on two grounds. In the first place, utilities must cover large fixed costs of operation. In electricity, for example, the maintenance of a line from a pole to a customer's meter is a fixed cost that may be attributed to that customer. In addition, there are costs that may not be so readily attributed to a particular customer such as the cost of maintaining storage facilities and a portion of the reticulation system in the case of a gas utility. Some of these costs are covered by fixed charges that a customer must pay regardless of usage. In many cases, though, only a portion of the fixed cost is recovered in this way. The remainder must be covered through the usage-sensitive part of the tariff. In order to ensure that all customers contribute to such fixed costs, regulators and utilities often design a declining block usage tariff in which residual fixed costs are met by the charges for each customer's first few units of consumption. The second rationale derives from the fact that many regulated firms benefit from economies of scale. Utilities often argue that declining block tariffs are justified because they encourage greater consumption, causing larger, more efficient plants to be constructed over time.

In recent years these justifications have come under attack from those who believe that the regulated firm's goal is profit maximization, whatever the avowed goals of regulation. In this view, declining block structures are simply a means of increasing profits through a subtle form of price discrimination. Depending on the case at hand, these critics assert that small users tend to have lower price elasticities of demand than do large users. Declining block tariffs allow the firm to extract high profits from the price-inelastic small user group by means of a high usage charge for low and moderate ranges of consumption. The price-sensitive large users pay a lower usage charge which is unavailable to small users. Thus the utility is merely "rationing by price."

Beginning in the mid 1970's economists began to develop a theory of nonuniform pricing, in which quantity discounts and quantity premia are allowed. The viewpoint of this theory is that quantity discounts can be thought of as equivalent to a set of optional two-part tariffs, wherein a consumer can select an option with a low fixed "entry" fee and a high usage charge if he or she is a small user, or one with a high fixed entry fee and a low usage charge in the case of a large user. In this context, one can show that if one were to propose a uniform tariff structure without the declining block feature, an alternative declining block tariff can be devised which would have all consumers and the firm better off then they would be under the uniform tariff structure.

This view of declining block tariffs is fundamentally different from the traditional view. If declining block tariffs were nothing more than a scheme to increase profits through price discrimination against small users, one could improve the lot of small users by requiring that the utility allow resale. Under the modern view, to allow resale reduces the set of optional two-part tariffs and could actually result in losses to small users. This issue motivates the development of nonuniform pricing theory in Chapter 4 and 5.

An equally important policy issue is that of cross subsidization. When rate changes of a sweeping nature are proposed in a rate hearing, it is common for users facing increased prices to argue that under the new rates they would be subsidizing other users and, therefore, that the rate increases should be disallowed. In cases where the utility faces a fringe of competitive suppliers, these suppliers commonly allege that the utility is unfairly competing against them by means of predatory prices financed by cross subsidies from other areas of the utility's business. During this kind of debate it is common for the opposing parties to advance widely differing definitions of cross subsidy and to propose different tests for its existence. Typically, regulatory bodies choose some form of Fully Distributed Cost (FDC) standard to test for cross subsidy.

Beginning in the 1970's economists began to formulate a more careful theory of cross subsidy. Under this theory, a cross subsidy is said to exist where there is an incentive for one or more groups of customers of a public utility to desert the public utility and choose to be served by a firm catering to their demands, on a stand-alone basis. A subsidy-free set of prices is one such that no group of customers is paying more than its stand-alone cost and the regulated firm covers all its fixed costs. An equivalent statement is that the regulated firm break even with each customer group paying at least the incremental cost of serving it. In this framework, economists have shown that FDC cost standards have no meaning as tests for cross subsidy. As we note in Chapter 3, however, FDC approaches do have one point of interest: in some cases, they are themselves subsidy-free.

A third area of policy debate concerns the magnitude of likely efficiency gains to efficient pricing rules such as Ramsey pricing and optimal nonuniform pricing as compared to FDC pricing rules. For some years economists studying the postal service, railroad and telecommunications industries have pointed out that FDC rules have no claim to economic efficiency and urged that Ramsey prices be used, instead. Generally speaking, the use of Ramsey pricing would appear to lead to drastic changes in prices. This book describes these studies and simulates the effects of Ramsey pricing in the interstate telecommunications market as compared to the use of FDC pricing rules. On the whole, the estimated efficiency gains to Ramsey pricing appear to be small, on the order of two to three percent of revenue. Optimal nonuniform prices are also calculated and lead to substantially larger efficiency gains.

A final policy problem area concerns the design of optional tariffs. In the area of local telephone service optional tariffs offer a way of maintaining universal service as the interstate service subsidy is gradually phased out. Optional tariffs can be viewed as nonuniform price schedules and the theory of nonuniform pricing mentioned above is applicable here, too. In addition, suppose that the optional tariff is designed to generate the same revenue as an existing tariff. To the extent that it is indeed optional, it can be designed to benefit both consumer and the firm.

Our goal is to appeal to a readership ranging from the non-technical general reader to professional economists. Chapters 1 through 5 contain a non-technical presentation of public utility pricing theory integrated with policy discussions of the sort that motivated the theory. No mathematical background is needed beyond Algebra I. A course in introductory economics will be helpful, but not essential; Chapter 2 contains a self-contained discussion of the economic concepts necessary to follow the development in Chapters 3 through 5. Neither the policy issues nor the economic principles are transparent, but the discussion should be easy to grasp for any non-technical reader with a serious interest in pricing issues. For the professional economist, there are a number of new results. We derive in Chapter 6 efficient pricing rules where consumers are themselves business firms and where one must take account of effects of changes in the utility's prices which flow through to final consumers of the goods and services produced by the utility's business customers. Our results show conditions under which the analyst can set the correct prices using the usual Ramsey and nonuniform pricing rules, based on knowledge of equilibrium demand functions for the utility's services. Chapter 7 computes optimal nonuniform price schedules. We analyze the properties of these optimal prices for the cases of interstate telephone service. A minor point, but one of some interest, concerns the properties of FDC prices, discussed in Chapter 3. As mentioned above, in certain instances, FDC prices turn out to be subsidy-free. One of these methods, known as the Attributable Cost Method, is also consistent with the recent axiomatic approach to cost-based pricing.

This book is an exercise in normative regulatory economics. It is concerned with increasing economic efficiency and consumer welfare. It is not intended to be a realistic description of how regulators actually operate. Recent work on the positive theory of regulation,[1] although preliminary, paints a complex picture of economic regulation. Regulators are assumed to be interested in maximizing political support for their incumbency and do so through their regulatory decisions. Interest groups attempt to influence these decisions through a complicated process of coalition-building. This positive theory bids fair to be able to answer fundamental questions concerning the forms that regulation takes and in which industries it takes hold.

Normative economics is not the central issue in regulatory decision making. Nonetheless, its role is important. The authorizing legislation for many regulatory bodies frequently contains exhortations in favor of "cost-based" pricing, and against "undue" price discrimination. To define these terms and apply them to actual cases, the tools of normative economics are used. Recent Interstate Commerce Commission (ICC) proceedings[2] have undertaken a searching review of ICC ratemaking practices in light of tools such as marginal cost pricing and Ramsey pricing. Furthermore, when regulation violates efficiency criteria seriously enough, not only economists become concerned. Peak load pricing in electricity, for example, was taken seriously in the U.S. when it became clear that excessive use of electricity was contributing to an energy crisis that alarmed many people. Hence, normative

---

[1] See, for example, Stigler [1971], Peltzman [1976] and Posner [1974].

[2] See ICC Docket 347 (Sub 1).

economics plays an important, though not preeminent, role in the regulatory process.

Throughout this book we will employ the simple paradigm of a large regulated firm facing a fringe of competitive suppliers. This accords reasonably well with the relationship between AT&T and other common carriers in the interexchange telecommunications market and with local telephone operating companies and their competitors who offer bypass alternatives. Electric and gas utilities probably have no competitive fringe, although they face indirect competition from alternative fuels. We will assume that firms in this competitive fringe take the tariff structure as given and maximize their own profits accordingly. Faced with this market structure the regulator is assumed to choose tariffs which maximize economic efficiency over the set of customers served by the regulated firm, ignoring the competitive fringe except as it affects the demand curves for the services of the dominant firm. The work of Braeutigam [1979] and Ebrill and Slutsky [1984] suggests strongly that to do otherwise will lead to policies which are so complex as to be unworkable in any practical sense.

CHAPTER 2

Basic economic principles

2.1 Introduction

The aim of this chapter is to introduce basic concepts of welfare economics and industrial organization that shall be used throughout the book, and to introduce the paradigm of the regulated firm that we use throughout our discussion. We intend neither a full and complete treatment of these concepts nor an elementary textbook treatment of the material. Such is available elsewhere.[1] Our intent is to provide a brief and nontechnical introduction to those ideas used most frequently in chapters subsequent to this.

We assume that the objective of regulators in setting prices is to maximize social welfare, broadly defined. Pricing policy serves this function in two ways: directly, by redistributing wealth in society, and indirectly, by signalling a reallocation of resources in society.

So called *lifeline service* that offers minimal service at low rates to poor people and the elderly is often a redistribution to these groups from the company and other consumers. It achieves the social purpose of providing public utility service to those who would not otherwise be able to afford it. This is an example of the redistributive function of pricing policy. As an example of the reallocative effect of pricing, imagine that the utility were to offer an optional day/night tariff constructed to yield the same revenue to the company as some existing tariff. Consumers cannot lose by such an offering to the extent it is indeed optional. The company gains however, to the extent that facilities may be less heavily used during the peak day period. We call a change that makes one person or group better off at the expense of no

[1]
We highly recommend the recent texts by Just, Hueth and Schmitz [1982] for their particularly lucid treatment of issues in welfare economics, Baumol, Panzar and Willig [1982] and Sharkey [1982] on industry structure and Zajac [1982] on the equity/efficiency discussion.

one else, a *Pareto improvement*.[2] In the day/night tariff, the gain comes from inducing consumers to utilize the more favorable night tariff. This reallocation allows the company to utilize the existing plant more efficiently. This efficiency gain would arguably make the company better able to afford a lifeline service offering.

This example shows that the maximization of economic efficiency is not necessarily at variance with the maximization of a more broadly defined measure of social welfare. Economic efficiency is said to be maximized where no Pareto improvements are possible. In such a situation there is no alternative pricing policy that will make one individual or group better off and no one worse off.

The gain in economic efficiency resulting from the provision of an optional tariff is reasonably easy to see. What is not so clear is how to quantify this gain. This becomes important where the utility may offer only one tariff. Which should it choose? If all optional tariffs generate a gain in economic efficiency, which generates the most gain? In the case of a particular tariff, one might ask how much the consumer would be willing to pay for the tariff. In other words, suppose we were to tax the consumer who adopted the new tariff. At what tax would the consumer be no better off than before the new tariff offering? Similar monetary measures can be developed to guage the value to the utility of the new tariff.

Since the gains to consumers and producers can be quantified in this way and reduced to a common monetary base, it is tempting to argue that the economic efficiency argument can be extended to cases where some are actually hurt by the new tariff — if in fact there are some features in it that are not optional. The argument is that since the welfare measures have been reduced to monetary terms, the "winners" could *potentially* compensate the "losers." This leads to a measure of welfare as the sum total of the monetary benefits accruing to every individual and group as a result of the tariff. What if the compensation does not actually occur?

In some cases, individuals who are hurt in one way by a proposed change may also benefit in other ways by the change. Suppose we were to consider changes in postal rates. Households might be hurt by an increase in the cost of mailing a first class letter, but would also benefit by a corresponding reduction in the cost of mailing magazines and other printed matter. On net, households may not be affected by the change, but the Post Office might gain production efficiencies through a relative reduction in first class mail deliveries.

---

[2]
So named for the nineteenth century Italian economist and philosopher Vilfredo Pareto.

Unfortunately, such an example is not typical. For example, one argument in favor of low coin telephone rates is that public telephones provide essential service to those who could not otherwise afford it. However, public telephones are also used by relatively affluent business people and by commuters. Suppose the telephone company were to argue for higher coin telephone rates on the grounds that such service is very expensive to provide and that it could meet the social objective more cheaply through a lifeline service offering. It would then pass on the savings in the form of lower residential rates. The public utility commission might object to such a plan on the basis of opposition from business and commuter groups even if it were shown to be the case that residential users gained more than the combined business and commuter interests lost.

The excess of benefits that society as a whole loses by failure to adopt a policy in question is called the *deadweight loss*. Recall that the benefit is measured as the willingness to pay for a proposed policy change. Failure to adopt the policy represents a true loss to society occasioned by the unwillingness to tax those who benefit from the policy in order to compensate those who lose. Actual compensation involves many difficult ethical and political questions. The measure of the benefits forgone — the deadweight loss — is a relevant quantitative measure of the cost to society of meeting these important ethical and political objectives.

In this chapter we consider how to define measures of the extent to which changes in price affect the well being of consumers and producers. In so doing, we define monetary measures of their willingness to pay for these changes. We then discuss how these measures are defined in the context of a market structure where cost conditions imply that the most efficient industry structure is less than fully competitive and where there may be more than one firm or industry affected by the price change. This leads to a discussion of our paradigm of the regulated firm.

2.2 The theory of consumer behavior

A first step towards comparing alternative public utility pricing options is to obtain an unambiguous measure, in monetary terms, of the benefit to consumers of a proposed change in prices. Such unambiguous measures do exist, but they are somewhat difficult to apply given the available data. Fortunately, Willig [1976] has shown that consumer surplus, a measure initially due to Dupuit [1844], is an adequate approximation for most practical circumstances. Since consumer surplus is a measure of welfare that is readily measurable using data typically available to both utilities and regulators, it is the measure of choice in most policy applications.

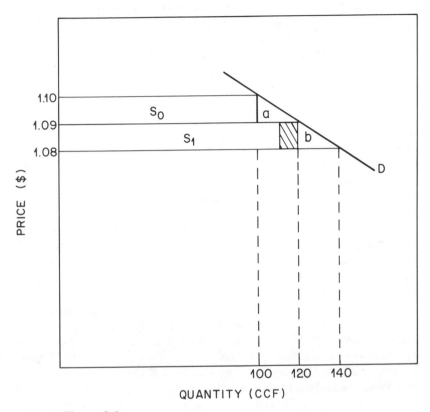

Figure 2.1

To motivate surplus as a measure of consumer welfare, consider
Figure 2.1. Suppose the current price per cubic combustible foot
(CCF) of gas were $1.10 and consumption of gas were 100 CCF's per
month at that price. If the price were to fall to a $1.09, then the
consumer could buy the 100 CCF's at the new price and realize a net
saving of $1.00. The dollar saving is the benefit of the reduction in
price — the area S_0 in the figure. In many practical situations where
the price change is small (a cent in this example) it suffices to measure
the benefit as the old consumption level times the change in price.
However this simple calculation will typically understate the benefit due
to a reduction in price if that reduction causes consumers to buy more
gas. At a price of $1.09 suppose that price experiments indicate that
the typical consumer would tend to consume 120 CCF's per month.
What happens if the price were further reduced to a $1.08? One would
conclude from the above discussion that the benefit of the additional
cent reduction is $.01 × 120 or $1.20, the area S_1 in Figure 2.1.
Overall then, one might argue that the benefit to the consumer of the
reduction in price from a dollar ten cents to a dollar eight cents is $1.00

plus $1.20 or $2.20. This amount is termed the change in *consumer surplus* due to the change in price. It is measured geometrically as the area between the two prices to the left of the demand curve - the schedule of quantities demanded as price falls from the old price to the new price.[3]

However, this definition of benefits involves an element of double counting. On the reduction in price from $1.10 to $1.09, the consumer is better off by the amount of one dollar. This is the same as money in his or her pocket, and can be used for many purposes: to buy chocolates, to be put aside towards the down payment on a fast sports car and, potentially, to be used to pay the higher heating bills that will result from raising the thermostat a notch in winter. It is this latter use of the money that is the cause of concern. The money spent to buy the 120 CCF's will come in part from the benefit the consumer obtains from the initial reduction in price. The $1.20 figure includes *both* the benefit due to the reduction in the price of gas *and* the extent to which the initial gain of $1.00 is spent on additional gas. Thus the $1.20 amount cannot be regarded as a pure gain to the consumer, and the $2.20 total overstates the benefit of the reduction in price from $1.10 to $1.08.[4] This degree of overstatement is measured by the shaded area of the figure. If only we could measure the shaded area, we could adjust the consumer surplus number to obtain an unambiguous measure of the extent of the benefit due to the reduction in price. Hicks [1943] refers to this benefit as the *compensating variation* of the price change. This compensating variation is the amount of money the consumer could be taxed at $1.08 per CCF and be no worse off than if the price were in fact $1.10 per CCF. This measure of welfare is unambiguous, but unfortunately it is impossible to measure unless one can obtain an accurate assessment of the shaded area in Figure 2.1.[5]

[3]
This definition of consumer surplus would include the areas marked "a" and "b" in Figure 2.1 — which are excluded from the $2.20 amount only because we did not consider price changes in fractions of a cent in the example.

[4]
There are certain types of goods considered to be of low quality which the consumer buys only because he or she could not afford better. For such an *inferior* good consumption may actually fall with a rise in income. In such a case, the $2.20 number will actually understate the benefit due to the fall in price.

[5]
There is another measure of welfare — the *equivalent variation* that uses as the welfare comparison point the new price of $1.08 and asks how much would the consumer have to be bribed to accept the old price of $1.10. Typically this will be *greater* then the surplus number by an amount roughly equal to the shaded area in Figure 2.1 for small price changes. Like the measure of compensating variation it, too, is not directly observable.

However, the shaded area is small in most typical applications. How big could it be? Suppose we were to take from the consumer the dollar that resulted from the reduction in price from $1.10 to $1.09. By how much would the consumption of gas actually fall? This is an empirical question, but we should expect that the consumption of most utility services not be too sensitive to small changes in income. The measure of this sensitivity is termed the *income elasticity* of demand. This elasticity is measured as the percentage change in consumption $\Delta Q/Q$ (the "Δ" represents "change in") as a result of a given percentage change in income $\Delta m/m$, or

$$\eta = \frac{\Delta Q}{Q} \Big/ \frac{\Delta m}{m} \tag{1}$$

where η represents the income elasticity of demand.

Given the income elasticity of demand, typically in the region of .5 for many public utility services, we are in a position to determine the magnitude of the shaded area in Figure 2.1. Suppose we define S as the total surplus resulting from the reduction in price $S = \$1.00 + \$1.20 = \$2.20$. Then, if m represents the consumer's income, it is possible to show[6] that the shaded area is at most $1/2\ (S^2/m)\ \eta$. Suppose we were to use the $2.20 surplus measure as a monetary measure of the effect of the reduction in price. Then this overstates the "compensating variation" by an amount at most $1/2\ (\$2.20)^2/m \times .5$ or $1.21/m$. Another way of stating this is that the compensating variation, C, may be approximated by $C \simeq S(1 - \epsilon)$ where $\epsilon = 1/2\ (S/m)\ \eta$. Willig [1976] shows that this error formula is quite general.[7] It shows that where

---

[6]

Suppose we were to tax consumers by the amount of $1.00 that represents the benefit due to the initial reduction in price. If the income elasticity were in fact .5 and 120 CCF's were consumed at the price of $1.09, to determine the change in consumption (ΔQ) resulting from this tax we can solve the equation

$$.5 = \frac{\Delta Q}{120} \Big/ \frac{(-\$1.00)}{m} \text{ or } \Delta Q = -\frac{120 \times \$1.00 \times .5}{m} = -\frac{60}{m}$$

which would be trivial for large incomes, m. Translating this into a general expression yields $\Delta Q = -Q_1 \cdot S_0/m \cdot \eta$. The shaded area in Figure 2.1 is simply the change in price ΔP times the increase in demand ΔQ due to the increase in disposable income Δm resulting from the change in price. Using our expression for ΔQ we have

$$\Delta P \times \Delta Q = \Delta P \cdot Q_1 \times \frac{S_0\eta}{m} = \frac{S_1 S_0\eta}{m} < \frac{1}{2} \left[S_0 + S_1\right]^2 \frac{\eta}{m}.$$

The quantity $S_0 + S_1$ is the total consumer surplus, $S = \$1.00 + \$1.20 = \$2.20$.

[7]

The results can also be extended, with some degree of difficulty, to the multimarket case. See MacKenzie [1979] and Willig [1979].

surplus of the price change is small relative to income (S/m is small) or the income elasticity of demand is small, consumer surplus is a perfectly adequate measure of the welfare generated by a change in price. Both conditions are reasonable approximations in the case of public utility service offerings.

To this point we have considered the benefit to consumers of changes in price. The current price of gas could be compared to a price so high that our typical consumer would consume no gas at all. The benefit associated with a reduction from this very high price to the current price is referred to as the total consumer surplus. We may think of this consumer surplus as a measure of the total benefit or consumer *utility* of the current consumption of gas over and above the amount paid for the gas. If we let P represent the current price of gas and Q represent the consumption of gas, then consumer surplus S is given by

$$S = U - P \times Q + Y$$

where U represents a monetary measure of the utility to the consumer of consuming an amount of gas equal to Q, and Y is income left over for other purposes. Needless to say, such an interpretation requires that surplus is an adequate welfare measure: that it is small relative to income and/or that the income elasticity is negligible.

The analysis can be extended to the case where the change in price affects the demand for the services of other utilities. Suppose that the gas utility also provides electric service to a given locality. If both gas and electric prices change then as above to a first approximation surplus is given by the sum of the quantities consumed times the respective changes in price. This is analogous to the price change of a cent considered above. If price changes are substantial one needs to account for the effect of a change in the price of gas might have on gas *and* electricity consumption. In the simplest case, such a change will have no effect on the demand for electricity — the two markets are said to be *independent*,[8] and the measure of aggregate consumer surplus is the

----

[8]

The general measure of how sensitive demand is to a change in price is termed the *price elasticity of demand* or where there is no possible confusion, simply the *elasticity* of demand. It is defined analogously to the income elasticity of demand as minus the percentage change in quantity demanded as a result of a percentage change in price: $-[(\Delta Q(Q)/(\Delta P/P)]$. The measure of the extent to which the price in one market affects the demand in others is termed the *cross elasticity of demand*. In the example above, the case of independent demands exists when the cross elasticities are zero:

$$\frac{\Delta Q_E}{Q_E} / \frac{\Delta P_G}{P_G} = 0 = \frac{\Delta Q_G}{Q_G} / \frac{\Delta P_E}{P_E}$$

(where E and G refer to electric and gas respectively). Of course, if the consumer spends all his or her income, all markets cannot be independent in this way. Here it suffices that the markets *in question* are independent.

sum of consumer surplus resulting from the gas and electric markets. The case of dependence is obviously more difficult. In the following chapters we show that the definition of surplus as consumer utility minus expenditure is useful in this context.

2.3 The theory of producer behavior

It would appear to be much more straightforward a matter to calculate the loss to a producer of a potential reduction in price. If a utility were compensated for the reduction in price from $1.10 to $1.08 per CCF by a lump sum payment equal to the loss in profits, the utility should be indifferent to the change. This loss of profits is measurable and so the profit measure would appear an unequivocal measure of the benefits lost by the utility in agreeing to go along with the price reduction. But what should happen if the reduction from $1.10 to $1.08 were sufficient to force the utility to go out of business? What would it take to make the utility indifferent to shutting its doors?

To answer this question, it is appropriate to break down profit, assumed to be the objective of firms, into its component parts of revenue (R) and cost (C):

Profit $= R - C$.

Costs can be broken down into those costs that depend on the scale of production, or *variable* costs (VC) and those that do not depend on the scale of production, or are *fixed* (F):

Profit $= R - VC - F$.

A test of whether a producer in fact maximizes profit is whether any variation in the observed scale of operations leads to an increase in profits. This leads to the well known condition that for a profit maximizing firm, marginal revenue (MR) - the increase in revenue per unit increase in the quantity sold - equals marginal cost (MC) - the corresponding change in variable costs.

Suppose that the current price of gas were $1.10 per CCF. Revenue from sales is simply $1.10 times the amount of gas sold. Our gas utility assumes (somewhat unrealistically) that it can sell any amount of gas at the going price, so that the marginal revenue is also $1.10. Suppose further that it is producing 80,000 CCF's and that the cost of producing an extra CCF at that level of output is $1.09 - the marginal cost of production. If the utility were to increase production it would make one cent on each additional CCF sold. At 100,000 CCF's the marginal cost is $1.10 and at that point it no longer will be advantageous to increase production. The situation is depicted in Figure 2.2.

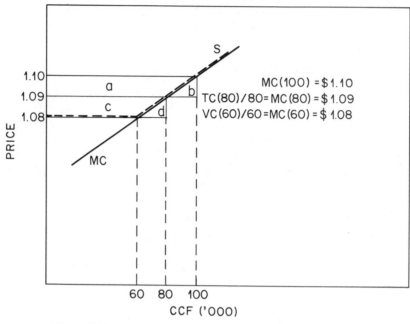

Figure 2.2

Suppose the price were to fall to $1.09 per CCF, increasing demand to 100,000 CCF's. The loss in profits would be $1,000.00. However, at this new price the gas utility would only be willing to supply 80,000 CCF's, so that an additional drop in price of one cent per CCF would induce a loss of profits of $800.00. The total loss in profits resulting from the reduction in price from $1.10 to $1.08 is $1,800.00. This analysis suggests a measure of *producer surplus* analogous to consumer surplus. Producer surplus has the geometric interpretation of the area to the left of the marginal cost curve below the current price. (The areas "b" and "d" would be eliminated if we were to conceive of the price reduction as a service of smaller price changes in fractions of a cent.) This interpretation follows if

1. The utility stays in business both before and after the price change.
2. The utility does indeed believe it can sell all it wants at the current price.

We shall return to the second point later in this chapter.

Presumably there is a price sufficiently low that the utility would go out of business. If the revenues of the utility were derived solely from gas, with limited liability the benefit to the firm is exactly equal to the profit from sale and distribution of gas. In this extreme case, the amount of utility would pay to avoid going out of business is the profits it earns at the going price of gas. Suppose the total (fixed plus variable) cost of supplying gas were $87,200 when 80,000 CCF's are distributed, or $1.09 per CCF. At $1.10 per CCF there is a profit to be made equal to the area marked "a"; this profit represents the benefit to the utility of the price set at $1.10. The price $1.09 is termed a *breakeven price* and the constraint that the utility earns at least a positive profit is termed the *breakeven constraint*.

However, the above scenario is not necessarily reasonable. For a utility that produces more than one product, the allocation of overhead that defines fixed cost is necessarily arbitrary. If the utility wants to stay in business it will of necessity cover fixed costs over all lines of production. If an activity contributes at least in part to its fixed cost allocation over and above the variable costs which by definition are zero if the activity were terminated, the activity has a positive value to the corporation. Alfred Marshall [1930] defined this benefit as the *quasi rent* of the activity equal to the difference between revenue and total variable cost, or (equivalently) profit plus fixed costs.

Suppose at a production of 60,000 CCF the variable costs were computed as $64,800, or $1.08 per CCF. At a price of $1.09 the utility would just break even on the sale and distribution of gas, yet already gas contributes an amount equal to the area "c" towards covering the fixed costs of the utility. At a price of $1.10 the value of the gas sale and distribution would be the quasi rent given as the sum of the profit (area "a") plus the coverage of fixed costs (area "c"). The dotted line Figure 2.2 represents the supply curve of this producer. At any price in excess of $1.08, supply would be given by the quantity for which price equaled marginal costs — but for any price less than $1.08 the utility would go out of business and the supply would be zero. Defining the supply curve in this way, quasi rent has the geometric interpretation of being the area to the left of the supply curve below the current price. Quasi rent makes sense as a measure of the change in benefits due to short run changes in prices. Typically a utility would not incur fixed costs if it did not expect to at least break even. From this *ex ante* perspective, the measure of benefit would still be the area to the left of the supply curve below the current price, the profit at that price. However quasi rent would overstate the benefit. In this longer term perspective, the definition of fixed costs are somewhat ambiguous.

In the very short term, all costs are fixed. Costs are defined by contracts with the pipeline companies and with the unions and by the need to maintain the reticulation system. The pipeline contracts and the workforce can be varied on the near term, and on the somewhat longer term the scale of the reticulation system can be varied. Indeed, it could be argued that for a sufficiently long period of time *all* costs are variable. Moreover, the marginal cost will itself depend on the scale of production defined by the fixed cost commitment. When computing the benefit due to a given price change, it is very important to specify the period for which the benefit is to be defined. Generally speaking, throughout this book we will assume that markets are in static equilibrium, with all "long run" adjustments completed. In this interpretation one minute is like the next, and no careful choice of time period is called for.

2.4 Individuals, firms and the market

The advantage of focussing on monetary or compensation measures of welfare of individuals and of producers is that such measures can be aggregated across individuals in a market setting. Since the responses of individuals to price changes are not observable using aggregated market data, the aggregation of individual responses to market prices implies that the measures of welfare are potentially measurable at the aggregate level. However, these measures need to be interpreted with some care.

A. Aggregation of consumers

The market demand for gas, to take the example of the first section, is readily computed as the sum of demands at each price. In Figure 2.3 we illustrate this process. At $1.10, consumer A would consume 100 CCF's whereas consumer B would consume 30: a total of 130 CCF's at that price. Similarly at $1.08, consumer A would consume 140 and B, 50 giving a total demand of 190. Since the aggregate demand of each price is simply the sum of individual demands, the area to the left of the aggregate demand curve is the sum of the areas to the left of the disaggregated demand curves. For this reason aggregate consumer surplus is well defined. However, whether this aggregate surplus is a meaningful measure of welfare is another matter.

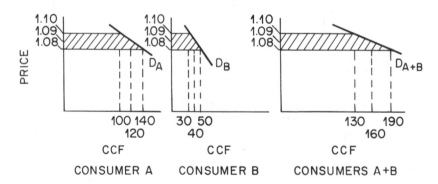

Figure 2.3

For aggregate surplus to be a meaningful measure of consumer welfare two conditions must be met:

1. The error using surplus to approximate compensating (or equivalent) variation must be small for all consumers.
2. The measure of welfare assumes all consumers are treated equally, so that the welfare of society is a simple summation of the welfare of each individual in society.

The first condition is a satisfactory approximation for most public utility service offerings. The second condition presents a problem where, for a given policy individual consumers are differentially affected by that policy and those who are hurt are not actually compensated by those consumers who are actually better off by the change.

B. Aggregation of producers

If supply curves for each producer (defined as marginal cost above the point where revenue covers the variable costs) are summed across producers, as in Figure 2.4, then the quasi rent, or producer surplus defined as the area to the left of the aggregated supply curve, is the sum of quasi rents for each individual producer. Since individual producers can have very different cost structures it is important that firms be viewed symmetrically or that if some firms are helped by a given policy and others hurt, that the winners actually compensate the losers.

C. Implications for the market

We are now in a position to examine the impact of price changes in the context of a market where there are (potentially) many consumers and producers. In Figure 2.5 we interpret the supply curve S as the aggregation across producers of their individual supply curves and the demand curve D as aggregated across consumers.

In the previous section we assumed that the utility could sell all that it wished at the current price. This would appear somewhat unrealistic in the gas example, but it might be more realistic for a small firm offering bypass services in a telecommunications market. If the demand curve is downward sloping as in Figure 2.5 it must be that such a firm considers that any increase in its output q merely affects relative market shares leaving total industry supply, Q, essentially unaffected. In other words, it believes that $\Delta Q/\Delta q$, the *conjectural variation*, is for all intents and purposes zero.

If all suppliers in the industry shared such conjectural variations, the price of 1.09 cents per message unit would be a viable price for telecommunications services; at that price demand equals supply. The

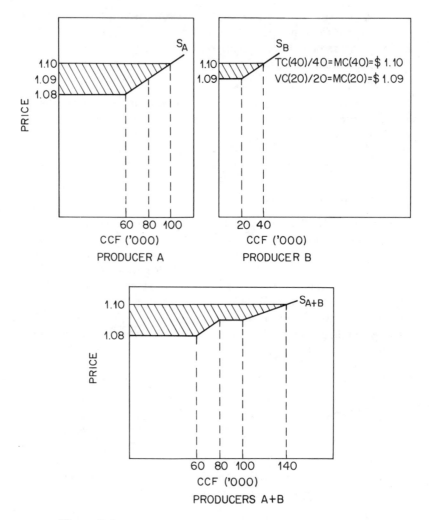

Figure 2.4

benefit to consumers of such a price is measured as the area "a" plus
"b" plus "c", the consumer surplus. The benefit to producers can be
measured by the area "d" plus "e" plus "f".

Suppose there were only one supplier: the case of a monopolist. In
this case the firm output q is the industry output Q so that the
conjectural variation $\Delta Q/\Delta q$ is unity. The monopolist recognizes that
the amount per unit that consumers are willing to pay depends on the
quantity consumed, according to the demand curve. So long as the

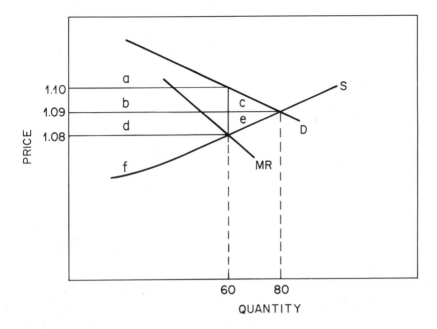

Figure 2.5

demand curve is downward sloping the marginal revenue is always less than the average revenue — the price.[9] Suppose that the marginal revenue were given as *MR* in Figure 2.5. Then the condition that marginal revenue equal marginal cost would imply that the monopolist would provide 70 million units at a price of $1.10 cents per unit. At that price, the consumer surplus is reduced to the area "a" while the producer surplus is equal to "f" plus the profit equal to areas "b" plus "d".

We are now in a position to measure the costs associated with the exercise of monopoly power. Relative to the zero conjectural variation case, there is a wealth transfer equal to area "b" from consumers to producers, as well as a net loss to society equal to the sum of areas "c" plus "e". This observation leads to the popular policy prescription that would curtail the existence of monopolies in favor of competitive firms

9
   Revenue, R is price P times quantity Q. Thus the change in revenue is $\Delta R = P_1 Q_1 - P_0 Q_0 = P_1(Q_1 - Q_0) + Q_0(P_1 - P_0)$, or $MR = \Delta R/\Delta Q = P_1 + Q_0 \Delta P/\Delta Q$. Since the last term is negative with a downward sloping demand curve, MR is less than the price, P.

which would behave as if they had zero conjectural variations. However, as we shall see, the competitive model is not always a viable alternative for the provision of utility services, so that we must consider policy alternatives that allow for conjectural variations greater than zero.

2.5 Single market equilibrium

In the previous section, the number of producers (and consumers) was taken as given, and the behavior of firms was determined by their conjectural variations. If with many firms the areas "d" plus "e" in Figure 2.5 represent profits above fixed costs, then one might expect entry of new firms into the industry to take advantage of these profits. The supply curve would move out from S_0 to S_1 and the price would fall from 1.09 to 1.08. The mere threat of entry might suffice to force the price down to $1.08. In this instance a competitive equilibrium that implies zero industry profits is viable, and price equals marginal cost. However such a zero profit industry equilibrium is not necessarily viable.

A particular firm, contributing to industry output Q in Figure 2.6 may make zero profits by threat of entry. However, if that firm has decreasing average costs due to a large fixed cost component, marginal cost will be less than average cost and the firm can increase profits by increasing the scale of its operations. Such increasing returns to scale necessarily imply that the competitive solution is not viable.

To be more precise, if the costs of producing 100 units of Q are less for the monopolist than they would be for any group of firms acting independently — that is to say, if costs are *subadditive* — then not only is the competitive solution not viable but it is more efficient to allow the monopolist to produce the total industry output.[10] In such a situation the monopoly is termed a *natural monopoly*.

If average costs fall for all levels of output, then not only is it more efficient to have the natural monopoly produce the entire industry output, but the natural monopoly is said to be *sustainable* in the sense that no potential entrant could enter the industry and make positive profits. However, not all natural monopolies are sustainable in this sense. Suppose average costs first fall and then rise for large levels of output. It may be that even though there is no reorganization of industry output that would lower total costs — costs are subadditive —

10
  Sharkey [1983] shows that while economies of scale imply subadditivity the converse is not true. He shows that subadditivity is a useful construct for the definition of natural monopoly in a multiple output case.

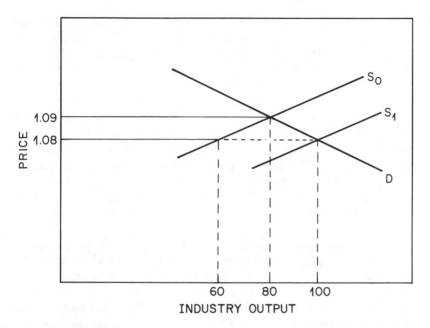

Figure 2.6

a particular entrant may make short run profits by undercutting the cost of the monopolist and so challenge its position.[11] To fully analyze this case requires a theory of entry and monopolist response, outside the scope of this chapter.

If the utility in question either is a natural monopoly or is close to being one, the policy issue is then to devise a pricing scheme that takes advantage of the cost efficiencies of having one firm produce the industry output yet minimizes the welfare distortions associated with profit maximizing behavior of the monopolist. One solution is to have the monopolist mimic the competitive solution, and set price equal to marginal cost. However, at such a price the monopolist may not cover fixed costs and will therefore choose not to produce. Later in the book we consider pricing schemes that maximize consumer surplus subject to the monopolist staying in production — a *breakeven constraint*.

---

[11] For discussions of sustainability in this context see Sharkey [1982] Ch. 5 and Baumol, Panzar and Willig [1982].

2.6 Multimarket equilibrium

To this point we have considered welfare measures that presume the industry in question sells all that it produces to final consumers. This model is not descriptively accurate for many public utilities. Any change in the price of electricity will affect those who use electricity in the home. It will also affect those who consume the products made possible by the provision of electricity. In addition the firms which produce using electricity will also be affected. Thus any welfare analysis of public utility pricing must consider not only the direct but also indirect or *flowthrough* effects of any change in the price of the utility's services. It will turn out that the evaluation of consumer and producer surplus proceeds much as before, provided that the demand and supply curves are so-called *equilibrium* demand and supply curves, which reflect industry response to changes in the prices of the utility services.

A simple example of flowthrough effects is given by the example of resale of telecommunications services. In this example we may consider the telephone company as a wholesaler of telephone message units, and the reseller as a retailer of the same units. Assume also that the resale message unit market is competitive in the sense that the reseller takes the wholesale and retail prices as given.

If the wholesale price were to fall from P_w^0 to P_w^1 then, given the retail price P_R^0, retailers would wish to sell a quantity Q_1. However, the price would have to be discounted to sell this many message units and would eventually fall from P_R^0 to P_R^1, and in equilibrium the number of message units produced and sold would be Q_1^*.

To evaluate the welfare implications of the reduction in wholesale price from P_w^0 to P_w^1, consider Figure 2.7. The consumer surplus associated with the price reduction is evidently the area "a" plus "b" in the lower panel of the figure. However, that is not the only welfare implication of the price change. At the initial wholesale price, producer surplus of retail production is areas "a" plus "c". After the change it is "c" plus "d". Thus producer surplus increases by an amount of "d" minus "a". If retailers and consumers shared this gain, the net increase in welfare would be the area "d" plus "b".

In a typical application it will prove very difficult to compute the areas "d" plus "b" across all industries which use the utility services as an input. Fortunately, this is not always necessary. The bottom panel of Figure 2.7 implies a "derived demand" for the utility's services given in the top panel of the figure. If our telephone company were to assume the retail price as given, it would face a demand curve for message units that reflects the fact that the marginal cost of providing retail service is given by the wholesale price of message units. However,

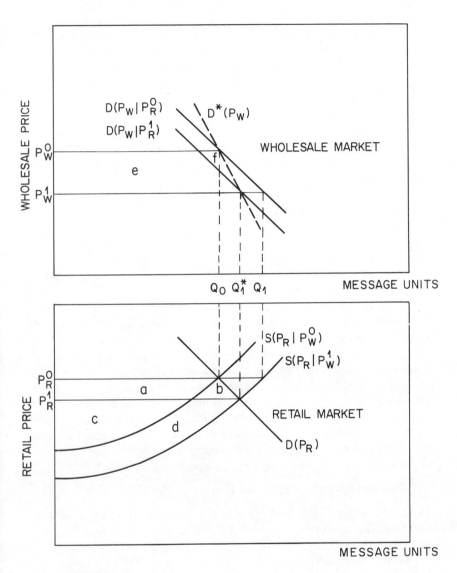

Figure 2.7

if the wholesale price were to fall from P_w^0 to P_w^1 the retail price would also *in equilibrium* fall as would the demand for message units by the resellers. The dotted line, which reflects the demand for message units by resellers is termed the *equilibrium demand* curve.

It is reasonable to consider the surplus given as areas "e" plus "f" to the left of the equilibrium demand curve as a measure of welfare. Indeed, it can be shown that areas "e" plus "f" will exactly equal "d" plus "b". Consumers could presumably purchase message units directly from the telephone company. If they faced the same costs as the competitive supplier of resold message units, the consumers would capture the entire benefit "b" plus "d". As far as the telephone company was concerned, the demand for message units by such consumer cooperatives would be identical to the resellers, but now, the dotted line is the demand curve of final consumers. The areas "e" plus "f" is now a direct measure of consumer surplus and is thus equal to "b" plus "d".

The conclusion then is that the analysis of the previous sections continues to apply even if the utility sells to producers as well as consumers. The only complexity is to ensure that the demand curves are *equilibrium* demand curves, defined so as to account for all adjustments in the downstream industries that result from the change in price. Just, Hueth and Schmitz [1982] extend the analysis to consider the case where competitive suppliers provide inputs to the utility and show that the welfare comparison can proceed as before provided that the supply curves are *equilibrium* supply curves that account for all adjustments in the industries that supply inputs to the utility.

The competitive analysis of the utility industry proceeds precisely as in the previous section provided that the demand and supply curves are appropriately defined as equilibrium demand and supply curves. One should note, however, that this simple result does assume the downstream firms and input suppliers indeed earn zero profits. Without such an assumption, it is necessary to consider the price impact on each and every downstream firm and input supplier, as well as the possibility of strategic behavior on the part of those other industries.

2.7 The paradigm of the regulated firm

In the remainder of this book we consider alternative pricing policies for regulated firms. The objective is to maximize economic efficiency. Is it possible to make consumers or producers better off by any variation in prices that hurts neither group?

We assume throughout the book that the regulated firm is a natural monopoly in the sense that its costs are subadditive. However, it may not be an actual monopoly. While the regulated firm may supply a large part of the total industry supply — its conjectural variation is close to unity — there may in fact be a fringe of competitive suppliers whose conjectural variation is close to zero. In the United States telecommunications market the Bell System provided much of the local and long distance telephone service prior to 1984. However, there were many small independent companies providing long distance services between specific cities and other companies that provided service that bypassed the local telephone network. It is reasonable to suppose that these competitive firms made their pricing and output decisions conditioned on knowledge of the Bell tariff. In this paradigm the dominant firm subtracts fringe output from the market demand at each price and concerns itself with the residual demand for its service.[12]

The natural monopoly with a fringe of competitive suppliers or potential suppliers shall be the paradigm of the regulated firm used throughout the book. The objective of the firm (or regulator) shall be to choose prices that maximize the sum of consumer and producer surplus perhaps subject to a breakeven constraint. Such prices achieve the object of attaining a maximum feasible economic efficiency.

[12]

This assumes implicitly that constraints exist that prevent the expansion of the competitive fringe. In addition we assume no strategic interaction between the dominant firm and the competitive fringe (see Sharkey [1982]). An alternative paradigm is to consider a model of regulation that comprehends *both* the dominant firm *and* the competitive fringe. Such a model presents some considerable difficulties in application (Brauetigam [1979] and Ebrill and Slutsky [1984a, 1984b]). In such a case, regulation to maximize economic efficiency would lead, among other things, to an artificial division of the market between the fringe and the large firm. Such forms of regulation have proven to be complex and unworkable.

CHAPTER 3

Welfare and efficiency in pricing

3.1 Introduction

In this chapter we bring together the demand side and the cost structure of the regulated firm to start on our main theme: efficient pricing by the regulated firm for its services. The discussion is designed to bring out the main concepts as clearly as possible. These concepts are:

- Efficient prices are those which lead to the highest possible level of welfare, defined as the sum of consumer surplus and producer surplus.
- Moving from some given set of prices to efficient prices makes it possible for the "winners" from the price change to compensate the "losers" and yet still remain better off than before the change. Thus, potential economic welfare rises for all individuals.
- If the regulated firm must break even out of its own sales revenues, potential welfare of society is lower than if the regulated firm were not required to break even.

We first discuss these points in a simplified scenario where the demands for the services of the regulated firm are independent of each other, and where marginal costs are constant. Subsequently, the analysis is broadened to include cross-elasticities of demand between services and to consider non-constant marginal costs. The discussion will cover marginal cost pricing, so-called Ramsey pricing and the accounting-based methods known as Fully Distributed Cost (FDC) pricing. In addition, we will discuss the literature on cross subsidy and the recent axiomatic approach to the allocation of common costs.

3.2 Pricing and efficiency

In the previous chapter we presented consumer surplus and producer surplus, or quasi rent as useful dollar measures of the impact of price changes on the welfare of consumers and producers. Economists often use the sum of consumer surplus and producer surplus as an index of economic efficiency. In this section we will investigate the features of *efficient prices,* i.e., those which lead to a maximum of consumer surplus plus producer surplus. The initial discussion will deal with the special case in which the firm has constant marginal costs and independent demands. As explained in Chapter 2, the independence assumption refers to zero cross price elasticities among the goods produced by the regulated firm. In general, we do not mean to say that there are zero cross elasticities between those goods and unregulated goods produced elsewhere in the economy.

A. Welfare and efficiency

To begin with, we consider only a single commodity produced by a regulated firm with a marginal cost MC that does not vary with the level of output. On grounds of efficiency, where should the regulator set its price? In Figure 3.1 we depict the initial situation with a price P_0:

Initial consumption $= Q_0$

Initial consumer surplus $=$ area "a"

Initial producer surplus $= (P_0 - MC) \cdot Q_0 =$ area "b" + "c".

(If the firm has an overhead cost F, the producer surplus areas "b" plus "c" represents a contribution to cover that overhead.) Suppose that we lower the price to P_1. Consumer surplus rises by "b" plus "d"; producer surplus falls by "b", but this drop is partly offset by an amount equal to "e", which represents extra producer surplus that the firm earns by producing an incremental amount $Q_1 - Q_0$ at a price P_1 which, although lower than P_0, still exceeds marginal cost. Thus,

Area "b" $= (P_0 - P_1)Q_0$

Area "e" $= (P_1 - MC) \cdot (Q_1 - Q_0)$.

Consumers gain by "b" plus "d", whereas the firm only loses "b" minus "e" in producer surplus. Thus, the *total* of consumer surplus plus producer surplus *rises* by "d" plus "e";

Area "b" + "d" minus "b" $-$ "e" $=$ Area "d" + "e"

$$= \frac{(P_0 - P_1)(Q_1 - Q_0)}{2} + (P_1 - MC)(Q_1 - Q_0) .$$

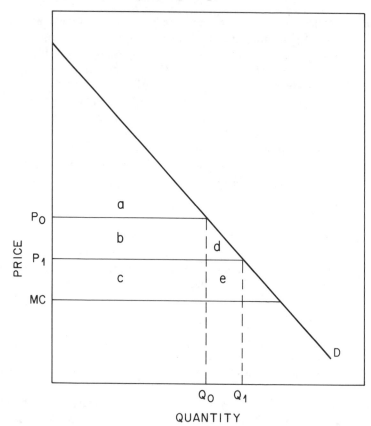

Figure 3.1

The fact that consumer surplus (*CS*) plus producer surplus (*PS*) rises means that it is possible to devise taxes and subsidies outside the pricing system that fully compensate the firm for the change, while leaving consumers on net better off. This compensation should be arranged so that it does not distort consumption or production. The simplest tax/subsidy which meets this requirement is the lump-sum, or poll tax. Because such a tax is unrelated to any agent's consumption or production decisions, it cannot distort them. We could tax away the lost producer's surplus "b" and return it to the firm if we wished, so that consumers gain "d" and the firm "e". Or, we could rest content with the distributional effects of the price change, so that consumer surplus rises by "b" + "d" and producer surplus falls by "b" − "e". Alternatively, suppose that initially the firm were barely covering its fixed cost, so that

$$\text{Area "b"} + \text{"c"} = (P_0 - MC) \cdot Q_0 = F.$$

That is, the firm earns a zero profit. After the price change, we could redistribute "b" from consumers to the firm and, simultaneously, transfer "e" from the firm to consumers. Then the firm would be returned to its *status quo ante* but consumer surplus would be higher by the quantity "d" + "e".

Clearly, we could bring about any distribution of economic welfare we wanted in this way. The important point to note is that welfare has in fact increased by the change. A measure of the the maximum increase in overall welfare is "d" + "e"; no parallel system of compensation can benefit either consumers or the firm by more than this amount.

Now consider Figure 3.2, where the price P_0 is less than marginal cost MC. In such a situation producer surplus is negative. What happens if price rises to P_1, where P_1 is also less than marginal cost? First, consumer surplus falls by "c" + "d" and producer surplus rises by "c" + "d" + "e" + "f", meaning that producer surplus is less negative with price P_1 than at price P_0 by precisely this amount. Once again, total surplus increases:

$$\Delta(CS + PS) = -[\text{"}c\text{"} + \text{"}d\text{"}] + [\text{"}c\text{"} + \text{"}d\text{"} + \text{"}e\text{"} + \text{"}f\text{"}] = \text{Area "}e\text{"} + \text{"}f\text{"}.$$

As before, the net efficiency gain measured by the quantity "e" + "f" could be parceled out in a number of ways by a system of non-distorting lump sum taxes and subsidies. For example, if one wanted to allow the price to rise to P_1, but at the same time keep consumer surplus from falling, we could tax the firm the amount "c" + "d" and still leave producer surplus higher by "e" + "f". Alternatively, without such a tax the regulator might allow producer surplus to rise by the entire amount "c" + "d" + "e" + "f". Once again, the increase in total surplus has made it possible to increase social welfare, no matter how the increase in welfare may be distributed.

Because producer surplus plus consumer surplus rises as price moves toward marginal cost from either direction total surplus is maximized when price is set equal to marginal cost. Any deviations of price from marginal cost can only *reduce* total surplus, $CS + PS$, so that if either the producer or consumer gains by the deviation, such a gain can only come at the expense of the other. To see this better, consider Figure 3.3, where $P_0 = MC$; $CS = \text{Area "}a\text{"} + \text{"}b\text{"} + \text{"}c\text{"}$ and $PS = 0$. If one were to raise price to P_1, above marginal cost, consumption falls to Q_1. Consumer surplus falls by the amount "b" + "c" and producer surplus rises by "b". Even if all of the gain in producer surplus were redistributed to the consumer, leaving producer surplus at zero, consumer surplus is still lower than it was initially by the amount "c".

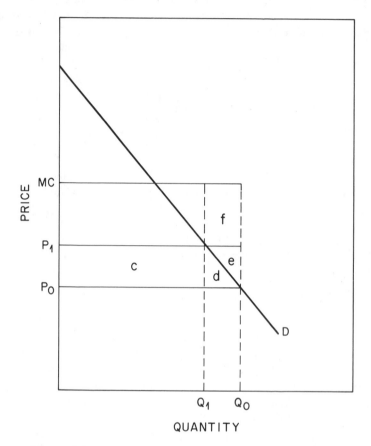

Figure 3.2

We refer to the change in *PS* + *CS* as *deadweight loss*. This loss is given by the triangle "c", which represents the net value by which society values the decrement in consumption $Q_0 - Q_1$, a loss that cannot be made good by parallel taxes or transfers. If the price fell below marginal cost, a similar loss would occur. In this context, the deadweight loss measures the cost to society of a decision not to set prices equal to marginal cost.

In the single commodity case, total surplus is maximized when price is set equal to marginal cost. The price which maximizes total surplus is said to be efficient. If the current price is set equal to the efficient price so defined, a system of poll taxes and subsidies can make *both* consumers *and* producers better off.

Now let us expand the discussion to the case of several commodities: what are the efficient prices in this context? With independent

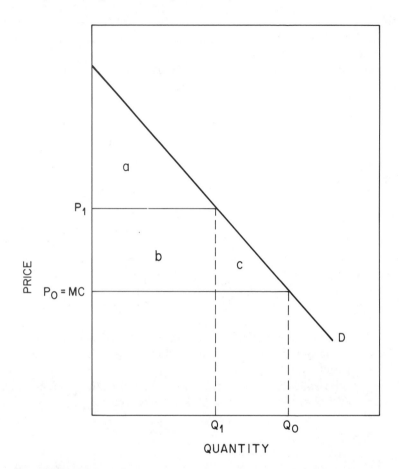

Figure 3.3

demands and constant marginal costs, it should be clear that nothing changes. The efficient price in each market can be determined in isolation from other markets since demand and supply in those markets are not affected. In this case the single market discussion applies. If this is so, consumer surplus plus producer surplus aggregated over *all* markets is maximized by setting price equal to marginal cost in each market independently.

This result holds true even when we allow for non-zero cross-elasticity of demand between services and when we allow for marginal costs that vary with the level of output. The basic intuition is the same. If the price in some market exceeds marginal cost, consumers are willing to pay more to get an extra unit of output than it costs to produce that unit. Thus consumers could compensate the rest of the economy for the value placed on the resources used to produce the extra output, and still remain better off than without the increment. When price is less than marginal cost, the rest of the economy can compensate consumers of the commodity in question for the loss of a unit of consumption and still remain better off than before. At the risk of seeming repetitious, we state in full the principle of efficient pricing:

> Consider a regulated firm producing M outputs at prices $P_1, P_2, ..., P_M$. The efficient set of prices is that which maximizes total surplus across all M markets and is given by:
>
> $P_i = MC_i$
>
> $i = 1, 2, ..., M$
>
> where MC_i is marginal cost in market i.

We can apply this result to the classic problem of peak load pricing for a public utility which is not — or, need not be — concerned with breaking even. Suppose that there are two relevant production periods for the utility. The first period is defined as a peak period, when all the productive capacity of the firm is utilized. The productive capacity in the second "off peak" period is underutilized. The marginal variable cost of production in either period is a constant b, and the marginal cost of extra capacity is β. Under these conditions the efficient prices are $P_1 = b + \beta$ and $P_2 = b$.[1]

Let us illustrate the multimarket case with an example taken from electricity pricing. Consider two services, peak and off-peak electricity supply. The demand curves for each service are:

$$Q_1 = 720 - 4000\, P_1$$

$$Q_2 = 180 - 1000\, P_2$$

where

> Q_1 = consumption of peak period electricity in kwh/month
>
> Q_2 = off-peak consumption (kwh/month)
>
> P_1 = price in peak period ($/kwh)
>
> P_2 = price in off-peak period ($/kwh)

[1]
  These results are contained and extended in a number of well known articles, such as Houtakker [1951], Steiner [1957], Hirshleifer [1958], Williamson [1966], Turvey [1968] and Littlechild [1970].

Initially, $P_1 = P_2 = \$.08$ and at this price $Q_1 = 400$ and $Q_2 = 100$. The off-peak marginal cost is $\$.02$ and the peak marginal cost is $\$.09$. The firm has overhead costs of $2.00, and earns a contribution (producer surplus) just equal to that amount:

$$(P_1-MC_1) \cdot Q_1 + (P_2-MC_2) \cdot Q_2$$

$$= (\$.08-\$.09) \cdot \$.00 + (\$.08-\$.02) \cdot 100$$

$$= \$2.00 .$$

Clearly, price differs from marginal cost in both periods.

Now set prices at their efficient levels: $P_1 = \$.09$, $P_2 = \$.02$. What happens? First, peak consumption falls to 360 and off-peak consumption rises to 160. Consumer surplus in the peak period falls:

$$\Delta CS_1 = (\$.08-\$.09) \times 360 + (\$.08-\$.09)(400-360)/2$$

$$= -\$3.80 .$$

Surplus associated with off-peak consumption rises, however:

$$\Delta CS_2 = (\$.08-\$.02) \times 160 + (\$.08-\$.02)(100-160)/2$$

$$= \$7.80$$

Consumer surplus rises by $\$7.80 - \$3.80 = \$4.00$, and the effect on total surplus is given by

$$\Delta(CS + PS) = \Delta CS_1 + \Delta CS_2 + \Delta PS$$

$$= -\$3.80 + \$7.80 - \$2.00 = \$2.00 .$$

Therefore, total welfare has gone up by $2.00 to the extent that lump-sum taxes/subsidies can make both consumers and the firm better off then they were at the old prices. For example, we could tax $6.00 away from off-peak consumers and give $2.10 to the firm and $3.90 to peak period consumers. This would increase peak period consumer surplus and producer surplus by $\$.10$ over their initial levels and leaves off peak consumer $1.80 better off than before.

To further illustrate the principle at work here, suppose we have two consumer types: rich consumers and poor consumers. Rich consumers have the same demand curves as before:

$$Q_1^R = 720 - 4000 \, P_1$$
$$Q_2^R = 180 - 1000 \, P_2$$

Poor consumers buy *absolutely* less electricity than the rich in *both* periods and use *relatively* less off-peak electricity:

$$Q_1^P = 216 - 1200 \, P_1$$
$$Q_2^P = 18 - 100 \, P_2$$

which is thirty percent and ten percent of the rich consumers' demand respectively.

At the old prices $P_1 = P_2 = \$.08$, $Q_1^P = 120$ and $Q_2^P = 10$ so that the firm loses $\$.60$ on sales to poor customers. Under the new price structure, $Q_1^P = 108$ and $Q_2^P = 16$, with a net loss in the consumer surplus of poor consumers equal to $\$.36$. But because P_1 has risen, the firm breaks even on the peak-period consumption of the poor. Therefore, it could give back the $\$.36$ to poor consumers and still remain $\$.24$ better off than before. Or, we could take the $\$.36$ from the rich consumer, leaving the poor consumer no worse off, the firm just covering its variable costs, and the rich consumers with a net increase in their consumer surplus of $3.64.

Apart from illustrating how efficient pricing works, this discussion brings out the link between efficiency and social welfare. Efficient pricing makes it possible for a social planner to use a system of non-distorting taxes and subsidies to maximize his ethical notions of social welfare. If he wants to make consumers as a group as well off as possible, the first step is to set efficient prices for the utility. The same holds true if he wants to benefit any *particular* group of consumers or the firm itself. Put crudely, by setting prices efficiently, we can maximize the size of the welfare "pie" — the sum of consumer and producer surplus — which we can then (in principle) divide up as we please.

B. *The breakeven constraint*

So far, we have concerned ourselves only with maximizing total surplus, and have not worried about either consumer surplus or producer surplus by itself. It is possible that a pricing scheme that maximizes surplus will cause the firm to incur a loss. For example, we just saw that a marginal cost pricing regime will not cover any overhead (fixed costs). More generally, whenever average costs are declining with increased output, marginal cost is less than average cost and marginal cost pricing will fail to break even. In addition, the operating franchise of the utility may require one group of services to support another group of services. For example, for many years the interstate services of AT&T were required to make a contribution to local telephone service through a procedure known as the separations process. Here too, setting prices equal to marginal cost across the board will induce the company to make a loss on its overall operations.

In some European countries, such a loss is not of any particular concern, since deficits in utility budgets are met out of general tax revenues. The United States, however, has a different tradition of regulation: utilities' revenues are expected to cover their costs, including a fair return on investment. In this institutional setting, prices must be set at least to allow the firm to break even.

This breakeven constraint implies that when a fixed cost exists — or, indeed, in any situation in which marginal cost is less than average cost — marginal cost pricing is not feasible. Prices must differ from marginal cost. Clearly overall welfare, as measured by total surplus, declines when we move away from marginal cost pricing. How do we quantify this welfare loss? (Again, for simplicity, we assume that marginal cost is constant.)

Once again, consider the single commodity case in Figure 3.4. Suppose that the firm must cover a fixed cost F, in addition to all variable costs. Initially, price equals marginal cost, so that sales revenues do not cover F. Now raise price to P_1, a level which cuts consumption from Q_0 to Q_1 but which just covers the fixed cost. Consumer surplus falls by the quantity $F + $ "d", where F is simply a transfer from consumers to the firm and "d" is a drop in total surplus, $CS + PS$. We can view "d" as the net valuation which society places on the foregone consumption $Q_0 - Q_1$. Thus, "d" is the deadweight loss to society of requiring that the firm break even out of its own sales revenue.

Consider the same problem in the context of our two period electricity pricing example. In that example, the demand curves of the peak and off-peak periods are

$$Q_1 = 720 - 4000\, P_1$$

and

$$Q_2 = 180 - 1000\, P_2$$

respectively. The marginal costs in the two periods are $c_1 = \$.09$ and $c_2 = \$.02$ and there is a positive fixed cost of $2.00. Many combinations of prices for the two services will allow the firm to break even. Such prices must meet the condition that total revenue equal total cost:

$$\textit{total revenue} = P_1 \times (720{-}4000\, P_1) + P_2(180{-}1000\, P_2)$$

$$= \$.09 \times (720{-}4000\, P_1) + \$.02 \times (180{-}1000\, P_2) + 2$$

$$= \textit{total cost} \ .$$

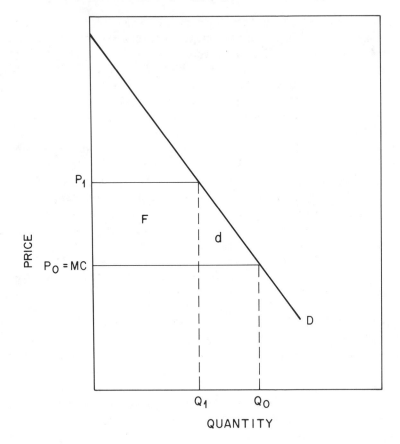

Figure 3.4

Three such pairs of prices are

$$\begin{cases} P_1 = \$.09 \\ P_2 = \$.0337 \end{cases} \quad \begin{cases} P_1 = \$.1740 \\ P_2 = \$.02 \end{cases} \quad \begin{cases} P_1 = \$.08 \\ P_2 = \$.08 \end{cases}$$

Since all three pairs of prices allow the firm to break even, we can choose between them by selecting the pair of prices with the lowest deadweight loss, or, equivalently, the high total surplus. Performing the relevant calculations, and realizing that producer surplus is equal to $2.00 for each of these three pairs of prices, we find that

Total Surplus:

	$P_1 = $	\$.09	$P_1 = $	\$.1740	$P_1 = $	\$.08
	$P_2 = $	\$.0337	$P_2 = $	\$.02	$P_2 = $	\$.08
		\$28.90		\$14.88		\$27.00

so that the first pair of prices, $P_1 = \$.09$ and $P_2 = \$.0337$ is preferred.

This approach underlies the modern economist's approach to public utility pricing, and in the rest of this book we will explore it in detail. For this reason, we state it in some generality:

Efficient public utility pricing: Given a regulated firm that must break even and which serves M markets, the efficient set of prices $P_1, P_2, ..., P_M$ is that set which maximizes total surplus subject to the constraint that the firm earns zero profit.

C. *The efficiency effects of price changes*

Having stated the principle of efficient public utility pricing, we can begin to address the question of how the analyst can compute prices which maximize total surplus. One way to start is to ask how to tell whether or not a *given* set of price changes is likely to increase total surplus. The price changes may be specified by a regulator, the management of the regulated firm, or by the analyst and may have no claim to any kind of optimality. Our aim is to arrive at a simple test for the effects of these price changes on total surplus.

1. Residential Customers

We begin with a simple case. The monopolist sells M services to a market of residential consumers. The services could be electricity in different times of day, telephone calls in different mileage bands, or different classes of mail service. The utility, which we shall assume is a monopolist, changes prices $P_1, P_2, ..., P_M$ for these services and the effects of price changes $\Delta P_1, \Delta P_2, ..., \Delta P_M$ are to be considered. The utility is constrained to break even and we will suppose first that both the new and the old prices allow this to occur. For this to be the case the induced change in the producer surplus of the monopolist is zero and the change in total surplus is simply the change in consumer surplus. From our discussion in Chapter 2 we recall that for small price changes, the net effect of a set of price changes is equal to the change in the consumer's bill at the old consumption level:

$$\Delta TS = \Delta CS = -X_1 \Delta P_1 - X_2 \Delta P_2 - \cdots - X_M \Delta P_M .$$

Needless to say, this test expression is easily computed by the analyst.

2. Business Customers

It is more difficult to construct such a test when the monopolist is selling to business customers. In such a case account must also be taken of what were termed in Chapter 2 the *flowthrough* effects of price changes. That is, changes in $P_1, P_2, ..., P_M$ will show up as changes in the business customers' costs of doing business and will affect output prices in the industries in which they sell. These changes in output prices will induce demand changes in the output markets

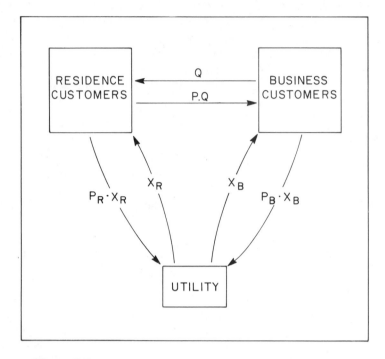

Figure 3.5

served by the monopolist's business customers, which will feed back on business customers' demands for the monopolist's services. If the monopolist's customers are intermediate goods manufacturers, this process will repeat itself through the entire vertical production chain until the flowthrough effects of the monopolist's price changes reach final product markets.

To see what can be done in this more complicated situation, suppose that the monopolist sells both business and residential services (in practice, each service may be thought of as a broad aggregate of different offerings such as peak/off peak, short- and long-haul telephone calls, etc). The business customers are all firms in a single industry which produces an output Q and sells it at a price P to the same residential customers who also buy the residential service of the monopoly. This paradigm is depicted in Figure 3.5. We devote business and residential outputs by X_B and X_R and their prices by P_B and P_R, respectively.

Now suppose that the regulator tells the firm that the prices P_B and P_R must change. For the purpose of illustration, suppose further that the residential price goes up and the business price falls. To some extent, the reduction in P_B will benefit consumers through its effect on lowering P, the price in the downstream industry. To determine whether this effect outweighs the increase in the residential price, think of the downstream industry as a "filter" between consumers' purchases of the downstream output Q, and the regulated monopolist's business sales. If the downstream industry is perfectly competitive, this "filter" is non-distorting, and we can visualize matters as if the residential customers posed as business customers, bought X_B from the monopolist, and produced Q for themselves. As we show in Chapter 6, using a mathematical approach, this way of looking at things is correct; that is, we can think of residential consumers buying X_R at a price P_R and X_B at a price P_B and deriving consumer surplus therefrom. From our discussion above, then, the effect on consumer surplus of changes in the prices of X_B and X_R can be calculated from the ordinary formula for a change in consumer surplus: $-X_R \cdot \Delta P_R - X_B \Delta P_B$.[2]

3.3 Ramsey pricing — efficient pricing subject to a breakeven constraint

Our previous discussion leads us to the analysis of the efficient prices which cover the total costs of the regulated firm. Because the breakeven constraint prevents the imposition of the fully optimal, so-called *first-best*, marginal cost prices, we refer to prices which maximize total surplus subject to breaking even as optimal *second-best* prices. Such prices can, of course, take on infinite variety, such as quantity discounts, quantity premia, hookup charges, etc. In this section, we ignore quantity discounts and premia, and confine our attention to *uniform* prices which maximize total surplus subject to a breakeven constraint ($PS = 0$). (Uniform prices, by definition, are prices which do not vary with the level of consumption.) Symbolically, the most efficient uniform second-best prices are those which

$$\text{maximize } [\ CS + PS\ ]$$
$$\{P_1, P_2, ..., P_m\}$$

$$\text{subject to } PS = F$$

or, equivalently,

2
   Chapter 6 also shows that under certain conditions this formula hold true even when the downstream industry is not perfectly competitive and acts according to the conjectural variation model with free entry. The same results go through in contestable markets in the case of flat bottomed average cost curves analyzed by Baumol, Panzar and Willig [1982].

maximize CS
$\{P_1, P_2, ..., P_m\}$

subject to $PS = F$,

where F represents the fixed costs of the firm.

For ease of exposition, we shall maintain our assumption that marginal costs are constant and that demands are independent. Under these assumptions we can analyze pricing in each market virtually in isolation from the other markets.

To best understand the principle of second-best pricing, suppose that we began with a situation in which all prices are set to marginal cost. Where a fixed cost exists, the firm will fail to break even. Is it possible to modify prices to include a markup over marginal cost in such a way as to perturb the situation as little as possible? It would seem reasonable to impose high markups in those markets where they will matter least, where quantity demanded is not too sensitive to price changes. That is, increase prices in markets where price elasticities of demand are relatively low. Markups should be lower in those markets with relatively high price elasticities. By following this strategy, we alter markets as little as possible from the price-equal-marginal cost equilibrium, which provided the highest possible value of total surplus. This suggests that a reasonable formula for the second-best markup of price over marginal cost in each market can be given by

$$\text{Markup} = \frac{P_i - C_i}{P_i} = \frac{\lambda}{\epsilon i}$$

where P_i is the price in market i, C_i the marginal cost, and ϵ_i the price elasticity of demand. In this formulation, the low elasticity markets get high markups and the highly price-elastic markets get low markups. The proportionately constant λ adjusts markups in *all* markets uniformly to the point where the firm breaks even. (This result is derived mathematically in the Appendix to this Chapter.) This pricing rule is, perhaps, the best known result of the entire literature on efficient public utility pricing, apart from the first-best rule of setting price equal to marginal cost. It has become known as the Inverse Elasticity Rule, or IER. An alternative way of expressing the IER is that

$$\lambda = \left[\frac{P_i - C_i}{P_i} \right] \cdot \epsilon_i = \left[\frac{P_j - C_j}{P_j} \right] \cdot \epsilon_j , \quad j \neq i$$

In other words, for any pair of markets served by a regulated firm, the percentage deviations from marginal cost, weighted by the price elasticities of demand, should be equal for both markets to the markup λ.

The IER was anticipated in 1926 by Frank Ramsey,[3] who was concerned with optimal excise taxation, and showed that when the effects of change in the taxes on the government's budget can be ignored (analogous to our assumption of negligible income effects), then the tax on each commodity should be inversely proportional to that commodity's price elasticity of demand. Because Ramsey's work is so closely related to public utility pricing theory, prices which maximize total surplus subject to a breakeven constraint are often called Ramsey prices. The constant λ is often called the Ramsey number.

The numerical solution of Ramsey prices can become quite complicated. There is one case, however, in which they can be expressed quite simply. Suppose that the price elasticity of demand in each market, ϵ_i, is constant, so that quantity demanded in each market takes the form

$$Q_i = k_i P_i^{-\epsilon i}$$

where ϵ_i is the constant price elasticity and k_i is a scaling term. In this case, from the IER the Ramsey prices can be rewritten in terms of the underlying constants C_i, ϵ_i and k_i as

$$P_i = \frac{\epsilon i C_i}{\epsilon i - \lambda} \ .$$

For such Ramsey prices, the markup fraction λ is set so that total revenues equal total costs:

$$\sum_{i=1}^{M} (P_i - C_i) Q_i - F = \sum_{i=1}^{M} \frac{\lambda k_i}{\epsilon i} \left[\frac{C_i \epsilon i}{\epsilon i - \lambda} \right]^{1-\epsilon i} - F = 0 \ .$$

Thus, to compute Ramsey prices in this case, one can simply set prices with different values of λ until a value of λ is found which sets $PS = F$.

We can extend Ramsey pricing to the case where demands are not independent and where marginal costs are not constant. Unfortunately, the analysis becomes somewhat more complicated, and the simplicity of Ramsey pricing disappears. Nonetheless, some discussion of the problem will prove instructive.

As we showed in Chapter 2, when demands are not independent and when income effects are unimportant, consumer surplus maximization amounts to maximizing the following utility function:

Ramsey [1926].

$$U(Q_1,Q_2,...,Q_M) - \sum_{i=1}^{m} P_i Q_i + Y \ .$$

U is the monetary benefit of consuming the quantities $Q_1,Q_2,...,Q_M$ and Y is income left over for expenditure on other goods. Therefore, total surplus is simply written as

$$TS = U(Q_1,Q_2,...,Q_M) - C(Q_1,Q_2,...,Q_M)$$

where $C(Q_1,Q_2,...,Q_M)$ is the regulated firm's joint cost function. The firm's pricing problem is to maximize TS subject to breaking even:

$$\sum_{i=1}^{m} P_i Q_i - C(Q_1, Q_2, ..., Q_M) = 0$$

The mathematics involved are unnecessary to go through here, and are covered in the appendix to this chapter. To give some idea of how the results look, let us consider the two market case ($M = 2$). In that case, the Ramsey prices must satisfy the condition

$$\lambda = \left[\frac{P_1 - C_1}{P_1} \right] \cdot \left[\frac{\epsilon_{11}\epsilon_{22} - \epsilon_{12}\epsilon_{21}}{\epsilon_{22} - \dfrac{P_2 Q_2}{P_1 Q_1} \epsilon_{21}} \right]$$

$$= \left[\frac{P_2 - C_2}{P_2} \right] \cdot \left[\frac{\epsilon_{11} - \epsilon_{22} - \epsilon_{12}\epsilon_{21}}{\epsilon_{11} - \dfrac{P_1 Q_1}{P_2 Q_2} \epsilon_{12}} \right] .$$

The marginal costs C_1 and C_2 in this more general model are not constant and are those which hold at the set of outputs generated by the Ramsey prices. The terms

$$S_1 = \frac{\epsilon_{11}\epsilon_{22} - \epsilon_{12}\epsilon_{21}}{\epsilon_{22} - \dfrac{P_2 Q_2}{P_1 Q_1} \epsilon_{21}}$$

$$S_2 = \frac{\epsilon_{11}\epsilon_{22} - \epsilon_{12}\epsilon_{21}}{\epsilon_{11} - \dfrac{P_1 Q_1}{P_2 Q_2} \epsilon_{12}} .$$

have been called price "superelasticities" by Rohlfs.[4] They include the

[4] See Rohlfs [1979]. See also the Appendix for derivation.

own price elasticities for each good, ϵ_{11} and ϵ_{22}, but also the cross price elasticities ϵ_{12} and ϵ_{21}, weighted by relative revenues, P_1Q_2 and P_2Q_2. We can write the price rule when cross elasticities are present in a manner reminiscent of the IER:

$$\lambda = \left[\frac{P_1 - C_1}{P_1}\right]S_1 = \left[\frac{P_2 - C_2}{P_2}\right]S_2$$

That its, percentage deviation of price from marginal cost, weighted by the superelasticity should be equal across markets. Clearly, when the cross-elasticities ϵ_{12} and ϵ_{21} are both zero, so that demands are independent, this rule reduces to the IER.

This is a much more complicated set of conditions than the simple IER which we obtained with independent demands. Instead of the simple own elasticity terms ϵ_{11} and ϵ_{22}, the markups in the two markets are weighted by the superelasticity terms S_{11} and S_{22}, which include correction terms depending not only on the cross elasticities ϵ_{12} and ϵ_{21}, but also on the prices and quantities themselves. Intuitively, however, the result has the same flavor. Markets are assigned high markups where the effect of a small change in price is to perturb consumption a relatively small amount relative to where they would be under marginal cost pricing. The effect of cross elasticities is that even if the price elasticity of demand in a given market is quite low, when a rise in that price exerts a large distorting effect in other markets then a low markup is in order.

At this point it is appropriate to return to the problem of flowthrough effects, broached in the previous section. When some of the regulated monopoly's customers are business firms producing "downstream" from the utility, they are purchasing the services of the regulated monopoly as inputs which they use to produce in their own outputs markets. Consequently, changes in the regulated firm's output prices represent changes in the cost of doing business for these customers, which will flow through to their final output markets. For example, such a set of services might be peak and off-peak electricity for industrial customers. If the regulated monopolists' business customers are selling in perfectly competitive industries, the Ramsey pricing *formulae* are unchanged. The only point to keep track of is that the price elasticities which appear in them must be calculated from the equilibrium demand curves for the relevant services of the regulated monopoly,[5] i.e., those which

---

[5]
In Chapter 6 we analyze efficient pricing when the downstream industry is governed by the conjectural variation model, which includes the posibility of imperfect competition. For the ordinary Ramsey pricing formulae to be correct with imperfect competition, it is both necessary and sufficient that the downstream demand curve be linear in price. The same results hold true in contestable markets when average cost curves are U-shaped with flat bottoms.

take account of the feedback effects of changes in the prices in downstream industries which were induced by changes in the monopolist's prices.

3.4 Allocation of common costs

One of the everyday regulatory problems in countries where public enterprises must break even is to allocate costs to services for ratemaking purposes. This is not a straightforward task and is the source of many of the most muddled, lengthy and unsatisfactory proceedings in regulatory history. The root of the problem is that prices must be set for each service offered by the firm but substantial amounts of cost represent facilities used in common by several or all services and cannot be allocated in a clear cost-related way to any single service. In the electric utility industry an example of a common cost is the cost of baseload generating capacity. Baseload capacity operates continuously and is used by all customer classes in both peak and off peak time periods. Electricity tariffs are usually broken down by some or all of these categories. This has led to a regulatory tradition of long standing that to obtain a cost of service for each market, the baseload capacity must be allocated by customer class and time period. In telecommunications, switching capacity is used by a number of voice grade and data services and in regulatory proceedings strenuous efforts are made to allocate switching costs between all of them. It is standard practice to break the cost of the firm down to the attributable cost of each service and common costs, unattributable to a particular service. Generally, common costs are thought of as a fixed cost.

In Ramsey pricing the common costs are also covered, but the relevant cost concept is the *marginal* cost of usage for each service. Depending on its price elasticity of demand, each service makes a contribution to covering common costs so that the firm will break even. However, the only way that common costs enter in is in setting the level of contribution that the services collectively must generate.

Much of regulatory practice takes a different point of view from that of Ramsey pricing. It is traditional to require that each service be assigned a portion of the common cost and that its revenues equal the cost figure given by the sum of its attributable cost and its share of the common costs. Such approaches are generally known under the rubric of "cost-based pricing."

In this section we will describe three different approaches to the allocation of costs each of which differ from Ramsey pricing. The first is the approach known as Fully Distributed Costs. Under this approach common costs are allocated to service based on their relative shares of quantities such as output, peak demand, revenue or attributable cost.

This general approach has been used in U.S. regulatory ratemaking for decades. The second approach uses simple concepts from the theory of cooperative games. The object here is to allocate responsibility for common costs among services so as to avoid cross subsidy. This approach dates from the early 1970's and has common into fairly frequent use in policy discussions. Third, we discuss a fairly recent area of research known as the axiomatic approach to cost allocation. In this work, the object is to start by specifying reasonable properties that an allocation mechanism should satisfy, and then deduce what price structures are consistent with the axioms. None of these three approaches is concerned primarily with economic efficiency, although, as we will see there is a connection between what is termed *subsidy-free pricing* and economic efficiency.

A. Fully distributed cost pricing

Fully Distributed Cost (FDC) pricing consists of a whole set of approaches to allocating common costs to services. Once this allocation is done, prices are set so that each service just covers its fully distributed cost. The distinguishing feature of FDC pricing is that the allocation of common costs is done without much reference to what one would regard as economically meaningful criteria. Although allocations have been done in literally dozens of ways in different regulatory proceedings, there are three approaches which have been used most frequently: the relative output method, the gross revenue and the attributable cost method.[6] Under the Relative Output Method (ROM) the allocations of common cost to different services is made based on each services' share in the total output of the firm. Under the Gross Revenue Method (GRM) the allocation is based on each service's share in total revenue, and under the Attributable Cost Method (ACM) on its share of the total attributable cost over all services. Algebraically, we write the fully distributed cost of a service i as

$$FDC_i = \text{Attributable Cost of } i + f_i \times \text{Common Cost}$$

where f_i is the fraction of Common Cost attributed to service i. This fraction is calculated without any thought of economic efficiency considerations. In the present context, the fraction is given by the term

---

[6] The terminology here is taken from Braeutigam [1980].

$$f_i = \frac{Q_i}{Q_1+Q_2+\cdots+Q_m} \quad \text{under the ROM}$$

$$= \frac{\text{Rev}_i}{\text{Total Revenue}} \quad \text{under the GRM}$$

$$= \frac{\text{Attributable Cost of } i}{\text{Total Attributable Cost}} \quad \text{under ACM .}$$

In practice, FDC also involves numerous conventions regarding depreciation rates, valuation of assets at book vs. replacement cost, construction work in progress and hundreds of other items. We will ignore these complicated facts of life so as to concentrate solely on the effects of different allocation methods. All assets are assumed to be valued at replacement cost and we will treat common costs as a fixed cost F.

Apart from the allocation method, it is necessary to specify which quantities are to be used. Until the 1970's it was common to use recent test period data to get the cost, output and revenue data to be used in the allocations. The prices set by the FDC methods were unlikely to be consistent with the quantities used in the allocation. To see this denote the test period by t and assume that new FDC prices are to be set in period $t+1$. The outputs, revenues and costs used in period t are, of course, generated by the prices being charged in period t. When price in period $t+1$ is set it will generally differ from price in period t, so outputs will change from their period t levels. The effect is that since the FDC prices were set to break even on period t quantities and costs, the firm will have non-zero profits in $t+1$ as demands and, hence, outputs adjust to the new prices.

In recent years, some regulatory jurisdictions have begun to use price elasticities of demand in setting FDC prices. This means that prices and quantities are arrived at which are demand-compatible. If the firm and regulator use good estimates of price elasticities, the FDC prices should actually lead to zero profits. To illustrate further the contrast between these approaches, consider the ROM method. Assume that demands are independent. Denote the attributable cost of service i in period t by AC_{it}. Using test year data from period t the unit price for service i is computed as follows in period $t+1$:

$$P_{i,\,t+1} = \left[AC_{it} + \frac{Q_{it}}{(Q_{1t}+\cdots+Q_{Mt})} \cdot F \right] \cdot \frac{1}{Q_{it}}$$

whereas demand-compatible prices are given by:

$$P_{i,t+1} = \left[AC_{i,t+1} + \frac{Q_{i,t+1}}{(Q_{1,t+1} + \cdots + Q_{M,t+1})} \times F\right] \cdot \frac{1}{Q_{i,t+1}}$$

$$Q_{i,t+1} = Q_i(P_{i,t+1}) \quad \text{(Demand at ROM price)}.$$

A final property of FDC pricing that is of interest is that when the regulated firm is at zero profit, the GRM and the ACM are equivalent. This result is due to Braeutigam [1980] and is easily demonstrated. With demand compatible prices ACM average revenue is given by

$$P_i = \frac{AC_i}{Q_i} \times \left(1 + \frac{F}{\sum\limits_{i=1}^{M} AC_i}\right)$$

and under GRM

$$P_i = \frac{1}{Q_i}\left[AC_i + \frac{F \cdot R_i}{R}\right] - \frac{AC_i}{Q_i} \times \left(\frac{R}{R-F}\right)$$

where R = total revenue. Under zero profit

$$R = \sum_{i=1}^{M} AC_i + F$$

so starting with the ACM price

$$P_i\Big|_{\text{ACM}} = \frac{AC_i}{Q_i} \times \left(1 + \frac{F}{\sum\limits_{i=1}^{M} AC_i}\right) - \frac{AC_i}{Q_i} \times \left(1 + \frac{F}{R-F}\right)$$

$$= \frac{AC_i}{Q_i} \times \frac{R}{R-F} = P_i\Big|_{\text{GRM}}$$

which is the price under GRM.

FDC prices have been used by regulators in several ways. One use of them is to compute a "true" cost of service, used as a guide in resource allocation. The ICC made such a use of FDC methods in the so-called Ingot Molds case of 1963.[7] This proceeding involved the shipment of ingot molds between certain points in Pennsylvania and Kentucky,

---

[7] For a good discussion of *Ingot Molds*, see Owen and Braeutigam [1978], Chapter 6.

which was traditionally carried by combination barge-truck service at a rate of $5.11 per ton. In 1963, railroads lowered their rates from $11.86 to $5.11. The barge-truck operators complained to the ICC that this rate would divert traffic to railroads but would be less than the railroad's true cost. Hence, the "inherent advantage" of the barge-truck combination would be ignored, to the detriment of national policy. The railroads were able to show that their incremental cost of ingot transportation between the points at issue was only $4.69 per ton, so that the $5.11 rate covered the added costs of ingot service and also made some contribution to their common costs. The barge-truck operators calculated the railroads' fully distributed cost of the ingot service at $7.49 per ton. The ICC ruled in favor of the barge-truck operators, arguing that fully distributed cost was appropriate for use in judging the "inherent" advantage of a mode of transportation. Whatever the political factors which may have gone into the ICC's decision, the intellectual argument reflects a concern for economic efficiency, that the ingots should move on the transportation mode with the lowest economic cost.

The use of FDC methods reflects a related but somewhat different concern in the regulation of the domestic telephone industry: cross subsidy between the users of different services. In the consolidated FCC Dockets 18128/18684, the Federal Communications Commission undertook a series of investigations lasting from 1964 until the late 1970's concerning the impacts of different FDC methods applied to various message, private line and telegraph services offered by AT&T. The principal issue of the Docket 18128/18684 is similar to that in the Ingot Molds case. Non-Bell providers of private line services argued that AT&T private line rates were below cost. AT&T argued that its rates covered its incremental costs; therefore, they were compensatory. Competitors argued that FDC pricing constituted the appropriate methodology. In 1971, AT&T filed an exhibit known as the Fully Distributed Embedded Cost Study for its interstate services. This study explored no fewer than seven FDC methods, which varied in detail but can be grouped under our three allocation methods. Depending on the method used, there were wide variations in the FDC-based rates of return calculated for each service. FDC rates of return for Wide Area Telecommunications Service (WATS) varied from 9.4 percent when calculated on an ROM basis (known as Method 1 in the study) to 17.9 percent on an ACM basis (Method 3). The rate of return for TELPAK, a bulk private line service, varied from 5.4 percent to 10.3 percent, depending on the method of allocation used. Similar variations were calculated for other services. Nonetheless, the study showed, by and large, that the two services which faced no competition, Message

Toll Service (MTS) and WATS, had substantially higher rates of return on an FDC basis than did services such as private line, in which AT&T faced competition.[8]

This finding gave substance to the fear that AT&T was using revenues from its monopoly services to subsidize predatory prices (below marginal cost) in competitive services. The FCC consistently took the view that FDC methods provided an appropriate method to test for the existence of cross subsidy. This concern reflects the desire to avoid below-cost pricing, as in *Ingot Molds*, but focuses on the question of whether or not customers in monopoly markets were subsidizing the low rate.

Economist's criticisms of FDC have been scathing. They particularly single out the fact that different FDC allocation methods are essentially arbitrary, yet can lead to widely different results. Second, there is no effort in FDC pricing to increase economic efficiency; the important cost concept is not marginal cost, but an "average cost" with no clear rationale. Also, price elasticities of demand have no place in setting FDC rates, except perhaps in forecasting revenue, so FDC prices will generally be much different from Ramsey prices. Finally, economists have argued that FDC methods are utterly meaningless in one of their main uses, testing for cross subsidy. Cross subsidy, logically, should exist only when the deletion of a service benefits users of other services. Professor William J. Baumol puts the point clearly:

> ...the reason no FDC test will do the job is because an FDC test deals with only one circumstance, that is, it deals with the service as it is operated or has been operated. It involves no incremental comparison. It does not compare the circumstances of the user with the service and in the absence of the service.[9]

We will proceed to illustrate FDC pricing in a numerical example of peak load pricing. Subsequently we will address the issue of FDC's relevance for the detection of cross subsidy.

B. Numerical example: FDC and Ramsey pricing

We take this example from the market for message service on the AT&T interstate network. The background is covered in Chapter 7

---

[8]
See Docket 18128/18684, Exhibit 23 (March 16, 1972), pp. 1-13.

[9]
Docket 18128/18684, Tr at 10386.

below; for our purpose here a brief description will suffice. Message telecommunication service comprises all switched services on the network; that is, we exclude private line. All message services are aggregated into Day and Non-Day; the system peak occurs during the day. We will confine our attention to business customers and assume that monthly demand functions take on the constant elasticity form

$$Q_i = k_i \, P_i^{-\epsilon_i}, \, i = \text{Day (D), Non-Day (N)} .$$

where $k_D = 59.09$, $k_N = 7.97$, $\epsilon_D = .534$ and $\epsilon_N = .77$. Marginal costs are assumed constant at 13¢ per minute for Day and 6¢ per minute in Non-Day. Fixed costs F are assumed to amount to $20.42 per month. These parameter values are broadly characteristic of message service markets of the late 1970's.

Table 1 contains the results of each of the pricing regimes. The two FDC pricing methods arrive at roughly similar Day prices, but the attributable cost method has a much lower Non-Day price. This is due to the fact that the ACM gives more weight to the lower Non-Day marginal cost than does the ROM. It is differences such as this between the results of the various FDC methods which makes the use of any one of them seem arbitrary. The Ramsey pricing results are a somewhat higher Day price, but a much lower Non-Day price compared to either the ACM or the ROM. This is largely due to the fact that Non-Day has a higher price elasticity (.77) than does Day (.534), as well as because the Non-Day marginal cost is lower.

Table 1. Numerical Examples

1. Prices (¢/min)

	Day	Non-Day
FDC-ACM	28.28	13.05
FDC-ROM	26.99	19.99
Ramsey	29.40	9.8
Marginal Cost Pricing	13.0	6.0

2. Efficiency Gains

	$/month	Efficiency Gains As % of Revenue
Ramsey over ACM	.09	.23
Ramsey over ROM	.83	2.20
MC Pricing over Ramsey	24.84	65.25

NOTE: In each comparison, efficiency gains as a percentage over revenue are given by the gain in $/month divided by the monthly revenue of the less efficient pricing method.

Looking at the efficiency (total surplus) gains to Ramsey pricing we see that they are rather small, ranging from a .23 percent gain over the ACM method to a 2.2 percent gain over the ROM method. On the other hand, the gain of marginal cost pricing over Ramsey pricing is huge — 65 percent of the revenue generated under Ramsey pricing. This suggests that the deadweight losses due to the breakeven constraint may be quite large, if the numbers used in our example are at all close to reality (and also that Ramsey pricing does little to mitigate them). It also suggests that it is worthwhile to search for pricing structures which will narrow the efficiency gap between Ramsey pricing and marginal cost pricing. We undertake this task in subsequent chapters.

C. The game theoretic approach to cost allocation: cross subsidy

Many regulated firms have a high ratio of common costs to attributable costs, which leaves a large degree of indeterminacy in setting prices. This fact leads frequently to allegations of cross subsidy. Consumers dislike high prices and are often on the lookout to see that the services they use are not cross-subsidizing some other service. The fringe of competitive suppliers facing the regulated firm has the opposite concern: it dislikes low prices and is apt to appeal to the regulatory authority that it is the victim of predatory pricing. Put together, these groups can often muster considerable political muscle behind the argument that consumers of the regulated firm's less competitive services are paying excessively high prices to subsidize predatory pricing in the regulated firm's more competitive markets. In addition to the Docket 18128/18685 concern that AT&T's message services were subsidizing non-compensatory pricing of AT&T's private line services, a similar charge was later made with regard to the pricing of AT&T's two message services, MTS and WATS. In FCC Docket 19104 it was argued by private line competitors that WATS was sold at a bulk discount to compete unfairly with private line, and that this was financed by excessively high MTS rates.

For reasons such as this, economists, many of them employed by AT&T's subsidiary Bell Laboratories, began in the early 1970's to formulate a rigorous theory of cross subsidy. Based on the theory of cooperative games, the theory attempts to define carefully what is meant by cross subsidy, to compute prices which do not cross-subsidize or are *subsidy-free* and to provide tests for whether or not given prices are subsidy-free. This theory can be described briefly.

To start with, the theory of cooperative games has little to do with "games" as laymen understand the word. It is actually a theory of coalitions. We start with some situation in which there are potential gains to a set of N players if they form a coalition; for example, if technology is such that average costs diminish with the number of consumers, then there would appear to be potential gains to forming a large "coalition" of users to be served by a single firm. The crucial question is whether there exist sets of prices for membership which keep members from defecting from the grand coalition of N players to form other, smaller coalitions. If this is possible, the theory says how to find sets of prices which keep the coalition stable. Usually there will exist more than one such set of prices. The collection of all sets of prices which keep the grand coalition of N players from fragmenting is referred to as the *core*. Since the pioneering paper by Faulhaber [1975], economists have tended to equate subsidy-free prices with prices which are in the core. That is, a set of prices contains cross subsidy if some players can improve their lot by defecting and forming a smaller coalition.

The simplest kind of game to look at is one in which the N players can be thought of as consumers attempting to be served at minimum cost. Thus, off peak service would be considered a player, peak service a player, etc. For simplicity, assume that demands are completely price inelastic, so that outputs for each player are fixed. Suppose that there are N players and a cost function $C(S)$ which gives the minimum cost of serving a coalition S, where S is a subcoalition which can be formed out of the N-player coalition. All possible subcoalitions S are continually considering whether or not to defect from the grand coalition and be served by a specialty firm using the the same technology as the monopolist. Faulhaber [1975] defined $C(S)$ as the *stand-alone cost* of coalition S. Each possible subcoalition has its own stand-alone cost. To keep each coalition S in the grand coalition N, the subcoalition S cannot be charged more than its stand-alone cost. Denote by r_i, $i \epsilon s$, the price paid by any member of the subcoalition S to belong to the grand coalition. Thus, to prevent S from defecting

$$\sum_{i \epsilon s} r_i \leqq C(S) \tag{1}$$

for each possible subcoalition S which can be formed out of the grand coalition N. In addition, the monopolist serving the N players must break even:

$$\sum_{i=1}^{N} r_i = C(N) \tag{2}$$

When both of these sets of constraints are met, then no subcoalition S will want break away from the grand coalition and be served at a lower cost. In the language of game theory, when a set of prices $r_1, r_2, ..., r_N$ satisfies the constraints (1) and (2), we say that they are in the core of the cost game.

There is another interpretation of these conditions. Consider a subset S, which is paying less than or equal to its stand-alone cost:

$$\sum_{i \epsilon s} r_i \leqq C(S) .$$

Denote all other consumers by $N-S$; they, too, must pay no more than their stand-alone cost $C(N-S)$. Incorporate this into the regulated firm's breakeven constraint:

$$\sum_{i \epsilon N} r_i = \sum_{i \epsilon N-S} r_i + \sum_{i \epsilon s} r_i = C(N)$$

implying that

$$\sum_{i \epsilon s} r_i > C(N) - C(N-S) .$$

Thus, all groups in S must bring in at least their incremental cost, a condition which must hold for all such possible subcoalitions. Thus, when the monopolist is assumed to break even, prices r_i which are subsidy-free (i.e., in the core of the cost game) have the following two equivalent features:

— no group of consumers pay more than its stand-alone cost.
— each group of consumers pays at least its incremental cost.

In this cost game, players are contemplating forming coalitions so as to reduce the cost of producing their demands. We have ignored the benefit side of the market. If the solution to the cost game results in prices which exceed the benefits that players derive from consuming their outputs, then they will defect. To take account of this benefit constraint we add the following set of conditions which must be satisfied:

$$r_i \leqq b_i, i = 1, 2, ..., N \tag{3}$$

where b_i is the benefit that player i derives from concerning Q_i. When these constraints are met, in addition to the core constraints (1) and (2) for the cost game, then we have found a solution to what is known as the benefit game.[10]

At this point it is instructive to compare the results of FDC pricing to the cross subsidy conditions. The FDC pricing rules all come down to the following form:

[10]
See Sharkey [1982].

$$R_i = AC_i + f_i F, f_i < 1 \tag{4}$$

where f_i is the fraction of fixed costs paid by service i and R_i is the revenue to be paid by service i. To compare this with the core constraints, suppose for a moment that demands are all fixed. It is clear that FDC prices are all in the core of the cost game:

$$\sum_{i \in s} R_i = \sum_{i \in s} (AC_i + f_i F) \leqq \sum_{i \in s} AC_i + F, \quad \text{for } S \leqq N \tag{5}$$

$$\sum_{i=1}^{N} (R_i - AC_i) - F = 0. \tag{6}$$

Therefore, when the cost function takes the separable form with a fixed cost, the FDC methods result in subsidy-free prices.

The distinction between FDC prices based on test period data and demand-compatible FDC prices is relevant here. By holding quantities fixed in the cost game it is as if we are using test period quantities and costs. As pointed out above, when these prices are actually put into effect, quantities will change from their test period levels. When they do, the breakeven constraint will be violated and prices will not be subsidy-free. If demand-compatible FDC prices are arrived at, they will satisfy the subsidy-free constraints of the cost game and will not violate the benefit constraints, either.

This discussion confirms a central contention of economists: that FDC prices are not tests for cross subsidy. Since any FDC method is subsidy free, no single one can be used as a test for cross subsidy. On the other hand, the extensive critical discussion by economists about FDC prices seems to have missed the other point made in this discussion, which is also germane; that when the firm's joint cost function is additively separable, the FDC prices are themselves subsidy-free. Therefore, they are not entirely devoid of merit.[11]

---

[11] We should point out briefly a connection between absence of cross subsidy and economic efficiency. To be subsidy-free, revenues for each possible grouping of services must at least equal the incremental cost of that grouping. If this condition were violated, not only would cross subsidy exist, but our discussion of economic efficiency above indicates that total surplus could be increased by going to a subsidy-free set of prices. It should also be noted that Brown and Heal [1985] have proposed using a system of optimal excise taxes to combine efficient consumer prices with subsidy-free producer prices.

D. The axiomatic approach to cost-sharing prices

This approach to common cost allocation differs both from traditional FDC pricing and from the game-theoretic approach, although it is related to the latter. FDC pricing starts with arbitrarily chosen ways of dividing up the common costs and examines the effects of the different allocation schemes. The game-theoretic approach involves a careful definition of cross subsidy. The axiomatic approach is not concerned directly with the economic effects of different allocation schemes, but begins by listing intuitively desirable features of any allocation scheme. Taking these desirable features as axioms, this body of research then deduces the features of prices which are consistent with the axioms.

The precise axioms that one writes down depends in part on whether the firm's cost function has a positive fixed cost or not. The fixed cost issue is, in turn, determined in part by whether one is dealing in the short or long run. It is often argued that in the long run all costs are variable. Axioms for the case where fixed costs are zero are presented in Mirman and Tauman [1982], Billera and Heath [1982] and Samet and Tauman [1982]. On the other hand, the time periods that are relevant for regulatory action are usually quite short, so that one can never be sure that the firm's cost function is that which minimizes total costs at current output. Mirman, Samet and Tauman [1983] (MST) discuss this point and present six axioms for cost allocation where the cost function is not assumed to represent the long run efficient technology for the given level of output and where a fixed cost is present.

For this analysis we envision a joint cost function C where

$$C = F + V(Q_1, Q_2, ..., Q_N) . \tag{7}$$

$V(Q_1, Q_2, ..., Q_N)$ is the variable cost function of the firm; it depends in a general way on all N of the firm's outputs. There are assumed to be no set-up costs for each service. For simplicity we will denote the list of outputs $Q_1, Q_2, ..., Q_N$ simply by Q and the total cost function either by C or $F + V$, depending on convenience. Let P denote the full list of prices $P_1, P_2, ..., P_N$. MST propose the following axioms:

Axiom 1: Cost Sharing. An allocation mechanism which results in prices P for given set of outputs Q and cost function C must cover its total costs.

Axiom 2: Rescaling. If the scales of measurement of the commodities are changed, then a sensible allocation mechanism should result in prices P which change accordingly.

Axiom 3: Consistency. Suppose that for a subset M of outputs costs depend only on total output $Q_1 + Q_2 + \cdots + Q_M$. Then the prices of any two outputs in M should be the same.

Axiom 4: Positivity. Consider two alternative total cost functions C and $\tilde{C}$ where $C \geqslant \tilde{C}$ at zero output and the cost difference $C - \tilde{C}$ increases as outputs rise. A sensible allocation mechanism should result in higher prices under C than under $\tilde{C}$.

Axiom 5: Additivity of Allocations. Suppose that the costs of producing a given set of outputs $Q = (Q_1, Q_2, ..., Q_N)$ can be separated into K different "stages", each with its own variable cost $G_k(Q)$, where k labels the stage. Thus $V(Q)$ is the sum of costs from the K stages:

$$V(Q) = G_1(Q) + G_2(Q) + \cdots + G_K(Q) .$$

Then the allocation mechanism should assign a fraction f_k of the common cost to each stage and the allocation $f_k F$ should be added to each stage's variable cost. Also, total revenue for the outputs Q should be expressable as the sum of each stage's cost:

$$\text{Total revenue} = \sum_{k=1}^{K} \left[G_k(Q) + f_k F \right] .$$

Axiom 6: Correlation. For any two stages k and ℓ, if $G_k > G_\ell$, then $f_k > f_\ell$.

Discussion. Axiom 1 simply requires that the firm break even across all services. It is this axiom which says that we are to deal with complete allocation of the common costs. Axiom 2 seems innocuous. The consistency axiom (Axiom 3) really says that all goods with the same marginal cost should be priced the same. It refers to situations where cost depends on total output of some group of services. For example the capacity cost of an electric utility depends on total peak demand, which is the sum of the demands of all customer classes in the peak period. If cost depends only on the sum $Q_1 + Q_2 + \cdots + Q_M$, then a one unit increase in one output has the same effect on total output and, hence, on costs as a one unit increase in another output. This axiom makes it clear that the prices which we derive from the six axioms have no special claim to efficiency. Under the consistency axiom, goods with the same marginal cost get the same price, even when their price elasticities of demand are much different. As we saw above in our discussion of Ramsey pricing, services with relatively low price elasticities of demand should be priced higher than more price-elastic services, even if their marginal costs are the same. The positivity axiom also deals with marginal costs. In order for one cost function C to increase with output more quickly than another cost function $\tilde{C}$, it is both necessary and sufficient that C have higher marginal costs at every point that $\tilde{C}$. Positivity says, therefore, that if we have one cost function C with higher marginal costs than another $\tilde{C}$, then a reasonable allocation mechanism should assign C higher prices than $\tilde{C}$. Axiom 5 and 6 should be discussed together. They state that if total variable costs V can be written as the sum of additive components G_k, then each component should be assigned an additive share of the common costs which correlates with the relative size of G_k. Consider the special case where k denotes a service and where G_k depends only on output Q_k, so that $G_k(Q_k)$ can be interpreted as the variable cost of service k. Viewed in this light, Axioms 5 and 6 are saying that common costs should be allocated as add-ons to the variable cost of each service in such a way that the allocation to any two services correlate with their relative variable costs. In a loose sense, this says that services which are relatively costly in the short run (high variable cost) will account for a relatively high share of long run cost, too. Hence they should get a relatively high share of the fixed cost, too.

Given these axioms, Mirman, Samet and Tauman (MST) prove a very strong theorem about the prices for the various outputs which are consistent with the axioms. To understand their result we introduce the concept of the *Aumann-Shapley price*.[12] In Figure 3.6 we consider the two-service case. Notice the ray connecting the origin with specified output levels $(\hat{Q}_1, \hat{Q}_2)$. At each point along that ray we compute the marginal cost of an additional unit of each service and then average all of these marginal costs. The result, an "averaged" marginal cost, is the Aumann-Shapley price for service i, denoted by ASP_i. MST show that given their axioms, the only price mechanism which is consistent with all six is the following modified Aumann-Shapley price:

$$P_i = \frac{ASP_i}{Q_i} \times \left[1 + \frac{F}{V(Q_1, Q_2, ..., Q_N)} \right].$$

Equivalently, total revenue for service i is given by

$$R_i = ASP_i \times \left[1 + \frac{F}{V} \right].$$

---

[12] See Aumann and Shapley [1974].

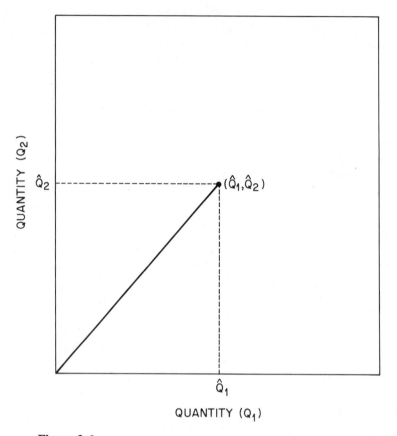

Figure 3.6

Thus, the prices which are consistent with the six MST axioms are the Aumann-Shapley prices multiplied by a factor which enables total costs to be covered.

The Aumann-Shapley price for a general variable cost V does not have a ready intuitive motivation. However, consider the special case where the variable costs are additively separable among services and where there are no special set-up costs particular to a given service:

$$C = F + \sum_{i=1}^{N} V_i(Q_i) \,.$$

This case is very restrictive, but in most applied work economists use a cost function of this form.[13] In this special case, the Aumann-Shapley price for service i is equal to $V_i(Q_i)$ and the MST axioms imply

$$R_i = V_i(Q_i) \times \left[1 + \frac{F}{\sum\limits_{i=1}^{N} V_i(Q_i)} \right].$$

But this is simply the revenue that is given by the ACM method of fully distributed costs. In other words, when the cost function is additively separable, the only price mechanism satisfying the six axioms of Mirman, Samet and Tauman is the ACM method of fully distributed costing.

E. Conclusions on FDC pricing

This discussion has aimed to bring out the salient points concerning the principal methods of common cost allocation which are not based explicitly on efficient pricing. Economists have long criticized FDC methods on three main grounds: (1) that they ignore pricing efficiency (2) that they have nothing to do with cross subsidy and (3) that they are arbitrary and lack a conceptual foundation. We have illustrated numerically the efficiency shortcomings of FDC pricing and our discussion indeed reveals that they are not tests for the presence of cross subsidy, in the sense that subsidy-free prices can differ from any one or all of the FDC allocations. All the same, the FDC methods may be less silly than they seem. Specifically, when the firm's joint cost function is additively separable with a fixed cost, the FDC methods are themselves subsidy-free. Also, because the ACM method is simply the modified Aumann-Shapley price when the cost function is separable, this method, at least, has a clear axiomatic foundation. Hence, it is not open to the charge of being arbitrary.

3.5 Conclusions

A main theme of this chapter is that economic efficiency can be increased by choosing the prices of a regulated monopolist so as to maximize the sum of consumer surplus and producer surplus. If this can be done in an unconstrained manner, the optimal set of prices is such that price is equal to marginal cost in each of the regulated monopolist's markets. If the regulated monopolist is producing under

---

[13] See, for example Willig and Bailey [1977], Griffin [1982] and Marfisi et al., [1980].

conditions of decreasing average cost and if the firm must break even out of its own sales, then we must calculate prices which maximize total surplus subject to a breakeven constraint. We call such prices Ramsey prices. In the special case where the monopolist's markets have independent demands, the Ramsey prices can be expressed in the famous inverse elasticity rule.

As an alternative to this approach to ratemaking we have FDC pricing. Although FDC pricing has no claim to economic efficiency and is to a large degree arbitrary, a practical difference between Ramsey pricing and FDC pricing is that FDC prices can be calculated from the regulated monopolist's books. Ramsey pricing requires this type of information but also uses estimates of price elasticities of demand. Because of the difficulty in estimating these elasticities precisely, practitioners of FDC pricing have often derided Ramsey pricing as impractical. The issue of practicality is not so easily decided, however. Because FDC pricing completely ignores price elasticity of demand, whenever a new set of FDC prices involves substantial deviation from a pre-existing set of prices, the firm is guaranteed not to break exactly even. A surplus or deficit must result. Indeed, for this very reason, adjustments for "repression" effects of prices changes (i.e., price elasticity of demand) are becoming accepted in many regulatory jurisdictions. If one grants that FDC pricing requires adjustment for "repression," some of the claimed advantage of FDC over Ramsey pricing disappears. On the other hand, there are plausible cases in FDC prices are subsidy-free and when the ACM method has a firm axiomatic foundation.

CHAPTER 4

Nonuniform pricing I

4.1 Introduction

In the previous chapter we developed the major theme of second-best pricing: to cover total costs of the regulated firm with minimum deadweight loss. The term *Ramsey prices* was used to refer to the set of uniform prices which maximize total surplus - minimizing dead-weight loss - subject to the breakeven constraint. Ramsey prices do this by charging different prices to the regulated firm's various markets with the aim of generating the largest amounts of contribution from markets in which a high markup of price over marginal cost will perturb consumption levels least from what would be achieved with full marginal cost pricing. In this chapter we will broaden the analysis to include price structures which permit us to vary prices not only between markets, but also between consumers in the same market.

The device for doing this is called the nonuniform price schedule. A *nonuniform price schedule* is a tariff for one or more goods in which the consumer's total outlay does not simply rise proportionately with the amounts of the goods he purchases; quantity discounts and quantity premia are permitted. Analogously, we call a tariff a *uniform price schedule* when total outlay is simply proportional to the amount purchased. Thus, Ramsey prices are the uniform prices which maximize total surplus subject to the constraint that the regulated firm break even. An example of a nonuniform price schedule is given in Figure 4.1, where we depict total outlay per month at different consumption levels under a residential electricity tariff used by the Commonwealth Edison Company in 1976.[1] This tariff consists of a monthly fixed charge of $1.20 and a usage charge of 4.18 cents per kilowatt hour (kwh) for the first 100 kwh and 3.14 cents per kwh for consumption in excess of 100 kwh.

---

[1] This tariff was taken from the *National Electric Rate Book* for 1976.

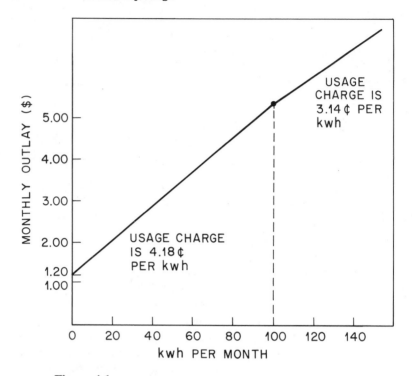

Figure 4.1

Under this tariff the consumer paid an outlay of $5.38 per month for monthly consumption of 100 kwh. For 200 kwh, total outlay was $8.52, which is less than twice the outlay for 100 kwh, indicating a substantial quantity discount.

The simplest type of nonuniform price schedule is the two-part tariff. Under a two-part tariff, the consumer must pay an entry fee E in order to buy any positive amount at a usage charge P which does not vary with the quantity purchased. Only by consuming nothing can he escape the entry fee. Therefore, at any positive consumption level Q, the consumer pays a total outlay $R(Q)$ equal to

$$R(Q) = E + PQ \ .$$

Figure 4.2 depicts a two-part tariff. In such a tariff, the amount a consumer must pay for an additional unit is constant at level P. It is common in regulated industries to encounter tariffs where the price for an additional unit varies with the amount consumed. These are called multipart tariffs. For example, the outlay function could take the form shown in Figure 4.3, where after paying the entry fee of $.60 a

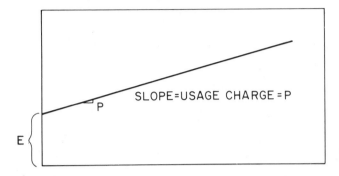

Figure 4.2

consumer pays $.02 per unit for the first 100 units, $.015 per unit for the second 100 units and $.01 per unit for any additional consumption. This is a four-part tariff of the declining-block type common to most regulated industries. More generally, an n-part tariff has an entry fee E and $n - 1$ rate blocks, each with its own usage charges. In the limit as the number of rate steps gets very large, a nonuniform price schedule

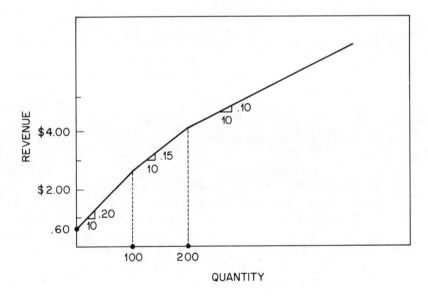

Figure 4.3

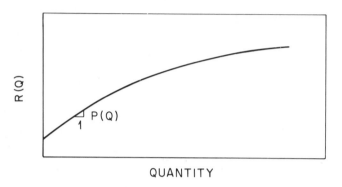

Figure 4.4

could be a smooth outlay function as in Figure 4.4. The usage charge at each initial consumption level Q is called the *marginal price at* Q, and we denote it by $P(Q)$. Mathematically, it is the change in total outlay R caused by increasing consumption from Q to $Q + \Delta Q$. Normalizing by the amount of the change,

$$P(Q) = \frac{R(Q+\Delta Q) - R(Q)}{\Delta Q}. \tag{1}$$

In the Commonwealth Edison Tariff the marginal prices are 4.18 cents per kwh for up to 100 kwh and 3.14 cents per kwh thereafter. For the two-part tariff, the marginal price is the same for all Q. In the case of the four part tariff,

$$P(Q) = .02 \ , \ 0 < Q \leq 100$$

$$= .015 \ , \ 100 < Q \leq 200$$

$$= .01 \quad \text{thereafter.}$$

A uniform price is simply a two-part tariff with a zero entry fee.

In this chapter we will introduce the theory of optimal nonuniform pricing in the case of a single product. The key ideas of the discussion are:

— In cases where marginal cost pricing will not cover the total costs of the firm, nonuniform prices can be used to increase total surplus above the level possible using only uniform prices.

— Nonuniform pricing is a method of tailoring prices in the same market to different consumers according to their underlying tastes for the good in question.

— The regulated firm cannot identify individual consumers by type and charge each consumer a separate price. Instead, the firm uses quantity consumed as a signal indicating a consumer's underlying taste for the good, and designs a nonuniform price schedule so as to price consumers differently according to the amount they buy.

— Relative to a uniform price regime where price exceeds marginal cost, an appropriately designed nonuniform price schedule can make all consumers and the firm better off. In a sense, then, there can be winners and no losers in a move from a uniform price to an appropriately designed nonuniform price schedule.

— In order to minimize deadweight loss (maximize total surplus) the regulator can design the nonuniform price schedule so that (a) most consumers buy at quantity levels where marginal prices are closer to marginal cost that they would be under Ramsey pricing and (b) total cost to the firm is covered by ensuring that consumers with the greatest demands make high contributions on their infra-marginal units of consumption.

4.2 Basic concepts

In discussing uniform pricing we assumed explicitly that all consumers in a given market were alike. In reality, of course, consumers differ between themselves in their taste for almost any good. For example, Pavarini [1979] analyzed usage of local telephone service in a number of localities, under tariffs in which usage charges were zero. Facing flat rate charges consumers' monthly calls varied widely. The average calling rate was 117 calls per month, while the median was only 93. This difference between mean and median results from the long upper tail of the distribution. Therefore, we must broaden our pricing analysis to account for diversity in taste.

To make the discussion simple, suppose that there are two consumers in the market, Big and Little. At any price, Big consumes more than does Little. The firm producing the commodity in question has a simple cost structure consisting of a fixed cost, F, and a constant marginal cost, c. At any price P, the firm must produce an amount $Q(P)$ which is equal to the sum of Big's demand, $Q_B(P)$ and Little's demand, $Q_L(P)$. Therefore, its total cost is given by

$$F + c \cdot Q(P) = F + c \cdot (Q_B(P) + Q_L(P)) \ .$$

Now, under uniform pricing, the only way the firm can break even is to set a price $\bar{P}$ so that at the resulting demand $Q(\bar{P})$, price is equal to

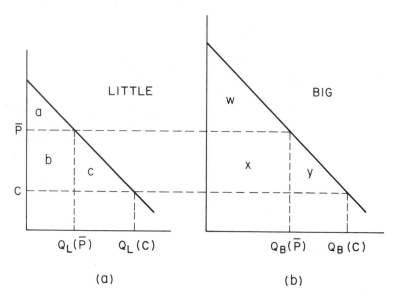

Figure 4.5

average cost. At this price the two consumers achieve surplus levels CS_L and CS_B given as areas "a" and "w" in Figures 4.5a and 4.5b, respectively. Including producer surplus, the total deadweight loss is given by the sum of areas "c" and "y". How can this deadweight loss be reduced?

In 1946 R. H. Coase suggested a special type of two-part tariff as a solution to this problem: set the marginal price (usage charge) equal to the regulated firm's marginal cost and set the entry fee at a level sufficient to cover the firm's total costs when it is paid by each consumer. By setting the usage charge equal to marginal cost, it was hoped that the correct amount of consumption would take place and that the entry fee would cover total costs without being itself a pricing distortion. In our two-consumer example, set E, an entry fee equal to $F/2$ and P equal to marginal cost, c.

Assuming that they can afford to pay an entry fee equal to $F/2$, Big and Little make their consumption decision based only on the marginal price (usage charge). The reason for this is that once the entry fee is paid it ceases to affect how much Big and Little pay for what they consume. Both consumers will buy up to the point where their willingness to pay is just equal to the marginal price P, where price equals marginal cost under the Coase two-part tariff; therefore Big buys $Q_B(c)$ and Little buys $Q_L(c)$.

It is easy to check that the firm will recover its costs under this tariff.

Little pays an outlay of $F/2 + Q_L(c) \cdot c$, Big pays $F/2 + Q_B(c) \cdot c$, so that the firm's total revenues are

$$\frac{F}{2} + Q_L(c) \cdot c + \frac{F}{2} + Q_B(c) \cdot c = F + c \cdot (Q_L(c) + Q_B(c))$$

which is exactly total cost. Most importantly, however, both consumers are buying the same amounts they would buy under straight marginal cost pricing. Deadweight loss is eliminated. The only difference from the outcome under marginal cost pricing is that an amount F is transferred from consumers to the firm. This transfer is only a distributional effect. It does not reduce total surplus below the level which would result from marginal cost pricing. In effect, Coase decoupled the problem of inducing the efficient level of consumption from the problem of covering the regulated firm's total costs.

The Coase two-part tariff seems to have brought about a simple, perfect solution. At times, however, it may go awry, because our discussion made the implicit assumption that with $E = F/2$ Little still found it worthwhile to go on consuming the good, when he could avoid paying the entry fee entirely by dropping out of the market and buying nothing. It could well be that the increase in potential consumer surplus occasioned by dropping the usage charge to marginal cost is more than cancelled out by the magnitude of the entry fee. In Figure 4.5a, if the quantity $F/2$ is greater than areas "a" plus "b" plus "c" then even with a marginal price equal to marginal cost, Little earns negative consumer surplus and could do better - i.e., earn a zero surplus - by ceasing to consume the good altogether. From the standpoint of total surplus over the two consumers, it might be better to find some price structure which will keep Little in the market, even if it is necessary to set a marginal price different from marginal cost (and accept some inefficiency in the consumption of the good) in order to do so.

Therefore, there are two problems which must be faced in pricing the output of the regulated firm: first, to price consumption efficiently and, second, to make sure the correct number of consumers participate in the market. Sometimes there will be a tradeoff between these two goals. If marginal prices are set at or close to marginal cost, so as to generate efficient consumption, the breakeven requirement on the firm may require an entry fee so high as to price too many consumers out of the market.

There is a possibility of avoiding this tradeoff and finessing the problem. If the regulators could identify the two consumers and determine prices for each of them separately, then they could charge each consumer a different two-part tariff. Each tariff would have marginal price equal to marginal cost, but Little's entry fee could be made small enough to keep him from dropping out of the market. Big's entry fee would be correspondingly higher. The two entry fees E_L and E_B would have to add up to F and obey the constraint that neither fee makes consumer surplus negative. In terms of Figures 4.5a and 4.5b E_L is no greater than the sum of "a", "b" and "c" and E_B is less than or equal to the sum of "w", "x" and "y". (If no such pair of entry fees can be found, then the product should be dropped, because it is not worth to consumers what it costs to produce.) Once again, deadweight loss has been entirely eliminated, total surplus is at the level which would be achieved under marginal cost pricing, and the firm has covered its costs.

The difficulty with this approach is that it may be impractical or illegal to charge different entry fees to the two consumers and keep Big from buying on Little's two-part tariff, thereby paying a lower entry fee. However, this suggests that there is some advantage from the standpoint of efficiency in sorting different consumers onto different tariffs if it could be done by non-coercive means. This constitutes the main theme of nonuniform pricing.

To see how this might be done, consider a "before-and-after" situation. Initially, the firm charges a uniform price equal to average cost

$$\bar{P} = \frac{F}{Q_L(\bar{P}) + Q_B(\bar{P})} + c = \text{average cost with price } \bar{P}$$

as before. The firm cannot identify and sort the two consumers, but it knows that two consumer types exist (even if it can't put names to them) and it knows their demand curves. Therefore, the firm can modify its price structure knowing how each consumer type will react to the change.

For example, the regulator can offer a two-part tariff as an alternative to buying at the uniform price $\bar{P}$: the marginal price (usage charge) is P^*, which is above marginal cost, but less than $\bar{P}$. The entry fee is equal to Big's initial consumption level at the average cost price $\bar{P}$ multiplied by the difference $\bar{P} - P^*$. That is

$$E = Q_B(\bar{P}) \cdot (\bar{P} - P^*)$$

$$c \leqslant P^* < \bar{P}.$$

The regulated firm gives each consumer the choice of the tariff package under which to buy. How will they choose?

Consider Figure 4.6. If Little buys at the uniform price $\bar{P}$ he earns consumer surplus equal to the area "a" in the figure. If he were to buy at the two-part tariff, the lower marginal price P^* would increase his consumption to $Q_L(P^*)$ and would expand his potential surplus by the

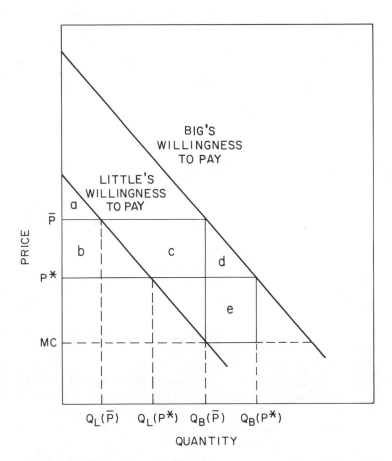

Figure 4.6

trapezoidal area "b". However, the entry fee which he would have to pay for the opportunity to take advantage of the lower marginal price is equal to area "b" plus "c". This means that the entry fee would cut into the triangle "a", so that Little's consumer surplus under the two-part tariff would be lower than if he stuck to the original uniform price. Therefore, the offer of the optional two-part tariff does not change Little's behavior; he is best off buying under the uniform price option $\bar{P}$.

For Big, though, the outcome is different. The lower marginal price P^* raises Big's consumption to $Q_B(P^*)$ and increases his potential surplus by areas "b," "c" and "d". The entry fee only taxes away "b" plus "c," leaving Big's surplus under the tariff higher than under $\bar{P}$ by the amount of the triangle "d". Therefore, Big will select the two-part tariff option over the uniform price option.

Finally, consider the position of the firm. It earns the same contribution from Little as before because Little's behavior has not changed. However, it is getting a higher profit from Big than under the average price regime. To see this, the first-round effect of the lower marginal price is to reduce contribution from Big by the amount of his old consumption times the price change. But this is just the rectangle "b" plus "c", which is restored to the firm because it is equal to the entry fee of the two-part tariff. In addition, since P^* exceeds marginal cost, the expansion of Big's demand from $Q(\bar{P})$ to $Q_B(P^*)$ must yield a profit to the firm equal to the rectangle "e". Therefore, since the firm was breaking even under the average cost price $\bar{P}$, it must make a positive producer surplus when the optional two-part tariff is offered.

By virtue of offering the optional two-part tariff, total surplus has gone up, and neither Big nor Little is worse off. Little's position is unchanged with the introduction of the two-part tariff, since he elects not to use it. Both Big and the firm are better off than previously.[2] We could make all parties strictly better off than under the simple price $\bar{P}$ by rebating some of the firm's extra profit "e" to Little, who would be identified to the firm simply as the consumer buying on the uniform price option.

In Figures 4.7 and 4.8 we see the precise connection between the offering of the two alternative tariff options and the nonuniform price schedule. In Figure 4.7 we depict total outlay under the uniform price $\bar{P}$ and the two-part tariff. Up to a consumption level $\hat{Q}$ the uniform price $\bar{P}$ dominates the two-part tariff, in the sense that for $Q < \hat{Q}$ the size of the entry fee in the two-part tariff makes it cheaper to buy under the uniform price option. For consumption greater than $\hat{Q}$ the lower marginal price P^* under the two-part tariff makes the latter cheaper than the uniform price, despite the entry fee. The edged portions of the two tariff options represent the undominated portions of each, and the effect of the two tariff options is as if the regulator were to have put into effect a single nonuniform price schedule $R(Q)$ given by the edged curve. In Figure 4.8 we see that the marginal price function $P(Q)$ of this nonuniform price schedule has two rate blocks.

Examples of such optional tariffs abound. In the car rental business a customer can usually decide whether to rent a car at a high charge per mile or to pay a flat rate. For short distances, it is cheaper to pay the mileage charge; for long distances, the flat rate is cheaper. Another

2

This discussion is a simplified version of the Pareto dominance result due to Willig [1978], who used a much more complicated technique. To the best of our recollection, the graphical illustration of Willig's result which we have used here is due to John Panzar.

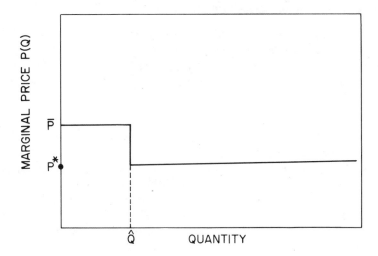

Figure 4.7

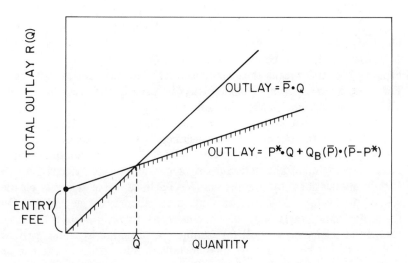

Figure 4.8

example is provided by local telephone service, where some local telephone companies provide several different tariff options ranging from a flat monthly rate to a lifeline tariff with a very low entry fee and high charges for usage.

4.3 A closer look at consumer behavior

Before exploring nonuniform pricing in any greater detail, it is necessary to develop a better way to characterize consumer demand and the fact that consumers have varying tastes for the products of the regulated firm. We will assume that consumer demand takes the form

$$Q_D = q(P, \theta)$$

where P is marginal price and θ is a taste variable. The economics literature treats the effect of θ in two different ways. First, the higher a consumer's taste for the good, as measured by θ, the greater his surplus from consuming it. This requirement seems fairly innocuous and the consumers preferences are called *weakly monotonic* in θ when it is met. Most of the results presented below depend on a stronger assumption: that *demand* increases with his taste parameter θ. This is referred to as *strong monotonicity*.

To see the relationship between weak monotonicity and strong monotonicity, see Figure 4.9. A consumer with a high value of θ has a demand curve which lies to the right of the demand curve of a consumer with a low value of θ (strong monotonicity). Therefore, at any given price P his consumer surplus is higher (weak monotonicity). On the other hand, Figure 4.10 shows that the high-θ consumer's consumer surplus can be higher than that of the low-θ consumer, but his demand less; this means the two consumers' demand curves must cross. For this reason, strong monotonicity is usually referred to as the *noncrossing assumption* about demands.

How would one measure the taste variable or determine its distribution in the population of consumers? In some cases, θ may be easily observable. In residential electricity demand, for example, family income is an important determinant of consumption of electricity. In telecommunications, the number of WATS lines leased depends on the size of the customer, as measured by sales, labor force, assets, etc. On the other hand, taste may be so elusive as to be unmeasurable. In residential telephone service, for example, a subscriber's calling pattern will depend on how much he likes to talk to other people, whether he needs to use the telephone for performing certain tasks for which he could also travel, where his best friends live, etc. These influences are so diverse that they are not directly measurable for practical purposes.

For the purposes of nonuniform pricing it is important to know the frequency distribution of θ. In the case where the taste variable is readily measured, such as income, it may be easy to construct the frequency distribution directly from observed data. For example, in the case of residential electricity demand, much is known about the

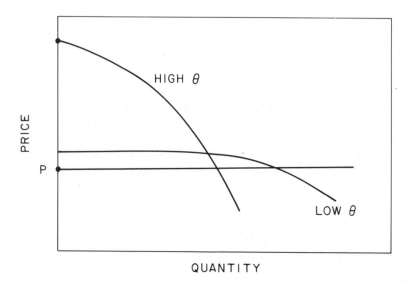

Figure 4.9

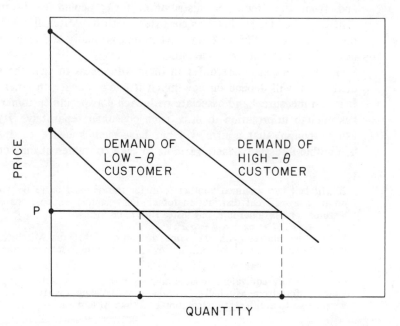

Figure 4.10

distribution of family income. In the case where θ is not directly observable, to construct a frequency distribution of θ usually requires strong assumptions and ingenuity. Bridger Mitchell [1978] used both in his study on the pricing of local telephone service. He had at his disposal the frequency distribution of consumption of local telephone service. He assumed that demand took the form

$$q(P,\theta) = (\alpha - P)\cdot\theta$$

where α is a constant and P is the usage charge. Thus, the demand function is linear in price and proportional to the taste variable θ. His consumption data came from areas in which local telephone service was priced at a flat rate, so that for anyone willing to pay the entry fee, P was equal to zero. Therefore, he regarded demand as being generated by the formula

$$Q = \alpha\theta.$$

From other considerations Mitchell was able to estimate α, so he could simply compute θ from

$$\frac{Q}{\alpha} = \theta$$

and from the frequency distribution for Q could easily infer the distribution of tastes that was consistent with it. Mitchell assumed that the natural logarithm of θ was distributed normally and estimated it to have mean 6.15 and variance .3025.[3]

Given that consumers differ in their willingness to pay, the response of the firm will depend on how much it knows about consumers' tastes. If it can measure θ and associate with each θ a specific customer, then it has enough information to price each consumer separately. It is more usual, though, that a firm will not have such knowledge. Instead of being able to assign a taste variable to each consumer, it may only have

---

[3]

If Mitchell had assumed another form for the demand curve he would have obtained a different distribution for θ. For example, suppose that demands were not proportional in θ, but instead took the form
$$Q(P,\theta) = \alpha_0 + \alpha_1\theta - \alpha_2 P.$$
Even if we started with the same distribution of Q as Mitchell did, the implied distribution of θ would not even be lognormal, let alone the same as Mitchell's. We can write $Q(P,\theta) = \alpha_0^* + \alpha_1\theta$ for $\alpha_0^* = \alpha_0 + \alpha_2\bar{P}$ which is observationally equivalent to assuming $\alpha_2 = 0$. In this case $\theta = [Q - \alpha_0^*]/\alpha_1$ which differs from Mitchell's formula. For the same distribution of Q, this would lead to a different distribution of θ than Mitchell's.

some idea of the distribution of tastes across the population of consumers. In our discussion of nonuniform pricing, we will assume that the firm only has access to the distribution of θ, and cannot classify specific consumers by type. With such information the firm can set a nonuniform price schedule knowing how many consumers will locate themselves at each point on it.[4]

To see this, assume that the firm knows the distribution of θ and also knows each consumer type's demand function $q(P,\theta)$. Let the firm offer a three-part tariff with entry fee E and marginal prices equal to P_1 for the first Q_1 units and $P_2 < P_1$ for consumption greater than Q_1. To see who will buy on the first rate block (at marginal price P_1), it is necessary to know if some consumers will buy none of the good at all because of the size of the entry fee. It may be that the entry fee will deter nobody from entering the market. That is, for the consumer with the least taste for the good of any consumer $(\theta = \underline{\theta})$ consumer surplus is positive even with the entry fee. This outcome seems likely in such cases as residential electricity consumption, where it is hard to imagine a consumer completely dropping off the local power company's distribution net even with a very high entry fee. On the other hand, in some regulated markets there is evidence that some consumers may be priced out of any consumption. The 1970 census indicated, for example, that about 13 percent of households[5] did not have telephones. As of the 1980 census, the comparable figure had dropped to about 7 percent, but the debate concerning the effects of the telephone access charges proposed in 1983 by the FCC indicates that the figure could rise again if local telephone rates rise sharply. In interstate telephone markets it is common to find customers who place no calls to certain mileage bands at peak periods. Therefore, there may well exist some consumer of type θ_0 greater than or equal to the lower limit $\underline{\theta}$ who is just indifferent between buying and dropping out of the market. Consumers with θ less than θ_0 buy nothing. Therefore, all customers with $\theta > \theta_0$ will make positive surplus and will stay in the market.

---

[4]

There is an alternate interpretation of this analytical framework. One could suppose that there is a single aggregate demand curve $Q(P,\theta)$ but where θ represents a random variable whose realization is unknown to the firm at the time its tariff is to be chosen. Thus, the different portions of a nonuniform price schedule would be interpreted as the optional buying plans that the consumer would select in different *expost* realizations of θ. Leland and Meyer [1976] derive optimal two-part tariffs under this interpretation.

[5]

See Mitchell [1976], page 50.

Next, the regulator needs to know how many consumers will buy on the first rate block and how many will locate themselves on the second block. To make the discussion easier at this point, we assume strong monotonicity of preferences, meaning that higher values of θ are associated with high levels of demand. Consider a consumer of type $\tilde{\theta}$ in Figure 4.11; his demand curve cuts P_1 at $\tilde{Q}$ units of consumption and just touches P_2 from below. Clearly, $\tilde{\theta}$ should stay on the first rate block, because from $\tilde{Q}$ to Q_1 he is paying P_1 per unit, which exceeds his willingness to pay for each unit in that range. Thus, in going from $\tilde{Q}$ to Q_1 customer $\tilde{\theta}$ *reduces* his consumer surplus by the amount "a" plus "c"; he is better off consuming $\tilde{Q}$ at a marginal price P_1. Now look at consumer type $\tilde{\tilde{\theta}}$, whose willingness to pay just touches P_1 from above at Q_1 and cuts P_2 at $\tilde{\tilde{Q}}$. From Q_1 to $\tilde{\tilde{Q}}$ this type of consumer adds "b" plus "d" to his consumer surplus, so he will buy $\tilde{\tilde{Q}}$ in the second rate block. Since $\tilde{\theta}$ is strictly better off on P_1 and $\tilde{\tilde{\theta}}$ is strictly better off on P_2, there must exist some θ_1 between $\tilde{\theta}$ and $\tilde{\tilde{\theta}}$ who is just indifferent between the two blocks. Figure 4.11 shows θ_1's willingness to pay curve cutting P_1 at Q_A and P_2 at Q_B. The triangle "a" represents the loss in consumer surplus which θ_1 incurs on consumption from Q_A to Q_1, where the marginal price P_1 exceeds his willingness to pay. Triangle "b" shows an equal gain from Q_1 to Q_B, leaving θ_1 indifferent between the first and second rate blocks. Therefore, all customers with taste indices between θ_0 and θ_1 will buy on the first rate block, buying according to their demand curves. All consumers with θ greater than θ_1 will buy on the second rate block. Writing a consumer's demand curve as $q(P,\theta)$, for consumers on the first block $Q = q(P_1, \theta)$ and for consumers on the second block $Q = q(P_2, \theta)$. Nobody will consume quantities between Q_A and Q_B.

A numerical example may make these points clearer. Mitchell estimated the distribution of θ for local telephone service to be lognormal with a logarithmic mean of 6.15 and standard deviation of .55. Mitchell used the following demand curve:

$$q(P,\theta) = (.202-P)\cdot\theta .$$

Now suppose that the following three-part tariff were offered:

$$E = 4.00$$

$$P_1 = .04 \quad \text{for} \quad 0 \leqq Q \leqq 110$$

$$P_2 = .03 \quad \text{for} \quad Q > 110 .$$

Since for given θ the demand curve is just a straight line, potential consumer surplus at any given price is a triangle with area equal to

$$(.202-P)^2 \cdot \frac{\theta}{2}.$$

Assume that θ_0, the consumer who is indifferent to consuming a small amount and not consuming at all, buys on the first rate block. The value θ_0 is given by setting consumer surplus equal to zero with an entry fee of $4.00:

$$(.202-.04)^2 \cdot \frac{\theta_0}{2} - 4.00 = 0$$

or

$$\theta_0 = \frac{8}{(.162)^2} = 304.83.$$

In order for "a" to equal "b" in Figure 4.11, θ_1's demand curve must cut the vertical line at Q_1 exactly in half. In terms of our example, this means that at $Q = 110$, the willingness to pay of θ_1 must be equal to .035. Knowing this, we can solve for θ_1 from the demand equation:

$$110 = (.202-.035) \cdot \theta_1, \quad \text{or } \theta_1 = \frac{110}{.167} = 658.68.$$

In terms of Figure 4.11, the consumers $\tilde{\theta}$ and $\tilde{\tilde{\theta}}$ are found by solving the following two equations:

$$110 = (.202-.03) \cdot \tilde{\theta}, \quad 110 = (.202-.04) \cdot \tilde{\tilde{\theta}}$$

so that $\tilde{\theta} = 639.54$ and $\tilde{\tilde{\theta}} = 679.01$. The corresponding borderline consumption level Q_A and Q_B are given by

$$Q_A = (.202-.04) \cdot \theta_1 = 106.71$$

$$Q_B = (.202-.03) \cdot \theta_1 = 113.29.$$

Thus, customers with taste indices lying between 304.83 and 658.68 buy in the first rate block at a usage charge of $.04. Their individual demands are given by $Q = .162\theta$ and the maximum consumption to take place in the first rate block is $Q_1 = 106.71$. Customers with θ greater than or equal to 658.68 buy in the second rate block and pay a usage charge of $.03, and the minimum consumption in this rate block is 113.29. Nobody consumes between 106.71 and 113.29.

Based on the underlying distribution of θ, we can now plot the frequency distribution of consumption which will occur under this

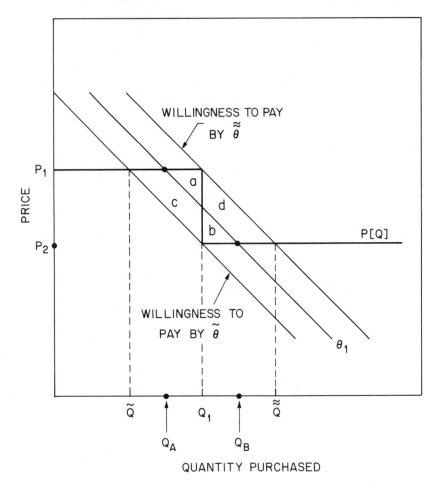

Figure 4.11

three-part tariff. For $Q \leqq 106.71$ consumption takes place according to the rule $Q = .162\theta$ For $Q \geqq 113.29$, $Q = .172\theta$. The distribution of θ is given in Figure 4.12. In Figure 4.13 we show the distribution of Q which results.

This example illustrates a critical step in the rate setting process. Given the distribution of tastes and individual demand behavior, to evaluate a particular tariff requires that we estimate the distribution of consumers along the different rate blocks of that tariff.

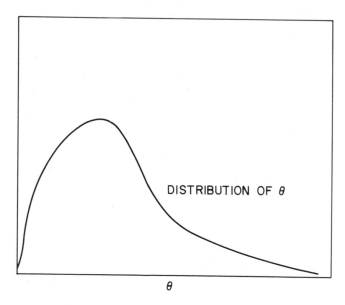

DISTRIBUTION OF θ

θ

Figure 4.12

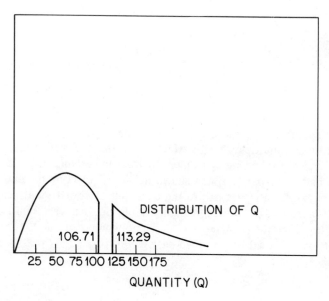

DISTRIBUTION OF Q

106.71   113.29

25 50 75 100 125 150 175

QUANTITY (Q)

Figure 4.13

4.4 Multipart tariffs

A. Preliminary

As we have seen, the economic efficiency of nonuniform prices stems from the fact that they induce consumers to sort themselves according to their taste for the firm's output. Multipart tariffs allow the regulator to achieve finer sorting of consumers by type than the very coarse sorting achievable with a two-part tariff. Hence, greater pricing efficiency is possible.

Formally, a multipart tariff is defined as a nonuniform price schedule with a finite number, n, of rate steps, where $n \geq 2$. Thus it consists of an entry fee E and a marginal price schedule:

$$P(Q) = P_1 \quad , \quad 0 \leq Q < Q^1$$

$$P_2 \quad , \quad Q^1 \leq Q < Q^2$$

$$P_3 \quad , \quad Q^2 \leq Q \leq Q^3$$

$$\vdots$$

$$P_n \quad , \quad Q^{n-1} \leq Q$$

and total outlay is written

$$R(Q) = E + P_1 Q \, , \, Q < Q^1$$

$$= E + P_1 Q^1 + P_2(Q-Q^1) \, , \, Q^1 \leq Q < Q^2$$

$$\vdots$$

$$= E + \sum_{i=1}^{n-1} P_i Q_i + P_n \cdot (Q-Q_{n-1}) \quad \text{for} \quad Q \geq Q_{n-1} \, .$$

Faulhaber and Panzar [1978] pointed out a link between two-part tariffs and multipart tariffs which illustrates the role of multipart tariffs as devices for sorting consumers by their underlying taste. Suppose that we had a five-part tariff as shown in Figure 4.14a by the outlay function $E_1 M_1 M_2 M_3$. It gives rise to the declining block marginal price schedule in Figure 4.14b. Notice in Figure 4.14a that one can think of the single outlay function $E_1 M_1 M_2 M_3$ as being composed of the undominated portions of a set of four two-part tariffs (E_1, P_1), (E_2, P_2), (E_3, P_3) and (E_4, P_4), where

$$E_1 < E_2 < E_3 < E_4$$

$$P_1 > P_2 > P_3 > P_4 \, .$$

In other words, if one two-part tariff has a higher entry fee than another, it must have a lower usage charge in order to be selected by some consumer. Clearly, when these two-part tariffs are juxtaposed as in Figure 4.14a, consumers will only select portions of them which are on the lower envelope of the set, which is $E_1 M_1 M_2 M_3$. Thus, when a multipart tariff shows quantity discounts, it can be viewed as the lower envelope of a set of two-part tariffs from which consumers select their optimal consumption points.[6] For this reason, the set of two-part tariffs can be referred to as a *self-selecting set* of two-part tariffs.

Looking back to Figure 4.1, the Commonwealth Edison three-part tariff was

$E = \$1.20$

$P_1 = \$.0418 , Q \leqq 100 \; kwh$

$P_2 = \$.0314 , Q > 100 \; kwh .$

This is equivalent to giving consumers a choice between one two-part tariff with $E = \$1.20$ and $P = \$.0418$ and a second two-part tariff with $E = \$2.24$ and $P = \$.0314$ The undominated portions of this pair of two-part tariff compose the three-part tariff we began with.

From this point of view, it is easy to see why a multipart tariff will achieve finer sorting than a single two-part tariff or uniform price. It is the equivalent of offering heterogeneous consumers a wider variety of tariff packages from which they can select, some of which will be better tuned to the needs of more different consumer types than any single uniform price or two-part tariff could be.

---

[6]

However, a nonuniform price schedule which displays quantity premia *cannot* be generated by self-selecting two-part tariffs. To see why not, consider the following hypothetical tariff for local telephone services which is an increasing block tariff:

$E = \$3.50$

$P_1 = \$.06 , \quad Q \leqq 30$

$P_2 = \$.10 , \quad Q > 30$

where Q is the number of calls per month. This price schedule can be generated by the following two-part tariffs:

Tariff 1: $E = \$3.50, \quad p = \$.06$

Tariff 2: $E = \$2.30, \quad p = \$.10$

If the firm tried to obtain the original price schedule by offering these two-part tariffs, consumers would foil it by buying on Tariff 2 for the first 30 calls and on Tariff 1 for more than 30 calls. In effect, then the firm will have charged a *declining* block three-part tariff, not an increasing block tariff. It is only by imposing the added restriction that for fewer than 30 calls the consumer *must* pay a marginal price of $.06, with $.10 thereafter, that the increasing black tariff remains effective.

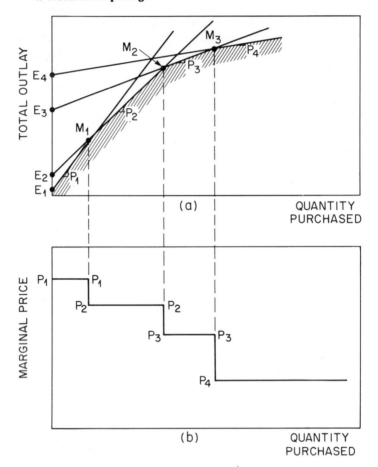

Figure 4.14

Faulhaber and Panzar [1978] proved an important result which follows naturally from this interpretation of multipart tariffs. They posit a continuous distribution of consumer types and show that under an optimal set of self-selecting two-part tariffs, the lowest usage charge exceeds marginal cost. They next consider the optimal set of $n + 1$ self-selecting two-part tariffs and show that the lowest usage charge in this larger set of tariffs lies closer to marginal cost than with the old set. Furthermore, the level of total surplus under the optimal set of $n + 1$ two-part tariffs is higher than with the optimal set of n two-part tariffs. This is the same as saying that the optimal $(n + 1)$-part tariff is more efficient than the optimal n-part tariff.

B. Pareto dominating block rate tariffs

In a sense, the result that the optimal $(n + 1)$-part tariff attains strictly higher surplus than the optimal n-part tariff is no more than one might expect. After all, since $(n + 1)$ two-part tariffs offer more degrees of freedom than n two-part tariffs, a policy-maker should be able to do better. With a continuous distribution of consumer types, each optional two-part tariff will be selected by more than one consumer type. Hence, there is always some consumer who can benefit enough by a tariff tailored to his or her needs so that the firm can generate more revenue and yet still leave him or her better off. In this section we will prove two further results on multipart tariffs which are in this general vein. In this discussion we will assume that there is a finite number N of consumer types. Because N can be as large as we want, this is no real limitation on the generality of the discussion in this section.

These results both stem from the "tailoring" feature of multipart tariffs. First, we show at some length that given any uniform price P_1 which exceeds marginal cost, an N-part tariff can be constructed based on P_1 so that no consumer is worse off than he would be under P_1, some consumers are better off, and the firm makes more profit than if all consumers were forced to buy at a single uniform price P_1. To describe such a situation we say that the N-part tariff Pareto dominates (PD) the uniform price. Second, we show that if initially all N consumers are buying on a k-part tariff, where $k < N$, we can find a $(k + 1)$-part tariff that Pareto dominates it.

The practical effect of this is that it is sometimes possible for the policymaker to take pre-existing tariffs and come up with PD modifications of these tariffs which increase economic efficiency, but do not require any messy balancing of gainers and losers. Such a course of action will be politically desirable in most cases and we will show in the discussion below that these Pareto dominating tariffs are computationally easy to find and require less data than do tariffs which go further and maximize total surplus.

Our starting point is a seminal result due to Willig [1978] which was touched on in the beginning of this chapter. Suppose that there is initially a uniform price P_1 which exceeds the firm's marginal cost. Willig showed that one can always construct a nonuniform price schedule based on this uniform price which hurts no consumers, helps some and makes the firm more money. To illustrate one way of doing this, let there be two consumer types where the demand curve for Mr. 1 exceeds that of Mr. 2 at any price: $Q_2(P) > Q_1(P)$. Now offer an optional two-part tariff (E_2, P_2) where P_2 exceeds marginal cost, c, but is less than P_1 and the entry fee, E_2, is given by

$$E_2 = Q_2(P_1) \cdot (P_1 - P_2).$$

In other words, the usage charge P_2 is less than P_1 so that Q_2 rises and E_2 is set so that the firm will make the same amount of money as it did initially on the first $Q_2(P_1)$ units of demand by the large user, Mr. 2. Because P_2 exceeds marginal cost, we can be sure that any incremental consumption by Mr. 2 beyond his initial level $Q_2(P_1)$ will yield the firm a profit. Mr. 1 may decide to buy under the two-part tariff or not, so his welfare can hardly fall as a result of offering it. The new tariff option allows Mr. 2 to increase his surplus by expanding his consumption from $Q_2(P_1)$ to $Q_2(P_2)$ so that Mr. 2 is sure to buy under the two-part tariff option.

Thus, the net effects of having two tariff options for two consumers are (a) Mr. 1 is no worse off than before the option was made available; (b) Mr. 2 takes the option and is better off; (c) the firm makes more money. In Figure 4.15a we depict total outlay under the uniform price option P_1 and under the two-part tariff. The edged portions of each are relevant and constitute a single nonuniform tariff. Figure 4.15b shows that this tariff is of the familiar declining block variety.

We will now generalize this result to the case where we offer N consumers N optional tariffs. Let us index consumers by i, i going from 1 to N. We will choose the i's so that they order consumers by their demands and assume strong monotonicity of demands in i:

$$Q_1(P) < Q_2(P) < ... < Q_N(P)$$

for all usage charges P. We do not need to know the distribution of consumer types at this point. We will begin with a single uniform price P_1, as before, and construct a set of N optional two-part tariffs in the same way as in the two-consumer case:

$$P_1 > P_2 > ... > P_{N-1} > P_N \geqq c$$
$$0 = E_1 < E_2 < ... < E_{N-1} < E_N$$
$$E_i = Q_i(P_1) \cdot (P_1 - P_i) \;, \quad i = 1, 2, ..., N \;.$$

As Figure 4.16 shows, this set of two-part tariffs is equivalent to the N-part declining block tariff given by the dashed lower envelope of the set of two-part tariffs.

By the argument just given, if consumer i were to select the two-part tariff designed with him in mind, $P_i \geqq c$ and $E_i = Q_i(P_1) \cdot (P_1 - P_i)$ then Mr. i is better off than he would be if he faced only the uniform price P_1, no other consumer is worse off, and the firm makes more profit. However, with N consumers a problem arises which did not exist in our two-consumer case: Mr. i might decide that he would be even better off to buy under the two-part tariff designed for a smaller user of type k,

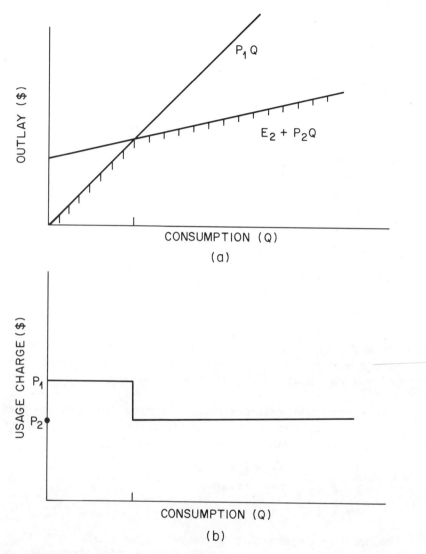

Figure 4.15

where $k < i$. There is nothing in the way we constructed the N two-part tariffs to guarantee that this will not occur. The two-part tariff (E_i, P_i) was only designed to be preferred by Mr. i to P_1, not to be preferred to any of the other two-part tariffs. If Mr. i chooses (E_k, P_k) where $k < i$, the difficulty arises that the firm might make less profit from Mr. i than when it charged Mr. i (and all other consumers) the uniform price P_1. Thus, the tariffs (E_i, P_i) must be *incentive compatible* with each other; if one were to offer a set of optional two-

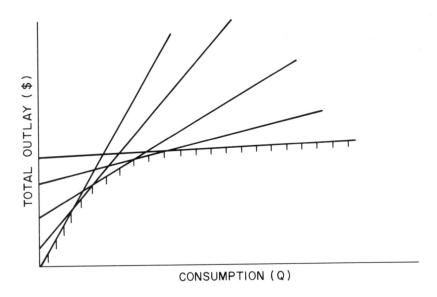

Figure 4.16

part tariffs such that the corresponding N-part tariff in place of the uniform price P_1 was not incentive compatible, one could no longer be sure that all parties (to include the firm) would gain from the new tariff.

An example will make this clearer. Suppose that there are three consumers, each with a unique demand curve. For simplicity, the demand curves are linear, differing only in the intercept:

Mr. 1: $Q_1 = 38.43 - 213.4P$

Mr. 2: $Q_2 = 48.93 - 213.4P$

Mr. 3: $Q_3 = 59.43 - 213.4P$

The firm has a constant marginal cost of $3.5¢$ and a fixed cost of \$5.38. Initially, the firm sets a price of $10¢$. At this price Mr. 1 consumes 17.09 units, Mr. 2 consumes 27.59 units and Mr. 3 buys 38.09 units. At this price, the firm just covers its total costs:

Profit $= (10¢-3.5¢) \times (17.09+27.59+38.09) - \$5.38 = 0$

Following the procedure above we design a two-part tariff for Mr. 2 and another for Mr. 3:

Mr. 2: $P_2 = 5¢$, $E_2 = 27.59 \times (10¢-5¢) = \$1.38$

Mr. 3: $P_3 = 4¢$, $E_3 = 38.09 \times (10¢-4¢) = \$2.29$

If Mr. 2 chooses to buy at (E_2, P_2) instead of at the uniform price of 10¢, he gains because of the reduction in usage charge from 10¢ to 5¢ and increases his consumption by 10.67 units, but has to pay back $1.38 out of the gain. Using the analysis of Chapter 2 to calculate the consumer surplus effect of a reduction in usage charge in the case where demand is linear, the first effect is

$$- \left[\Delta P \cdot Q_2 (P_1) + \frac{1}{2} \cdot \Delta P \cdot \Delta Q \right]$$

$$= 5¢ \times 27.59 + \frac{1}{2} \cdot 5¢ \times 10.67 = \$1.65 .$$

Subtracting the entry fee of $1.38, this leaves a net surplus increase of 27¢ to Mr. 2 if he buys under (E_2, P_2) instead of at $P_1 = 10¢$. Going through the same calculations for Mr. 3, if he buys on the two-part tariff

$E_3 = \$2.29$

$P_3 = 4¢$

instead of the uniform price $P_1 = 10¢$, Mr. 3 gains 38¢ in consumer surplus. As for the firm, it earns 16¢ more in profit from Mr. 2 and 6.4¢ more from Mr. 3 than if they could only buy at the uniform price of 10¢.[7]

However, Mr. 3 can get more consumer surplus buying under the two-part tariff (E_2, P_2). He faces a somewhat higher usage charge, 5¢ instead of 4¢, if he does and consumes 2.13 units less, but his entry fee would fall from $2.29 to $1.38, a substantial saving. The effect of the increased usage charge on consumer surplus is:

$$- \left[Q_3(P_2) \Delta P + \frac{1}{2} \Delta P \Delta Q \right] = - 50¢ .$$

However this loss is swamped by the saving of 91¢ due to the lower entry fee, so by selecting (E_2, P_2) instead of (E_3, P_3) Mr. 3 can increase his consumer surplus by 41¢. The firm no longer covers its total costs.

[7]

At $P_1 = 10¢$, the firm earns $(10¢ - 3.5¢) \times 27.59 = \$1.79$ from Mr. 2; under the two-part tariff

$E_2 = \$1.38 , P_2 = 5¢$

Mr. 2 buys 38.26 units and the firm earns $1.95, which exceeds $1.79. The calculation for Mr. 3 is similar.

Its profit on Mr. 1 and Mr. 2 is no different because Mr. 2 does not buy at $P_1 = 10\text{¢}$, preferring (E_2, P_2) as our calculations above showed. However, when Mr. 3 buys under (E_2, P_2) the firm earns

$$(5\text{¢} - 3.5\text{¢}) \times 48.76 + \$1.38 = \$2.11$$

whereas under the uniform price $P_1 = 10\text{¢}$ Mr. 3 contributed

$$(10\text{¢} - 3.5\text{¢}) \times 38.09 = \$2.48$$

or 37¢ more. Compared to the uniform price situation, the firm earns the same for Mr. 1 and an extra 16¢ from Mr. 2, so the net effect on the firm's profit of offering the optional tariffs

$$P_2 = 5\text{¢} \qquad P_3 = 4\text{¢}$$

$$E_2 = \$1.38 \qquad E_3 = \$2.29$$

is to reduce profit by 21¢. The optional tariffs have allowed Mr. 2 and Mr. 3 to increase their consumer surplus considerably, but the firm is no longer solvent.

How can this situation be avoided? We will proceed by leaving (E_3, P_3) alone, but trying out a new (E_2, P_2), that will still benefit Mr. 2 relative to $P_1 = 10\text{¢}$, but will not be quite such a good deal relative to (E_3, P_3). For example, suppose that

$$P_2 = 8.2\text{¢}$$

$$E_2 = 49.6\text{¢}.$$

Compared to (E_3, P_3) this two-part tariff offers a large reduction in entry fee, but at the cost of a 100 percent rise in the usage charge. If Mr. 2 buys under this particular (E_2, P_2) instead of at $P_1 = 10\text{¢}$, his consumer surplus rises by 3.5¢ and the firm earns 18¢ more on sales to Mr. 2. If Mr. 3 were to select (E_2, P_2), his consumer surplus would be 22¢ higher than under the single uniform price. But if he chose the two-part tariff designed for him, $E_3 = \$2.29$ and $P_3 = 4\text{¢}$ instead, his consumer surplus goes up by 38¢, so he will select (E_3, P_3). In other words, the consumer is better off by the amount of $38\text{¢} - 22\text{¢} = 16\text{¢}$ by selecting (E_3, P_3) instead of (E_2, P_2). Now the two-part tariff (E_3, P_3) is incentive compatible with respect to (E_2, P_2).

In general, for a two-part tariff (E_3, P_3) to be incentive-compatible with respect to (E_2, P_2) the gain to Mr. 3 from the saving $E_3 - E_2$ on the entry fee must be less than the loss from paying a higher usage charge. The saving from the lower entry fee is

$$Q_3(P_1) \cdot (P_1 - P_3) - Q_2(P_1) \cdot (P_1 - P_2) = [Q_3(P_1) - Q_2(P_1)] \cdot (P_1 - P_2)$$

$$+ Q_3(P_1) \cdot (P_2 - P_3).$$

The consumer surplus loss from the higher usage charge is

$$(P_2 - P_3) \cdot \left[Q_3(P_2) + \frac{1}{2} \cdot \left[Q_3(P_3) - Q_3(P_2) \right] \right].$$

For incentive compatibility, the loss must exceed the gain. Given any (E_2, P_2) and (E_3, P_3), if this constraint is met, Mr. 3 will prefer (E_3, P_3) to (E_2, P_2).

Suppose that the firm initially charges the single uniform price of 10¢, and then offers the two optional two-part tariffs

$$E_2 = 49.6¢, P_2 = 8.2¢; E_3 = \$2.29, P_3 = 4¢.$$

Because these tariffs are Pareto dominating (PD) and incentive-compatible (IC) we refer to them as PDIC tariffs. The effects of these tariffs are (a) that the firm earns 8¢ more profit from Mr. 1 and 6.4¢ more from Mr.2, for a total profit increase of 24.4¢ and (b) that consumer surplus rises by 3.4¢ for Mr. 2 and 38¢ for Mr. 3, for a total increase of 41.4¢. Total surplus rises by 65.8¢.

In Figure 4.17a we depict total outlay under each tariff option. The dashed lower envelope gives the equivalent block rate outlay schedule. This outlay schedule is equivalent to the following declining block schedule of usage charges:

$$P_1 = 10¢ \text{ , quantity} < 27.6$$

$$P_2 = 8.2¢ \text{ , } 27.6 \leqq \text{quantity} < 42.7$$

$$P_3 = 4¢ \text{ , quantity} \geqq 42.7.$$

This is depicted in Figure 4.17b.

In this example, we found a three-part tariff which is incentive-compatible and also Pareto-dominates the uniform price P_1. We can use this example in another way. Suppose, initially, that our three consumers faced only two tariff options, the uniform price of 10¢ and the two-part tariff with entry fee $E_2 = 49.6¢$ and a usage charge of 8.2¢. Clearly, Mr. 1 and Mr. 2 behave as we just found that they did. Mr. 3 prefers the two-part tariff (E_2, P_2) to the uniform price and selects it, along with Mr. 2. Now make available the third tariff option with $E_3 = \$2.29$, $P_3 = 4¢$. As we just showed, only Mr. 3 will take this

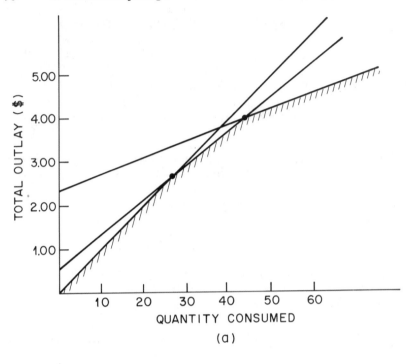

(a)

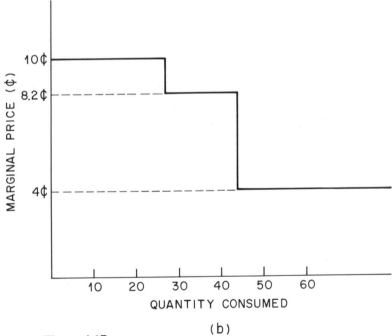

(b)

Figure 4.17

option, and by so doing he increases his surplus by 16¢. Starting with three consumers and two tariff options, we achieved a Pareto improvement by adding an appropriately-designed third tariff option.

Although this example assumes three consumers, it makes an important point which generalizes to the case of N consumer types. If the N consumer types are initially facing a k-part declining block tariff, where k is less than N then if $P_k > mc$ one can construct a $(k+1)$-part tariff which Pareto dominates the k-part tariff. To put this another way, if we regard the k-part tariff as being generated by k optional two-part tariffs, it is possible to find an additional optional two-part tariff which will lead to a Pareto improvement.

Consider consumer type N, the largest consumer, and offer him the following two-part tariff (E_{k+1}, P_{k+1}) where

$$mc \leq P_{k+1} < P_k$$

$$E_{k+1} = Q_N(P_k) \cdot (P_k - P_{k+1}) \, .$$

Using (by now) familiar reasoning, Mr. N will take the new tariff option and will contribute at least as much to the firm as he did buying on the original k-part tariff. Other consumer types may avail themselves of the new option, too. If so, they must also pay E_{k+1}, which is designed so that the firm makes at least as much money from Mr. N on (E_{k+1}, P_{k+1}) as it did on the original tariff. By strong monotonicity, smaller consumers contributed less to the firm on the original k-part tariff than did Mr. N. Therefore, if they select (E_{k+1}, P_{k+1}), the firm must make more producer surplus than if they stay where they are on the original k-part tariff. The introduction of the two-part tariff (E_{k+1}, P_{k+1}) has created a $(k+1)$-part tariff which Pareto dominates the original k-part tariff.

This discussion suggests that in some cases the competent analyst can enhance economic efficiency relative to some pre-existing tariff by designing a nonuniform price schedule which Pareto dominates it. This has the potential to ameliorate certain conflicts between regulatory authorities and the regulated firm because there are no losers from the new tariff. For example, suppose that a regulator proposes a particular uniform price P_1 or, perhaps, a k-part tariff. The firm can devise a PDIC tariff based on the regulator's tariff and make a politically compelling efficiency-based argument for its adoption.

Finally, it is important to notice that it requires comparatively little information on the part of the regulator to compute Pareto dominating block rate tariffs. It is not necessary, for example, to know the distribution of consumer types for the actual construction of the tariffs. It is necessary to know individuals' demand curves in order to check for incentive compatibility, but only for prices less than or equal to P_1. This is quite important because as we will see in Chapter 7 below, attempts to set prices to maximize total surplus — as opposed to merely increasing it — will usually involve setting extremely high prices for certain ranges of consumption. Such prices will often be completely outside the range of data on historical prices and thus little faith can be placed in estimates of demand at such price levels. The PDIC tariffs can be constructed from a price P_1 which is within the range of data and deserve confidence for that reason. To compute the total effect of such a tariff does require us to know the distribution of consumer types; but this information is not needed to construct the PDIC tariffs or to assert that they have the qualitative effects we have discussed.

C. Optimal PDIC tariffs

Thus far, the discussion of PDIC tariffs may seem unsatisfactory to the policymaker because PDIC tariffs only result in *improvements* to consumer surplus and profits. There has been no claim for optimality of any kind. In this section we examine tariffs constructed as described above that maximize profits (or, it could be, consumer surplus) subject to being PDIC. Tariffs of this sort combine a degree of optimality with the attractive fact that in going from a uniform price above marginal cost to a PDIC tariff, there are no losers. On the other hand, in general we must know the distribution of consumer types to do the optimizing. The discussion will follow the numerical example presented above, so that there is only one consumer of each type.

The objective of the firm is to choose price P_2 and P_3 to maximize producer surplus

$$PS = \sum_{i=1}^{3} \left[(P_i - c) \cdot Q_i(P_i) + E_i \right]$$

subject to the PDIC constraints:

PD: $E_i = Q_i(10\textit{c}) \cdot (10\textit{c} - P_i)$, $i = 1, 2, 3$.

IC: $(P_2 - P_3) \cdot \left[\dfrac{Q_3(P_2) + Q_3(P_3)}{2} \right] \geq 10.5 \times (10\textit{c} - P_2) + 38.09 \times (P_2 - P_3)$.

The incentive-compatibility constraint is taken from the discussion in the previous section and requires that the reduction in entry fee which 3 gets by buying under (E_2, P_2) instead of (E_3, P_3) is outweighed by the consequent increase in usage charge.

The solution to this profit maximization problem is the following pair of optional two-part tariffs:

$E_2 = 50.5¢$, $P_2 = 8.17¢$

$E_3 = \$1.76$, $P_3 = 5.38¢$.

At this solution, the consumers and firm all benefit relative to the initial situation with a single 10¢ uniform price. The firm increases its profit by 37¢ over the initial level of $5.38, a rise of 6.9 percent. Consumer 1 stays on the uniform price and is unaffected by the new tariff options; consumers 2 and 3 benefit by 3.6¢ and 22.8¢, respectively. The declining block tariff which is equivalent to the choice among these optional tariffs is:

Usage charge = 10¢ , 0 $\geq$ Quantity < 27.60

= 8.17¢ , 27.60 $\geq$ Quantity < 44.98

= 6.38¢ , Quantity $\geq$ 44.98.

We could equally well have maximized consumer surplus or total surplus subject to the PDIC constraints.

4.5 The optimal two-part tariff

Up to this point we have described how the regulated firm can attain higher total surplus using nonuniform prices than it can with uniform prices. In particular, we have discussed PDIC nonuniform tariffs. We will now begin the discussion of *optimal* nonuniform prices without PDIC constraints with an analysis of the two-part tariff[8] which maximizes total surplus subject to the breakeven constraint. We are no longer concerned to ensure that no consumers are injured by going to an optimal tariff. We are concerned only with maximizing total surplus over all economic agents.

Let n be the number of consumers, with $\underline{\theta}$ being the lowest value of the taste parameter in the population of possible consumers. If a consumer of type $\underline{\theta}$ earns a nonnegative consumer surplus with the Coase two-part tariff $E = F/n$ and $P = c$, then the Coase two-part tariff is optimal and achieves the same level of total surplus as does marginal cost pricing. The effect of the entry fee is only to redistribute surplus from consumers to the firm, and the job of efficient pricing is done.

When would this case be likely to arise? In certain regulated markets like electricity, water or natural gas it is extremely unlikely

---

[8]

The results in this section follows from choosing E and P to maximize total surplus subject to a breakeven constraint. See the appendix to this chapter for the derivation.

that a customer will drop out of the market, however high the tariff. In such cases, the usual declining block tariff is inefficient compared to the simple Coase two-part tariff. For example, consider the Commonwealth Edison tariff described at the beginning of this chapter:

usage charge $= 4.18¢/kwh$, $0 \geqq$ kwh < 100

$= 3.14¢/kwh$, kwh $\geqq 100$.

Suppose that there are two consumers, each with a constant price elasticity of demand equal to .8. It can be shown that a consumer with this kind of demand function experiences infinite disutility by leaving the market and, therefore, will be willing to pay any finite entry fee. Suppose that on the declining block tariff the smaller consumer buys 80 kwh per month and the larger buys 500 kwh per month. The electric utility's marginal cost is $2¢/kwh$. Together, the two consumers contribute $8.48 to the fixed cost of the firm:

$(4.18¢ - 2¢) \cdot 180 + (3.14¢ - 2¢) \cdot 400 = \$8.48$.

Now withdraw the declining block tariff and charge a single two-part tariff with a usage charge equal to $2¢/kwh$ and an entry fee of $4.24 per month. Clearly, this contributes $8.48 to the fixed costs of the firm, as before. The lower usage charge expands aggregate consumer surplus by $.50, net of the entry fee. (It should be noted that the smaller consumer is worse off than under the Commonwealth Edison tariff and the large consumer is much better off.)

However, if this entry fee would cause some consumer types to drop out of the market, the Coase two-part tariff would no longer be optimal. This case probably fits many telecommunications markets. This suggests that we think about the optimal two-part tariff problem as a problem in setting prices for two markets: participation and consumption. E is the price of participation and P is the price of consumption. Using this analogy, the results of Ramsey pricing suggest broad features of the optimal pair of prices (E, P) for these markets. If participation is highly inelastic relative to consumption, then the optimal two-part tariff will have a high entry fee and low usage charge. If the reverse is true, the entry fee will be relatively low, in order to increase participation, and the markup of P of marginal cost will be high so as to cover total costs.

The setting of E and P must take account of cross-elasticities between the two "markets" for participation and consumption. When the price of participation, E, rises it causes the initially marginal group to cease participating, which means that that group ceases to consume as well. When the price of consumption, P, rises this reduces consumption by all consumers and also induces the marginal group to drop out of the participation market. Hence, participation and consumption are complements and have a negative cross price elasticity.

The derivation of the optimal values of E and P is too complex to present here and are contained in of the Appendix to this chapter, but the "Ramsey" nature of the optimal two-part tariff comes through clearly. One condition which must hold for a two-part tariff to be optimal is

$$\frac{E - v + (P-c) \cdot Q(P,\theta_0)}{E} = \frac{M}{e}$$

where

e = elasticity of participation with respect to the entry fee E

M = a markup sufficient to allow the firm to break even

v = marginal cost of adding subscribers.

The term $E - v + (P-c) \cdot Q(P,\theta_0)$ is the amount of contribution made by a consumer of the marginal type θ_0. Any consumer who participates at all contributes at least this much. As intuition would suggest, the lower the elasticity of participation with respect to its price, the higher should be the contribution made by a marginal "unit" of participation. If participation were highly elastic, then the participation market would contribute less to the firm's total costs. A second condition which must be met by the optimal two-part tariff is

$$\frac{P-c}{P} = \frac{M}{\xi} \cdot \left[1 - \frac{\hat{q}(P,\theta_0)}{\bar{Q}} \right]$$

where ξ is the price elasticity of demand for total consumption (i.e., with respect to P), $\bar{Q}$ is mean consumption, and $\hat{q}(P,\theta_0)$ is the consumption of the marginal consumer. The usage charge P can be greater or less than marginal cost c depending on whether the consumption of the marginal consumer type θ_0 is smaller or larger than mean consumption. Under the strong monotonicity, or noncrossing, assumption discussed above, higher values of θ are associated with higher demands. With noncrossing, then $\hat{q}(P, \theta_0)$ is less than $\bar{Q}$ and the usage charge will exceed marginal cost. However, without noncrossing, it could happen that the marginal group θ_0 consumes more than does other groups which earns a positive consumer surplus. In such a case, the usage charge on the optimal two-part tariff will be less than marginal cost. In the commonly assumed case of noncrossing, the percentage difference between usage charge and marginal cost is higher, the lower is the price elasticity of demand, as in the Ramsey IER. The term

$$1 - \frac{\hat{q}(P, \theta_0)}{\bar{Q}}$$

is an adjustment term accounting for cross-elasticity between consumption and participation. The effect of this adjustment term is to force the planner to take account of the fact that when P is increased, not only does consumption fall, but participation declines, too. This keeps the usage charge P at a lower markup over marginal cost c than would otherwise be the case.

It should be noticed at this point that the optimal two-part tariff requires more information to compute than did the Pareto dominating tariffs that we discussed in Section 4.3 above. The terms e, ξ and $\bar{Q}$ all involve the distribution of θ, which was not needed earlier. The extra information is required when we aim to maximize, rather than merely increase, total surplus.

We can illustrate the optimal two-part tariff with a numerical example, adapted from Mitchell's study of local telephone service pricing. Following Mitchell, we will assume that θ is lognormally distributed with logarithmic mean 6.15 and standard deviation .55. The marginal cost of a call is 3.5 cents and a fixed cost of \$5.61 must be covered. We depart from Mitchell in assuming that individual monthly demands for calls take the form

$$Q = -3.57 + .21\,\theta - 213.4P$$

where Q is calls per month. In a regime of average cost pricing, the price comes out to be 9.7 cents per call. This is far above marginal cost, so that consumption is being priced inefficiently; on the other hand, virtually all consumers participate. The optimal two-part tariff has an entry fee of \$1.24 and a usage charge of 8.34 cents per call. Because 8.34 cents is closer to marginal cost that was the average cost price, consumption is being priced more efficiently. However, the \$1.24 entry fee causes 7.4 percent of the population of consumers to drop out of participation. The net effect is to raise total surplus by 5 cents per month over the level achieved with the average cost price.

4.6   Concluding remarks

This chapter has introduced the theory of nonuniform pricing. The rationale for nonunform pricing stems from the fact that a regulated firm producing under conditions of decreasing average cost cannot break even under marginal cost pricing. Whether or not this failure to break even ought to affect pricing depends on institutional arrangements. In Europe, it is sometimes accepted that public utilities should charge marginal cost prices, with revenue shortfalls made good by the government out of tax revenues. Regulatory tradition in the United States has always been that utilities cover their costs. In such cases there is reason to investigate nonuniform price structures.

Whether nonuniform price structures ought to be simple two-part tariffs or complex multipart tariffs depends on the elasticity of consumer participation. In the case of a market such as residential electricity consumption, it is almost inconceivable that any reasonable entry fee will cause any consumers to exit the market. In such a case, the Coase two-part tariff is the most efficient. Indeed, from this standpoint, the three-part tariff of Commonwealth Edison which we discussed above cannot be optimal. In markets which consumers may realistically be expected to exit, multipart tariffs offer the policymaker opportunities to increase efficiency above the level possible with a two-part tariff. Examples of such markets are local and long distance telephone service.

The most interesting contrast between nonuniform and uniform pricing is that nonuniform prices make it possible to make each economic agent better off than he would be under a single uniform price which exceeds marginal cost. We extended this notion to analyze Pareto dominating incentive compatible tariffs and optimal tariffs of that type. The nonuniform price schedules which seek to maximize total surplus subject only to an overall breakeven constraint will surely attain greater total surplus, but some consumer types will almost certainly lose by comparison to their positions under a uniform price. It is also important that Pareto dominating tariffs require less information do compute than to fully optimal nonuniform tariffs.

Finally, we note a point which we explore more fully in Chapter 7. When multipart tariffs with quantity discounts are advocated in actual regulatory proceedings, the argument in their favor is that large consumers are cheaper to serve than smaller consumers. For example, large industrial users of electricity often do their own transforming, whereas small users do not. In telecommunications, the unit labor cost of installing a PBX with many lines is said to be lower than installing one with only a few lines. Quantity discounts are justified as recognizing these cost differences. Our discussion has shown that the economic case for nonuniform pricing does not rest solely on these cost arguments. In fact, throughout this chapter we have assumed that all customers are equally costly to serve. The economic efficiency of nonuniform prices comes from their function of sorting diverse consumer types into tariff packages designed for them. The surplus gains made possible by this consumer sorting provide a case for nonuniform prices which is wholly different from the line of argument used in traditional regulatory proceedings.

CHAPTER 5

Nonuniform pricing II

5.1 Introduction

In the last chapter we showed that a properly chosen set of $n+1$ self-selecting two-part tariffs could Pareto dominate a set of n self-selecting two-part tariffs. The reason for this welfare dominance is that the set of $n+1$ two-part tariffs gives each type of consumer the ability to find a two-part tariff more closely attuned to his willingness to pay than under the original set of n two-part tariffs. Because of the relationship between a set of n self-selecting two-part tariffs and a single nonuniform price schedule with n rate steps, this result suggests that welfare can be made progressively higher by constructing nonuniform price schedules with more and more rate steps, each one progressively smaller in length, obtaining in the limit a continuously varying nonuniform price schedule.

In the upper panel of Figure 4.14 we depicted four self-selecting two-part tariffs which form the shaded piecewise-linear outlay schedule. The associated marginal price schedule is the declining block schedule in the lower part of that figure. If we were to let the number of optimally chosen self-selecting tariffs tend to infinity, then the resulting outlay schedule would be the smooth lower envelope of the two-part tariffs given as $R(Q)$ in Figure 5.1. The corresponding smooth marginal price schedule is given as the curve $P(Q)$ in the lower panel.

In this chapter we will explore the properties of smooth nonuniform price schedules which maximize total surplus, subject to the firm breaking even. The main points of the discussion are:

— Optimal nonuniform price schedules can display a variety of shapes, including quantity discounts and quantity premia.

— Whether or not quantity discounts are optimal depends on the distribution of tastes across consumers and not simply on possible cost differences between serving large and smaller customers.

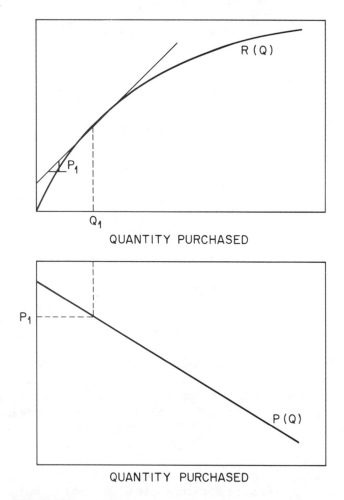

QUANTITY PURCHASED

Figure 5.1

— The marginal prices corresponding to optimal nonuniform outlay
  schedules follow a special form of the Ramsey Inverse Elasticity
  Rule which we discussed in Chapter 3.

5.2 Consumer choice on a smooth nonuniform price schedule

We will begin with the single market case,[1] such as local telephone
service. As before, let $R(Q)$ denote the total outlay a consumer pays

[1] For treatments of this problem, see Goldman, Leland, Sibley [1984], Roberts
[1979], Spence [1977] and Mirrlees [1971, 1976].

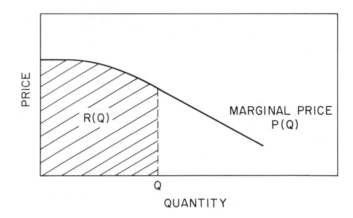

Figure 5.2

the regulated firm if he consumes an amount Q of the good. Derived from the outlay schedule, the marginal price schedule is $P(Q)$, where the marginal price gives the added outlay a consumer must pay the firms if he varies his consumption from Q. In the last chapter we discussed the block rate tariff, wherein $P(Q)$ remained constant within rate steps which could be substantial in size. With smooth nonuniform price schedules, the rate steps are infinitesimally small, so that the marginal prices can change substantially even over very small variations in consumption. Therefore, $P(Q)$ only gives a reliable indication of added outlay for very small changes in consumption. The marginal price is to be interpreted as the "price" of a very small increment in consumption.

Total outlay at a given consumption level is the sum of the individual prices for small increments in consumption which add up to the given level. Geometrically, total outlay at a point is equal to the area under the marginal price curve up to that point. Figure 5.2 illustrates this. Total outlay is given as the shaded area $R(Q)$.

Given the outlay and marginal price schedules, the consumer of type θ will select a consumption level so as to maximize his consumer surplus. This is illustrated in Figure 5.3 for a particular consumer with $\theta = 35$. In line with our analysis in earlier chapters, he chooses a consumption level at which his willingness to pay for an extra (small) increment of consumption is equal to the marginal price which gives the price of that increment of consumption. In Figure 5.3, this occurs at seven units. Total outlay is given by the shaded area $R(7)$ under the marginal price curve, and consumer surplus by the unshaded area between marginal price and willingness to pay, up to seven units.

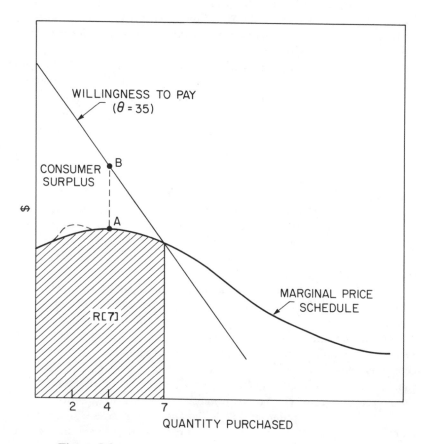

WILLINGNESS TO PAY
($\theta = 35$)

CONSUMER
SURPLUS

B

A

$

MARGINAL PRICE
SCHEDULE

R[7]

2   4   7

QUANTITY PURCHASED

Figure 5.3

Notice that we have drawn the marginal price curve so that it cuts the consumer's willingness to pay curve from below. This is necessary for the situation to make sense. If it cuts the willingness to pay curve from above, the consumer would be earning negative consumer surplus and should, on that score, consume nothing at all.

Three features of this model of consumer choice will be useful to note for the discussion below. First, if the marginal price curve increases in some range of consumption less then 7 units, it does not affect how much the consumer decides to buy. This is because such a price increase over the consumer's inframarginal units does not alter the fact that willingness to pay equals marginal price only at 7 units. For any consumption level less than seven units, willingness to pay is more than marginal price, so that by increasing consumption to seven units, consumer surplus still rises. Naturally, if the marginal price rises for a consumer's inframarginal units of consumption, his total outlay goes up and his consumer surplus goes down. However, as long as his consumer surplus remains positive, his consumption decision does not change. (If he earned negative consumer surplus, he could do better — a zero surplus — by buying nothing.) This is illustrated in Figure 5.3, where the marginal price curve rises by the dashed amount in the neighborhood of two units of consumption. Since this does not affect the marginal price at 7 units, it is still optimal for the consumer to buy 7 units.

The second point to bring out is that for any consumption level less than 7 units, the vertical distance between willingness to pay and marginal price represents the addition to his surplus which a consumer can achieve by consuming an additional small increment. Thus, in Figure 5.3, at four units of consumption, the consumer adds an amount equal to the difference between points A and B to his surplus by increasing his consumption from 4 to $4 + \Delta Q$, where ΔQ is a very small increase in quantity consumed.

Third, the discussion below assumes throughout that consumer preferences obey the requirement of strong monotonicity. Most of the results of nonuniform pricing theory depend on this assumption.

Key to the theory of nonuniform pricing[2] is the concept of the *marginal consumer type* at a given level of consumption. The marginal consumer type at some level Q is the consumer whose level of θ is such that he finds Q to be his surplus-maximizing level of consumption given the marginal price at Q. To put it another way, the marginal consumer type at some consumption level Q is the consumer whose willingness to pay at Q is equal to the marginal price at Q. For example, in Figure 5.4, the marginal consumer type at $Q = 7$ has a θ level of 35. All consumer types with values of θ greater than 35 have a willingness to pay at $Q = 7$, which is greater than $P(7)$. This means that the marginal group at $Q = 7$, with $\theta = 35$, makes a consumer surplus of zero for any small increment of consumption past 7, and customers with higher values of θ make positive consumer surplus from incremental consumption beyond 7 units. In Figure 5.4, two groups with θ's higher than 35 are shown: $\theta = 40$ and $\theta = 50$. The $\theta = 40$ group make a surplus equal to the difference between A and B on a move from $Q = 7$ to $Q = 7 + \Delta Q$ where ΔQ is a very small increment of consumption; the $\theta = 50$ group makes the difference between A and C on such a move. Clearly, no consumer type with θ less than 35 will buy an increment of consumption located at $Q = 7$. The group with $\theta = 40$ is the marginal consumer type at 10 units of consumption; each member of the group

---

[2]   This discussion follows that of Goldman, Leland and Sibley [1984].

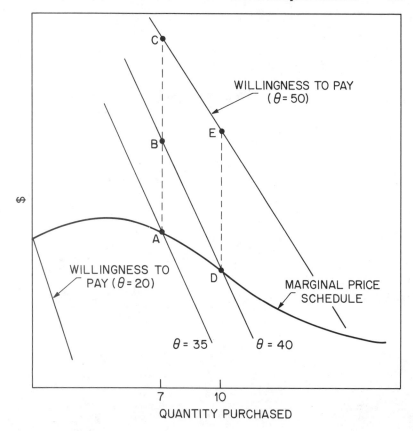

Figure 5.4

with $\theta = 50$ makes a consumer surplus gain of the difference between D and E for a small incremental movement beyond 10 units, and will become the marginal consumer type at some higher level of consumption.

To generalize, then, given some consumption level Q and the marginal price at that point, $P(Q)$, the marginal consumer type is the consumer whose θ value makes his willingness to pay at Q equal to $P(Q)$. Finally, the marginal consumer type at zero consumption is the borderline consumer type, whose willingness to pay for a small amount of the good is just equal to the price changed for the first small amount of consumption, $P(0)$. In Figure 5.4, the marginal consumer type at $Q = 0$ is $\theta = 20$. People with θ-values lower than 20 are priced out of the market altogether by the marginal price schedule shown there.

It is important to understand the effect of marginal price on the marginal consumer type at a given consumption level. In Figure 5.5,

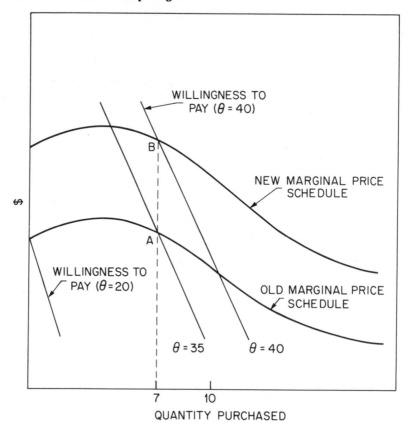

$ $

WILLINGNESS TO
PAY ($\theta = 40$)

B

NEW MARGINAL PRICE
SCHEDULE

A

WILLINGNESS TO
PAY ($\theta = 20$)

OLD MARGINAL PRICE
SCHEDULE

$\theta = 35$ $\theta = 40$

7   10

QUANTITY PURCHASED

Figure 5.5

suppose that the marginal price at $Q = 7$ jumps upward by the amount
AB. The $\theta = 35$ group would now increase its consumer surplus by
cutting back consumption below 7; hence, it is dropping out of the
"market" for incremental consumption located at $Q = 7$. The new
marginal consumer type is $\theta = 40$. All consumers with θ lying between
35 and 40 drop out of the market for incremental consumption at 7
units. If $P(0)$ rises, then more consumers are priced out of the market
for incremental consumption located at $Q = 0$, and do not consume the
good at all. If $P(0)$ falls, additional consumers are brought into the
market, since there will be some whose willingness to pay for the first
small increment of consumption is less than the old marginal price at
$Q = 0$, but at least as high as the new $P(0)$. If the marginal price rises
at a given consumption level, it takes a higher value of θ to be the
marginal consumer type at that consumption level. We will denote this
relationship by writing the marginal type at Q by $\hat{\theta}$ where $\hat{\theta}$ is an
increasing function of the level of consumption, Q, and the marginal
price $P(Q)$; $\hat{\theta} = \hat{\theta}(Q, P(Q))$, for short.

An algebraic example will help to cement this idea. Let willingness to pay be given by the formula

Willingness to pay $= 100 + 2\theta - 4Q$

and let the marginal price schedule be given by

$P(Q) = 50 - Q$.

To find the marginal consumer type $\hat{\theta}$ at 20 units of consumption, we use the definition of $\hat{\theta}$ to write

Willingness to pay at $20 = 100 + 2\theta - 4 \times 20 =$ marginal price at $20 \equiv P(20)$

$$= 50 - 20 = 30,$$

so that

$$\hat{\theta} = \frac{30-20}{2} = 5.$$

For a consumer with $\theta = 10$, an incremental increase in consumption from $Q = 20$ to $Q = 20 + \Delta Q$ will raise his consumer surplus by

$$(100 + 2 \times 10 - 80) - 30 = 10.$$

If the marginal price at $Q = 20$ rose to \$32, then the marginal consumer type rises from $\hat{\theta} = 5$ to $\hat{\theta} = 6$. Nobody with θ less than 6 will buy a consumption increment at $Q = 20$.

5.3 Markets for consumption increments

In previous discussions we described the marginal consumer type as the consumer who was just willing to pay for an increment at a particular consumption level. All consumers with a stronger taste for the good in question are more than willing to purchase the increment; those with a θ-value lower than that of the marginal consumer type are not willing to do so. This suggests that we can think of consumption increments as being bought in "markets" which differ depending on the point from which the increment is made. "Quantity" in such an increment market refers to the number of consumers willing to buy the increment. That is, if we look at the quantity axis in Figure 5.4, we can imagine a market for a ΔQ increment starting at $Q = 0$, another at $Q = 5$, another at $Q = 6$, etc., so that the whole quantity axis is really made up of increment markets located next to each other. Instead of viewing optimal nonuniform pricing as finding entire outlay and marginal price schedules, the analogy to a set of "markets" for increments suggests that we approach the problem by finding optimal prices for each of these multiple increment markets using the Ramsey pricing procedure.

Put together in their adjacent increment markets, the prices for these increment markets will make up the optimal marginal price schedule.

With this goal in mind, it is necessary to describe these increment markets in more detail. First, the aggregate demand for a consumption increment at Q is equal to the number of consumers with a value of the taste parameter θ which is at least as large as that of the marginal consumer type at that point. In other words, if N is the total number of potential consumers in the market and $N(\hat{\theta})$ is the number of consumers having θ values less than or equal to a given value $\hat{\theta}$, then the aggregate demand for a move from some level of Q to $Q+\Delta Q$ is given by the number of customers with $\theta \geqq \hat{\theta}$ and equals

$$N - N(\hat{\theta}(Q, P(Q)))$$

where $\hat{\theta}$ is the marginal consumer type at Q with marginal price $P(Q)$. An important feature of this demand function is its price elasticity, where the "price" here is the price of going from consumption level Q to $Q+\Delta Q$. When the increment price rises the former marginal consumer type in that increment market ceases to consume there, and drops back to become the marginal consumer type in an increment market located at a lower level of consumption. A consumer type with a higher taste level θ become marginal at the original consumption level. Thus, the elasticity of demand for a price increase is given by

$$\xi(Q, P(Q)) = \frac{\text{Number of consumers who drop out of the } \Delta Q \text{ market at } Q}{N - N(\hat{\theta}(Q, P(Q)))} \div \frac{\Delta P}{P(Q)}$$

For small changes in marginal price, the number of consumers who drop out of a particular increment market because of a rise in the price of that increment is given by the number of consumers with θ given by $\hat{\theta}$ multiplied by the change in $\hat{\theta}$ due to the change in $P(Q)$. Mathematically, the number of consumers with θ of $\hat{\theta}$ is simply the density function of θ evaluated at $\hat{\theta}$.[3] Therefore, we can rewrite $\xi(Q, (P(Q))$ to read

$$\xi(Q, P(Q)) = \frac{P(Q)}{N - N(\hat{\theta})} \times \begin{pmatrix} \text{change in } \hat{\theta} \\ \text{per unit} \\ \text{change in} \\ P(Q) \end{pmatrix} \times \begin{pmatrix} \text{density} \\ \text{of} \\ \hat{\theta} \end{pmatrix}.$$

[3]
  The density of $\hat{\theta}$ is the fraction of the population of all potential consumers who have a θ value of $\hat{\theta}$.

Having defined aggregate demand for an increment market and the price elasticity of demand for such a market, the next important feature of increment markets is that their demands are independent. If the price for an increment market located at Q_0 changes, it will not affect the demand for an increment market located at another consumption level Q_1. This is because the consumers willing to buy an increment at Q_1 look only at the price for an increment at Q_1. The price for an increment at Q_0 affects their realized level of consumer surplus, but does not affect the increment price at Q_1, so the demand for an increment at Q_1 is unaffected.[4] In Figure 5.6, with marginal price schedule as shown, the marginal consumer types at Q_0 and Q_1 are depicted. Suppose now that the marginal price at Q_0 moves upward as shown by the "blip." The old marginal consumer type now drops out of the increment market located at Q_0 and a group with a higher value of θ becomes the marginal type at Q_0. This price rise for the increment market at Q_0 does not affect the price of an increment at Q_1, and therefore does not affect the aggregate demand for an increment at Q_1.

A final point to be noted about increment markets concerns the marginal cost of such markets. An increase in demand for one increment market will increase the total costs of the firm by the same amount as in increase in demand at some other increment market. Both add to total output, and it is on total output that the regulated firm's marginal cost depends. Therefore, the marginal cost in any increment market is simply the marginal cost of a change in the firm's total output including all increment markets. Denoting the firm's total output by Q^T, its marginal cost is $MC(Q^T)$, where Q^T is the sum of all individuals' demands at the going nonuniform price schedule.

5.4 Inverse elasticity rule for nonuniform pricing

Thus far we have described how increments of consumption located at different quantity levels can be regarded as commodities unto themselves, each with a well defined marginal cost and aggregate demand. In this section we will show that a complete analogy exists between the pricing of these increment markets and Ramsey pricing. We will apply the best-known result of Ramsey pricing, the Inverse

---

[4]
For the reader with a background in economics, this important feature of the demand for an increment market comes from the assumed absence of income effects. If income effects are present, demands in different increment markets are not independent. It is partly for this reason that optimal tax equations are usually more complex and somewhat less intuitive than their counterparts in optimal pricing. In the tax context, consumer surplus is probably not an appropriate welfare measure because income effects cannot be assumed away. See Mirrlees [1971, 1976].

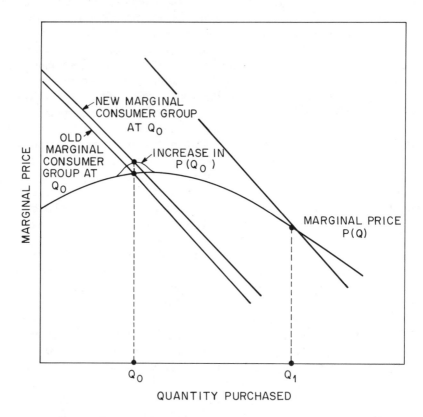

Figure 5.6

Elasticity Rule, to the pricing of increment markets and obtain the optimal nonuniform price schedule for a single commodity as a special type of Ramsey pricing.

We begin by defining consumer surplus and producer surplus in an increment market. Each consumer who is willing to buy an increment ΔQ at a given consumption level Q_0 earns an addition to his consumer on that ΔQ which is equal to the excess of his willingness to pay at Q_0 over the price for the increment at Q_0. Aggregate consumer surplus at that increment market is obtained by adding the consumer surpluses of all the consumers who participate in that increment market. Figure 5.7 illustrates this. We assume in this diagram that there is one consumer of each type.

The marginal consumer group at Q earns a zero consumer surplus by purchasing an increment ΔQ; by definition, his willingness to pay is equal to the marginal price. Consumers of type θ_1 earn a surplus given

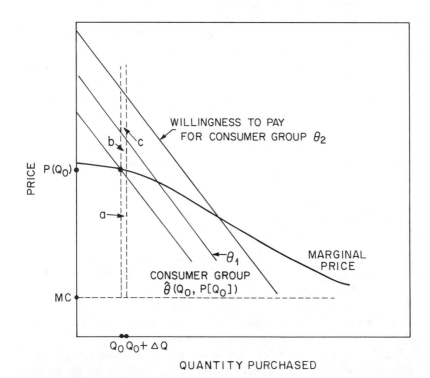

Figure 5.7

by area "b", and consumers of type θ_2 earn a surplus equal to "b" plus
"c" in the increment market at Q. Thus, aggregate consumer surplus in
that increment market is "b" + ("b" + "c") = twice "b" plus "c".[5]
Producer surplus in an increment market is equal to the price of the
increment minus marginal cost, summed over all consumers in that
increment market. In Figure 5.7, producer surplus is equal to three
times area "a". Thus, total surplus in the increment market is given by
three times "a" plus twice "b" and an additional "c".

Having obtained consumer surplus and producer surplus for an
increment market, we sum over all increment markets to get total
consumers' surplus and total producer surplus over all increment

[5] If there is more than one consumer of each type, then the consumer surplus
in this increment market would be $b \cdot g(\theta_1) + (b+c) \cdot g(\theta_2)$ where g is the
number of consumers at each θ.

markets. To price efficiently we pick prices for each one of the increment markets so as to maximize total surplus subject to the firm breaking even. By putting the optimal prices for adjacent increment markets together we will have constructed the optimal marginal price schedule, since the marginal price at a point is, by definition, the price for an incremental amount of consumption at that point. Because the set of prices for the increment markets maximizes total surplus, subject to breaking even, so must the marginal price schedule made up by stringing the increment market prices together.

With all of this superstructure built up, the form of the optimal marginal price schedule falls directly out of the Ramsey pricing theory presented in Chapter 3. Because the increment markets have independent demands, their prices must follow the Ramsey Inverse Elasticity Rule:

$$\frac{P(Q)-MC(Q^{T})}{P(Q)} = \frac{m}{\xi(q, P(Q))} .$$

(A constant m is set to achieve a break-even point.) The markup of price over marginal cost in each increment market is inversely proportional to the price-elasticity of demand in that increment market. Since this rule must hold in each increment market, the optimal marginal price schedule must follow it for all levels of consumption which are actually bought by some consumers.

The interesting feature of this result is that it links the seemingly different problems of nonuniform pricing and uniform pricing. Correctly interpreted, Ramsey pricing holds in both cases. It should be noted, though, that for the purpose of calculating efficient nonuniform prices numerically, other approaches are more convenient. Technical aspects are taken up in the appendix to this chapter.

This inverse elasticity rule for nonuniform pricing allows for quantity discounts and quantity premia, depending on the form which individuals' willingness to pay curves take and on the shape of the frequency distribution of consumer tastes. One feature of any optimal nonuniform price schedule is that marginal price must equal the firm's marginal cost for the last unit of consumption purchased by the largest consumer. In other words, if $\bar{\theta}$ is the highest possible value of the taste parameter, consumers with $\theta = \bar{\theta}$ must face a marginal price equal to marginal cost at the consumption level which maximizes their consumer surplus on the optimal nonuniform price schedule.

Using the intuition of Ramsey pricing, this result becomes plausible. Looking at the market for the final increment consumed by the largest users, by definition, only the $\bar{\theta}$ group is in the market for that increment. Therefore the price elasticity of demand for that final increment is infinite. By the inverse elasticity rule this means price must equal marginal cost in the market for the final increment consumed by the $\bar{\theta}$ group.

To gain further insight, suppose that it is not true, and that the maximal consumer type $\bar{\theta}$ faces a marginal price schedule $P_1(Q)$ which exceeds marginal cost at Q_1, the amount consumed by consumer $\bar{\theta}$ facing $P_1(Q)$. We can create a second marginal price schedule $P_2(Q)$ which dominates $P_1(Q)$ in the following way

$$P_2(Q) = P_1(Q), \quad Q < Q_1$$
$$= mc, \quad Q \geqslant Q_1.$$

where mc is the (constant) marginal cost. This new schedule is illustrated in Figure 5.8. In this way no consumer's behavior is affected except that of $\bar{\theta}$; he pays the same as before for up to Q_1 units of consumption. From Q_1 onward, however, $P_2 = mc$, so the $\bar{\theta}$ type will increase his consumption from Q_1 to Q_2 and gain in consumer surplus. The firm's producer surplus is unaffected by this change in the marginal price schedule because, in the first place, no consumers other than $\bar{\theta}$ have altered their behavior, and in the second place, the $\bar{\theta}$ group pays as much as it did before on the amount it consumed before and the increase in demand by $\bar{\theta}$ customers is priced at marginal cost. Figure 5.8 depicts the arrangement. Consumers with $\theta < \bar{\theta}$ still buy from the $P_1(Q)$ portion of the new price schedule. Type $\bar{\theta}$ faces the schedule $P_2(Q) =$ ABCD and consumes at D, increasing consumer surplus by the area "c" in the process. The firm continues to earn "a" plus "b" in contribution from the $\bar{\theta}$ consumers. Hence, total surplus rises by "c". By creating $P_2(Q)$, then, we have induced $\bar{\theta}$ to buy at marginal price equal to marginal cost, increasing the surplus of the $\bar{\theta}$ group at the expense of no one else. Therefore $P_1(Q)$ cannot have been optimal in the first place. This proves that the optimal marginal price schedule must have the property that it induces the highest users (those with $\theta = \bar{\theta}$) to consume at a point where the marginal price is equal to marginal cost. Figure 5.9 shows two marginal price schedules, $P(Q)$ and $\tilde{P}(Q)$. $P(Q)$ meets this necessary condition for optimality, but $\tilde{P}(Q)$ does not and, therefore, cannot be optimal. The Appendix to this chapter contains examples of how to solve for optimal nonuniform price schedules.

At this point, let us return to the main question of efficient pricing: how may a pricing scheme maximize total surplus while still enabling the firm to break even? The general approach is to try to locate levels of consumption which are price-inelastic, and try to make these regions

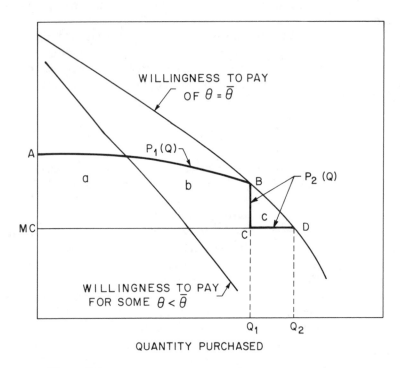

Figure 5.8

of consumption contribute as much as possible to the total costs of the firm. Consumers in price-elastic regions must be priced close to marginal cost. To try to extract a high level of contribution from price-elastic consumption would cause consumer demands to be cut so far back from the levels they would take on under marginal cost pricing that total surplus would fall excessively. In the case of Ramsey uniform pricing in Chapter 3 we endeavored to accomplish this with uniform prices which had high markups of price over marginal cost on price-elastic markets and low markup on highly elastic markets. Ramsey nonuniform pricing leads to greater pricing efficiency by going inside the individual markets and setting high markups on *ranges of consumption* in each market which are relatively unelastic. The inverse elasticity rule holds, in various forms, as a unifying principle throughout all of efficient pricing theory.

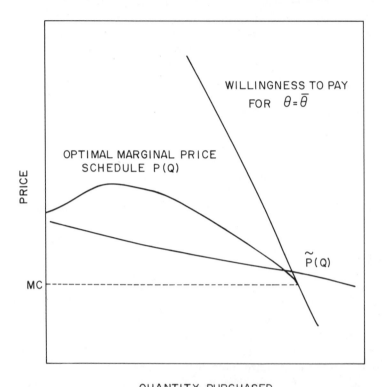

Figure 5.9

5.5 Properties of optimal nonuniform price schedules

In this section we will study in greater depth the behavior of optimal nonuniform price schedules. Recall the Inverse Elasticity Rule which governs the optimal marginal price schedules:

$$\frac{P(Q)-MC(Q^T)}{P(Q)} = \frac{m}{\xi(Q, P(Q))}.$$

The shape of the marginal price schedule is determined by the elasticity of demand for the increment market at each consumption level Q with respect to the marginal price. If $\xi(Q, P(Q))$ increases with quantity, then the marginal price schedule will display a quantity discount. If it falls for some levels of increasing consumption, then the marginal price schedule will show a quantity premium. Which outcome results depends on the willingness to pay function and the distribution of the taste variable, θ. We consider the seperate influences of each factor in turn.

To see the influence of willingness to pay, consider two alternatives. In the left hand panel of Figure 5.10 we show a set of willingness to pay curves for different θ levels wherein the price elasticity of demand is constant along each curve. These curves are flat up to a very low level of consumption $\hat{Q}$ and decline thereafter with constant elasticity, implying that for $Q > \hat{Q}$, the price elasticity of demand is constant. The horizontal segments from $Q = 0$ to $Q = \hat{Q}$ reflect the assumption that marginal utility does not decline until consumption reaches a minimal level $\hat{Q}$. For most consumers, willingness to pay is extremely high at $\hat{Q}$. All other things equal, this implies low price elasticities in the increment markets. at low levels of consumption. The inverse elasticity rule for nonuniform pricing suggests that high marginal prices should be set at low levels of consumption. In the right hand panel we depict a family of linear willingness to pay curves, which do not tend to infinity at low levels of consumption. In such a case, it is much easier to force consumers to zero consumption. The inverse elasticity rule suggests that it may be best to have low marginal prices for the first few units of consumption so as not to price too many consumers out of the increment market beginning at zero consumption. The firm's total costs could be made up by quantity premia at high levels of consumption.

The distribution of tastes is important because if the customers of the marginal consumer type in a given increment market are few in number relative to those in other increment markets, a rise in the increment price at that increment market may be accomplished at less reduction in total demand than would occur if the increment price were raised in some other increment market.

Numerical examples will illustrate these points. We will assume that θ is lognormally distributed; that is, the natural logarithm of θ is normally distributed, with mean 6.15 and variance .3025. The marginal cost of a call is 3.5 cents and a fixed cost of \$5.61 must be covered.

In order to see the effect of different demand curves, we will solve for optimal nonuniform prices under two assumptions about the form of the demand curve:

Linear demand: $Q = -3.57 + .21\theta - 213.4P$

Isoelastic demand: $Q = .0006\theta^{1.678}P^{-.625}$

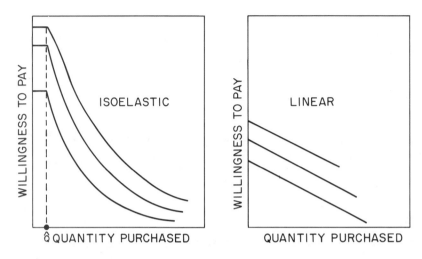

Figure 5.10

These two demand curves are tangent to each other at a price of \$.20 per call and a quantity of 68 calls, so that any differences in the resulting prices are due to differences in the shapes of the demand curves, and not to simple differences in scale of demand.

Figures 5.11 and 5.12 show the optimal marginal price schedules which occur under the two different demand assumptions. Figure 5.11 corresponds to linear demands, and Figure 5.12 to isoelastic demand. With linear willingness to pay curves, the optimal marginal price schedule at first declines with increased consumption. At about 200 calls per month the marginal price rises with consumption, and then takes a quantity discount ending at marginal cost, for the last call made by the largest user. With isoelastic willingness to pay, extremely high prices are charged for the first few calls, but the optimal marginal price function shows a steep quantity discount for all ranges of consumption.[6]

These results reflect two different strategies for attaining a high level of surplus. In the isoelastic case, consumers will pay a great deal for their first few calls, so the optimal pricing strategy is to cover the firm's

---

[6]
In the isoelastic case, for technical reasons, we cannot allow willingness to pay to become infinite. For this reason, we truncate it at a low consumption level Q_L and assume that willingness to pay is constant from zero to Q_L.

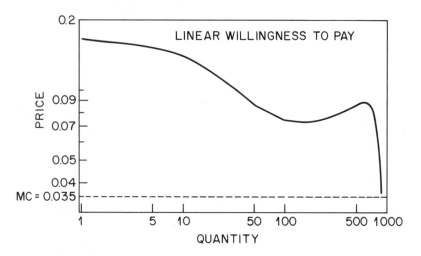

Figure 5.11

fixed costs by extremely high markups of marginal price over marginal cost for those calls, and to achieve pricing efficiency by a quantity discount which induces medium-sized and large customers to buy at marginal prices close to marginal cost. In the linear case, such a procedure would result in virtually the entire population of potential consumers dropping out of the market. Therefore, the optimal pricing strategy is to set a rather low marginal price at zero consumption and exclude a much smaller number of potential users. Marginal price declines toward marginal cost for consumption levels up to 200 calls per month and then covers the $5.61 fixed cost with a quantity premium which is faced only by the relatively large users.

Having examined the effects of willingness to pay on the optimal marginal price schedule, we will now examine the impacts of different distributions of θ in the population of consumers. In our continuing example, θ is lognormally distributed with logarithmic mean and variance μ and σ^2. For such a distribution of tastes, if we were to compare two different distributions of θ with different logarithmic means μ and the same σ^2, the distribution with the higher mean would contain a higher proportion of consumers with high levels of the taste parameter θ than would the distribution with the lower mean. Correspondingly, it would contain relatively fewer consumers with low values of the index θ. The effect of a higher variance is to make both very low θ's and very high θ's relatively more numerous than consumers with moderate levels of the taste parameter.

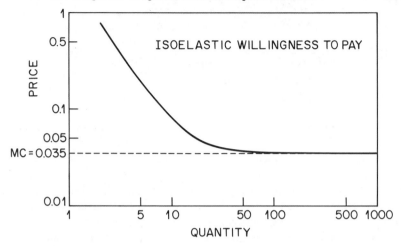

Figure 5.12

The optimal marginal price schedule corresponding to the base case values $\mu = 6.15$ and $\sigma^2 = .3025$ (with a revenue requirement of \$5.61) is given as the solid curve in Figure 5.13. We also show the uniform price of \$.0972 which would result from a policy of simple average cost pricing with the same revenue requirement of \$5.61. The marginal prices on the nonuniform price schedule start out at a marginal price much higher than the average cost price and decline in a quantity discount to levels very close to marginal cost, \$.035.

With a higher logarithmic mean of 8.61, with logarithmic variance σ^2 and revenue requirement still held at .3025 and \$5.61, respectively, the average cost price is equal to \$.039. The marginal price curve is tilted above the base case for low range of consumption and below it for medium and high levels. By about 25 calls per month, marginal prices under the revised price schedule fall below the base case schedule and by 130 calls per month converge very close to the marginal cost of \$.035.

The intuitive reason for this "tilt" effect of higher μ can be seen from the Inverse Elasticity Rule for marginal prices which was presented above.

$$\frac{P(Q) - mc}{P(Q)} = \frac{m}{\xi(Q, P(Q))}$$

where $mc = .035$ and

$$\xi(Q, P(Q)) = \frac{P(Q)}{\begin{pmatrix} \text{Number of consumers} \\ \text{with } \theta \geqslant \hat{\theta} \text{ before} \\ \text{the price change} \end{pmatrix}} \times \begin{pmatrix} \text{Change in } \hat{\theta} \\ \text{per unit} \\ \text{change in} \\ P(Q) \end{pmatrix} \times \begin{pmatrix} \text{Density} \\ \text{of} \\ \hat{\theta} \end{pmatrix}.$$

Imagine a situation in which the population demographics changed in such a way that the mean increased from 6.15 to 8.61. The first effect of the increase in the mean is to reduce the number of consumers with low values of θ. If we look at the increment market at zero, this means that the density of the marginal group at zero has fallen, so that $\xi(0, P(0))$ has gone down. From our inverse elasticity rule for nonuniform pricing, this means that the marginal price at zero must go up. This explains the fact that $P_2(0) = \$.223$ while $P_1(0)$ is only $\$.166$. By the same token, with the higher mean μ, the relative proportion of high values of θ has increased, making increment markets at high consumption levels more price-elastic than they are with $\mu = 6.15$. Therefore, marginal prices at high consumption levels must be closer to the marginal cost of $\$.035$ when $\mu = 8.61$ than when $\mu = 6.15$. To sum up, with a value of μ equal to 8.61 increment markets at low levels of consumption are less price elastic than when $\mu = 6.15$, and increment markets at high levels of consumption are more price elastic. From the Inverse Elasticity Rule, this accounts for the observed tilt to higher marginal prices for low consumption levels and lower marginal prices for high consumption levels.

The level of the logarithmic mean μ also affects the gain in total surplus which the regulator could achieve by going from average cost pricing to optimal nonuniform pricing. From Table 5.1 we see that with progressively higher values of μ the surplus gain of going from uniform to nonuniform pricing diminishes. With $\mu = 8.61$, the gain is almost nonexistent. To see why, notice that the average cost uniform price for higher levels of μ gets closer and closer to the marginal cost of $\$.035$ per call because with a high μ, the average level of consumption is high enough so that the revenue requirement per customer of $\$5.61$ is spread very thin. Thus, there is very little potential surplus gain available to be captured by a nonuniform price structure.

Figure 5.13 gives marginal price schedules for two values of the logarithmic variance, $\sigma^2 : \sigma^2 = .3025$ (the base case value) and $\sigma^2 = .4235$ with $\mu = 6.15$ in both cases. As before, the marginal price curve resulting from Mitchell's estimates of $\mu = 6.15$ and $\sigma^2 = .3025$ is

Table 5.1[*]

Level of μ	Uniform Price at Average Cost ($)	Surplus Gain ($)
5.85	.110	.240
6.15	.097	.090
7.38	.049	.022
8.61	.039	.002

Note: $\sigma^2 = .3025$ in all cases.

Table 5.2[*]

Level of σ^2	Uniform Price at Average Cost ($)	Surplus Gain ($)
.1815	.103	.230
.2420	.100	.145
.3025	.097	.090
.3630	.095	.060
.4235	.092	.023

Note: $\mu = 6.15$ in all cases.

[*] For both tables $mc = \$.035$, the revenue requirement is $5.61 and the individual demand function is $Q(P, \theta) = -3.57 + .21\theta - 213.4P$.

given by the solid curve, with an average cost price of $.097. The corresponding prices for $\sigma^2 = .4235$ are given as the dotted lines. The higher variance tilts the price schedule so that marginal prices at zero and low numbers of calls per month are lower and marginal prices at greater consumption levels are higher than when $\sigma^2 = .3025$. Once again, the intuitive reason for this follows easily from the Inverse Elasticity Rule. Since the increase in σ^2 increases the density of low θ consumers, the price-elasticity of demand for increment markets at zero

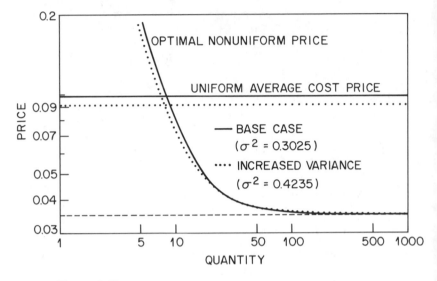

Figure 5.13

and low consumption levels is higher with $\sigma^2 = .4235$ than it is with $\sigma^2 = .3025$. Therefore, from the Inverse Elasticity Rule marginal prices in those ranges of consumption should be lower with higher variance. For large volumes of calls, the marginal price schedule for $\sigma^2 = .4235$ must compensate with higher marginal prices so as to cover the same revenue requirement of $5.61.

The level of variance σ^2 has a strong effect on the potential surplus gains from optimal nonuniform pricing. From Table 5.1, the higher σ^2, the lower is this surplus gain. This diminution occurs because the tilt towards bringing more consumers into the market which results from increased variance forces marginal prices for moderate and high levels of consumption up to levels which approach the average cost price.

Finally, it is useful to compare the effects of optimal nonuniform pricing to those of the optimal two-part tariff. At the end of the previous chapter we used the local service telephone pricing framework to compute the optimal two-part tariff in the case $\mu = 6.15$ and $\sigma^2 = .3025$. The entry fee was $1.24 and the usage charge $.0834. This tariff raised surplus by $.05 per month relative to the average cost price of $.097. Optimal nonuniform pricing for these parameter values increases surplus by an additional $.04 per month. Relative to the optimal nonuniform price schedule, the two-part tariff prices too many small users out of the market with the entry fee and fails to offer large users a low enough usage charge.

5.6 The multicommodity case[7]

We now expand the theory to include the case where the regulated firm sells more than one commodity and charges nonuniform prices for its services. This theory will allow us to address problems of pricing peak and off-peak services, telephone calls of differing distance, etc. We will retain the assumption that consumers differ by a single taste variable θ. It will turn out that the principles for the nonuniform pricing of a single good carry over to the multicommodity case and that the Inverse Elasticity Rule holds once again, in a somewhat different form.

As in Chapter 3, the firm offers M services, Q_1, Q_2, ..., Q_M; for brevity, we denote the entire list of services $(Q_1, Q_2, ..., Q_M)$ by Q. The firm offers the consumer an outlay function $R(Q)$ which depends on consumption of all M commodities. We denote by $P_i(Q)$ the marginal price of the ith service, given that the consumer is buying Q_1, Q_2, ..., Q_M. In other words, $P_i(Q)$ is the price of an increment of consumption of the ith good, holding purchases of all other services constant.

In the multicommodity case it is not as easy to depict consumer surplus graphically as it was in the single commodity case. Therefore, we will use the multicommodity surplus function where consumer surplus is given by the difference between utility and outlay:

$$\text{Consumer Surplus} = U(Q_1, Q_2, ..., Q_M, \theta) - R(Q_1, Q_2, ..., Q_M).$$

To maximize his consumer surplus, the consumer picks consumption levels $Q_1^*, Q_2^*, ..., Q_M^*$ so that willingness to pay for an increment of each good i is equal to P_i, the price of that increment. We will extend our assumption of strong monotonicity of preferences to the multicommodity case: a high value of the taste parameter θ leads to higher consumption of all M commodities.

A useful concept to the theory of multicommodity nonuniform pricing is the *menu path*. The menu path is the set of points in commodity space which is traced out by connecting the consumption bundles which are selected by consumers with different values of θ. We depict one possible menu path in Figure 5.14 for the two-commodity case. Point t_0 on the menu path represents the purchases of a consumer with a value of θ equal to θ_0, which are $Q_1^*(\theta_0)$ and $Q_2^*(\theta_0)$. Point t_1 on the menu path gives the purchases $Q_1^*(\theta_1)$, $Q_2^*(\theta_1)$ made by a consumer with a higher value of θ, θ_1. Thus, moving up on the menu path, we come to the consumption pairs selected by consumers with higher and higher

---

[7] This section follows the discussion of Mirman and Sibley [1980]. Although the presentation is not mathematical, the material is somewhat abstract. Therefore, readers who are not specialists may wish to skip this section. They can do so without serious loss of continuity.

values of θ.

The strong monotonicity assumption (that the demand curves of different types of consumers do not cross) plays an important part in the menu path. Because of this assumption, the curve must increase in both Q_1 and Q_2. To see why, look at point A with a taste value θ_A. Could the menu path be such that another consumer with $\theta_D > \theta_A$ consume at a point such as B, with more Q_2 but the same amount of Q_1? No, because by strong monotonicity a higher value of θ means that consumption of *both* commodities must rise with higher θ. For the same reason, the menu path could not move horizontally to a point such as C. Therefore, the menu path must rise in *both* Q_1 and Q_2, and the consumer with θ_D must be consuming at a point such as D.

A given menu path represents the individually optimal consumption points selected by the population of consumers for a particular outlay function, with its associated marginal prices. If the outlay and marginal price schedules are changed, the menu path will change (in general). If the outlay function generating the original menu path were changed in such a way that the marginal price of Q_1 were increased at every consumption level, then the menu path would shift upward to the dashed menu path, so that for every level of Q_2, consumers buy less Q_1.

With the concept of the menu path in hand we can reformulate the multicommodity problem in such a way that the single-commodity results which we discussed in the previous sections will give us the optimal nonuniform price schedule for the multicommodity case as well. Denote different points on the menu path by t, which represents distance along the path. Because each point, indexed by t, is associated with a unique consumption pair, t can be thought of as a sort of composite good, consisting of $Q_1, Q_2, ..., Q_M$ in the proportions given by the menu path. In the two-commodity case of Figure 5.14, for example, t_0 consists of $(Q_1^* (\theta_0), Q_2^* (\theta_0))$ and t_1 of $(Q_1^* (\theta_1), Q_2^* (\theta_1))$. In effect, then, we are dealing with a single commodity, t, which represents points on the menu path. $Q_1, Q_2, ..., Q_M$ are just functions of t.

We can write the outlay schedule which gives rise to a particular menu path as a function of t, the distance along that path:

$$R(Q_1(t), Q_2(t), ..., Q_M(t)) \equiv R(t) .$$

The marginal price of a movement along the menu path is given by

$$\frac{\Delta R}{\Delta t} = P_1 \cdot \frac{\Delta Q_1}{\Delta t} + ... + P_M \cdot \frac{\Delta Q_M}{\Delta t} \equiv P(t) .$$

In other words, a movement along the menu path from a point t to a point $t+\Delta t$ involves positive increments of all m commodities, by the strong monotonicity assumption. The prices of these changes in

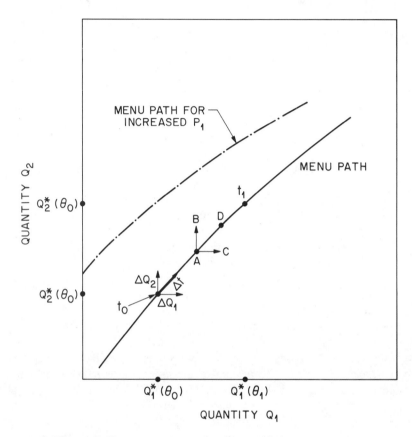

Figure 5.14

consumption of the m commodities are the marginal prices P_1, P_2, ..., P_M. Thus, the total extra outlay of an incremental move along the menu path is just the sum of the resulting incremental outlays in each of the M markets.

Going to the demand for points on the menu path, willingness to pay for an extra movement along the menu path is simply the sum of willingness to pay for each of the increments in the commodities $Q_1, Q_2, ..., Q_M$ which are induced by a movement along the menu path.

On the cost side, the cost to the firm of a consumer's moving from a lower to a higher point on the menu path is given by the extra cost of the increase in his consumption of $Q_1, Q_2, ..., Q_M$ which is implied by the movement along the menu path. To make this clearer, suppose that we have a two-commodity case with prices which generate the menu path $Q_1 = 3.5 \ Q_2$. For a one-unit change in Q_2 there is a 3.5 unit corresponding change in Q_1. If the marginal cost of Q_1 is 10 cents and the marginal cost of Q_2 is 20 cents, then a move from a point such as $(Q_1 = 35, Q_2 = 10)$ to $(Q_1 = 38.5, Q_2 = 11)$ involves a one-unit increase in Q_2, a 3.5 unit increase in Q_1 and costs the firm

$$(3.5)(10¢) + 1 \times 20¢ = 55¢.$$

This 55 cent figure can be thought of as the marginal cost of an extra consumer in the increment markets for Q_1 and Q_2 located at $(Q_1 = 38.5, Q_2 = 11)$ along the menu path. In general, let $MC(t)$ denote the marginal cost to the firm of an extra consumer in the increment markets located at point t on the menu path.

We have now reformulated the multicommodity pricing problem as the problem of pricing the single commodity t. Therefore, we can apply the results of our discussion in the single commodity case:

- At each point t along the menu path there is a marginal consumer type $\hat{\theta}(t, P(t))$.
- There is an aggregate demand at each t for an increment Δt and this demand is equal to the number of consumers with values of θ at least equal to $\hat{\theta}(t, P(t))$.
- The demands for different increment markets for movement along the menu path are independent of each other.
- There is a marginal cost $MC(t)$ to the firm of extra demand at a particular increment market.

We are now ready to apply the single commodity theory of nonuniform pricing to the pricing of movements along the menu path. Suppose now that we have found the menu path generated by the optimal multicommodity nonuniform price schedule.[8] Applying the Inverse Elasticity Rule for nonuniform pricing, the marginal price for points on the optimal menu path must satisfy the condition that at each point t on the menu path

$$\frac{P(t) - MC(t)}{P(t)} = \frac{m}{\xi(t, P(t))}$$

where $\xi(t, P(t))$ is the elasticity of demand for the increment market at t (on the menu path) with respect to the marginal price (of points on the menu path) at t. As before, m is a constant set so that the firm breaks even. Because consumers only pick points on the menu path, this expression represents optimal nonuniform pricing in the multicommodity case.

[8] As Mirman and Sibley [1980] note, the optimization takes place both over the prices of different points on the menu path and over the menu path itself.

Although this discussion shows the wide applicability of the Inverse Elasticity Rule, it may not be obvious to readers how we get from a nonuniform price schedule for points on the menu path to one for the commodities themselves. To do so we will start again with points on the menu path.

Each point on the menu path has associated with it a *set* of increment markets, one for each commodity. In Figure 5.14 at point t_0 there is a market for a ΔQ_1 increment at that point and a ΔQ_2 increment. (Added together, these increment markets for the individual commodities yield the incremental movement along the menu path, Δt, whose price we analyzed above.) At point t_1 on the menu path is another pair of increment markets. In an M-commodity analysis, there would be M increment markets for the commodities located at each point on the menu path.

If we raise the marginal price of one of the commodities at a point on the menu path, this lowers the demand for the entire *set* of commodity increment markets located at that point. The reason for this is that an increase in the marginal price of each good increases $P(t)$, the marginal price for a movement along the menu path. This induces the marginal consumer type at that point t to fall back to a lower point on the menu path. By doing this, he drops out of all of the commodity increment markets at the original point on the menu path.

Since the effect of raising one of the commodity marginal prices is to raise the marginal price for movement along the menu path, it should not be surprising that the rule governing optimal commodity marginal prices along the optimal menu path is similar to the rule for $P(t)$, namely:

$$\frac{P_i(Q) - MC_i(Q)}{P_i(Q)} = \frac{m}{\xi_i(Q(t), P(Q))}$$

where

$MC_i(Q) =$ marginal cost of the ith good given the total set of outputs Q

$\xi_i(Q(t), P(Q)) =$ elasticity of demand for the set of increment markets located at point t on the menu path with respect to the marginal price of the ith commodity at that point on the menu path.

By analogy with the single commodity theory, it is also true that marginal price must equal marginal cost at the surplus-maximizing consumption level of the consumer type with the highest value of θ, $\bar{\theta}$. Mathematically,

$$P_i(Q^*(\bar{\theta})) = MC_i(Q^T)$$

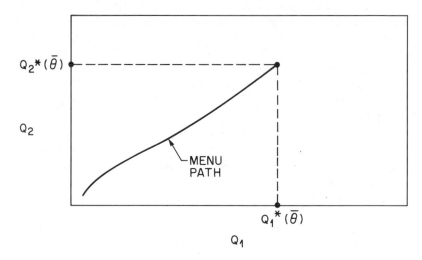

Figure 5.15

where $Q^*(\bar{\theta}) = (Q_1^*(\bar{\theta}), Q_2^*(\bar{\theta}),...,Q_m^*(\bar{\theta})$ is the optimal consumption bundle for the $\bar{\theta}$ group; in Figure 5.15 this is the upper endpoint of the menu path, labeled $Q^*(\bar{\theta})$. A numerical example for two goods will help to illustrate these concepts. We label the goods Q_1 and Q_2 and assume that consumers act according to the following utility function:

$$U(Q_1, Q_2, \theta) = .242\, Q_1 + .00136\, Q_1 \cdot \theta - .012 \cdot \frac{Q_1^2}{2}$$

$$+ .247\, Q_2 + .00139\, Q_2 \cdot \theta - .048 \frac{Q_2^2}{2}$$

$$- .0079 \cdot Q_1 \cdot Q_2 \,.$$

Faced with a particular outlay function for the two goods $R(Q_1, Q_2)$, the consumer chooses Q_1^* and Q_2^* to maximize his consumer surplus:

$$\underset{\{Q_1, Q_2\}}{\text{maximize}} \left[U(Q_1, Q_2, \theta) - R(Q_1, Q_2) \right].$$

This behavior generates the following two demand curves:

$$Q_1 = 17.79 + .103\theta - 90.48 P_1 + gP_2$$

$$Q_2 = 2.807 + .012\theta - 23.3 P_2 + gP_1$$

where $g = 15$. In this example the two commodities are substitutes for each other: a rise in the price of one good leads consumers to switch to the other. A \$1.00 rise in P_1 causes a 15-unit rise in the demand for good 2.

The firm's marginal costs are $c_1 = \$.096$ and $c_2 = \$.06$ and there is a fixed cost of $4.00 which must be covered.

From our discussion above we know that the optimal marginal prices must follow the rules

$$\frac{P_1(Q_1, Q_2) - .096}{P_1(Q_1, Q_2)} = \frac{m}{\xi_1}$$

and

$$\frac{P_2(Q_1, Q_2) - .06}{P_2(Q_1, Q_2)} = \frac{m}{\xi_2} \,.$$

Therefore, at each point Q_1, Q_2 it must be true that the deviations of marginal price from marginal cost, weighted by the increment market price elasticities, are equal to each other and to the constant m:

$$\left[\frac{P_1 - c_1}{P_1}\right] \cdot \xi_1 = \left[\frac{P_2 - c_2}{P_2}\right] \cdot \xi_2 = m \,.$$

From this expression we can calculate the menu path, which turns out to be

$$Q_2 = 1.747 + .11677 \times Q_1.$$

Our object is to find marginal prices P_1 and P_2 which maximize total surplus, subject to breaking even. In Figure 5.16 we depict that optimal marginal price schedules $P_1(Q_1, Q_2)$ and $P_2(Q_1, Q_2)$ which do this, where Q_1 and Q_2 are related by the menu path. The dashed curves are the optimal marginal prices for good 2 with $g = 0$ and $g = 15$. The solid curves are the marginal price schedules for good 1 with $g = 0$ and $g = 15$. The object is also to maximize surplus subject to the same breakeven constraint. The effects of the cross-elasticity are to raise the marginal price schedule in market 1 and to lower it in market 2.

5.7 Conclusions

This chapter has covered a great deal of material which the nonspecialist may have found difficult to understand.[9] Apart from the technical details of the theory, however, the main points to be kept in mind by the nonspecialist reader are two.

The first is that the Ramsey Inverse Elasticity Rule is a concept which unifies optimal uniform pricing with optimal nonuniform pricing.

[9]
The Appendix contains discussion of several technical issues not covered above, as well as examples of nonuniform price schedules in simple cases where closed form solutions exist.

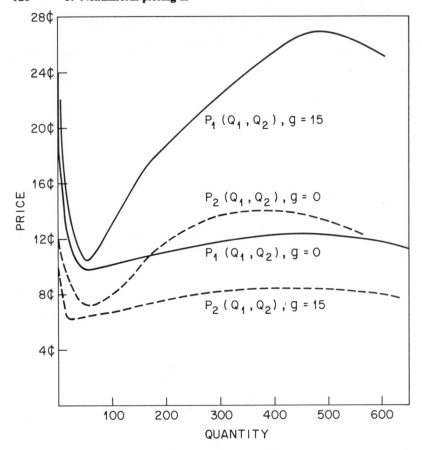

Figure 5.16

The Ramsey Inverse Elasticity Rule was originally developed as the most efficient means to discriminate between markets with uniform pricing structures where demands are independent. By the device of considering consumption increments as products unto themselves, we were able to apply the Inverse Elasticity Rule to the prices of these increments. Since the marginal price $P(Q)$ schedule of a nonuniform outlay function $R(Q)$ does nothing more than give the price of an incremental amount of a good, this meant that we got an Inverse Elasticity Rule for nonuniform pricing: at each point on a nonuniform outlay schedule, the percentage markup between marginal price and marginal cost is inversely proportional to the elasticity of demand for an increment of consumption at that point with respect to the marginal price at that point. This rule extends to the pricing of multiple commodities.

The second point to be retained is that the existence of quantity discounts and quantity premia on an optimal nonuniform price schedule is the result of designing the marginal price schedule so as to price discriminate efficiently among consumers. High marginal prices should be set at consumption levels where the elasticity of demand for incremental consumption is low, and marginal prices should be set close to marginal cost where the price elasticity of demand for incremental consumption is high. Going from low to high quantities on an optimal nonuniform outlay schedule, if increment markets become steadily more price elastic, the marginal price will fall, for a quantity discount. If the reverse occurs a quantity premium will be optimal.

Apart from its intellectual interest, this result is quite important because it challenges the basis on which declining block tariffs have traditionally been justified in the public utility arena. Traditionally, quantity discounts have been justified both in electricity and telecommunications pricing by arguments to the effect that large consumers are cheaper to serve than smaller ones. In rate proceedings, a great deal of time and effort is spent in establishing whether or not this condition is true in the case at issue. Indeed, in the Public Utilities Regulatory Policies Act of 11078.[10] Congress went on record as opposing declining block tariffs unless the public utility can demonstrate that the cost of energy component of total cost decreases as consumption increases. Our discussion shows that much of this discussion is beside the point: quantity discounts may be optimal even if large and small customers cost the same to serve. Whether or not quantity discounts or optimal depends in an important way on whether they are the best ways of sorting consumers onto different points of a nonuniform price schedule in a given market. If, in fact, large consumers *are* cheaper to serve than small ones, this may provide an additional reason for a quantity discount. But even if they are no cheaper to serve, our discussion shows that quantity discounts may still be economically efficient.

10
Public Law 95-617, 95th Congress.

CHAPTER 6

Efficient pricing and flowthrough

6.1 Introduction

A key ingredient in most discussions of efficient pricing theory is the assumption that the regulated monopoly's customers are independent of each other. That is, it is assumed that the amount consumed by one customer has no impact on the surplus which can be earned by another customer. For this reason, it is possible (and convenient) to ignore interactions between consumers in designing efficient prices.

In reality, there are many reasons why interactions between consumers could be important; in such cases, efficient pricing rules should take account of them. One especially important type of interaction occurs when the utility sells both to business customers and residential consumers. Residential consumers buy the utility's services as final products to be consumed. The business customers buy the utility's services as inputs into their own production processes, which produce outputs that they sell to other businesses and to final consumers, including, possibly, the utility's residential customers. The prices that the utility's business customers charge for the goods and services which they produce link their welfare to those of the utility's residential customers, who buy both the service of the utility and the outputs produced by the utility's business customers. Individual business users' profits are linked to the extent that they compete with each other. This type of interaction also occurs when a utility sets a nonuniform price schedule for business customers. Changes in marginal prices at given points on the schedule will affect total outlay for firms which consume larger amounts of the utility's services. This, in turn, affects prices in these industries. These "downstream" price changes

This chapter derives theoretical results not available elsewhere and is written for the technical reader. The results derived herein are interspersed throughout the other chapters of the book.

will affect the demands for the utility's services by still other downstream industries through cross-elasticity effects in final product markets.

In both of these cases the prices set by the public utility cause the fortunes of different customers to be interrelated through downstream market equilibrium relationships. We refer to this interrelationship as *flowthrough*. In this chapter we examine how to price efficiently when account is taken of flowthrough.

There is another feature of interest in taking account of the flowthrough effects of prices faced by business customers. In the preceding chapters we have pointed out that pricing changes in the direction of increased efficiency will usually hurt some customers, as well as benefiting others. For example, to go from FDC pricing to Ramsey pricing might easily mean that the peak period price would rise and the off peak price would fall. If overall consumer surplus rises as a result, this would be of small comfort to those who used primarily peak period service. Alternatively, efficient pricing might lead to a price increase for local telephone calls and a decrease for interexchange calls. Those customers who use primarily local service would be harmed by such an event. In these cases the economist can only point out to the policy maker that non-distorting lump sum redistributions out of the increased total surplus could in principle leave all parties at least as well off as before the pricing change, and nobody worse off. Unfortunately, mechanisms rarely exist to see that this actually occurs.

There is one important policy area, though, in which the required compensation may take place automatically. This is when the regulated firm's markets are segmented by customer class into business and residential markets, which is the case in virtually every regulated industry in the United States. It is often true that price changes proposed as leading to increased efficiency appear to hurt residential customers and help business customers. However, in such cases a reduction in the price at which a utility sells to its business customers shows up as a reduction in their costs of doing business. These cost reductions may flow through to residential consumers in the form of price reductions in the markets in which the utility's business customers sell their goods and services to residential consumers. In this chapter we consider two questions which arise in this context:

— Suppose that a utility proposes a set of price changes which increase total surplus, but include an increase in the residential price. How can we tell if the flowthrough effects of these changes compensate consumers by leading to price reductions in other markets which counterbalance the increase in the residential price?

— Taking into account flowthrough effects, how are our optimal pricing *formulae* affected?

To be useful, the answers to these questions must not drastically increase the amount of information they require a policy maker to possess. If efficient pricing principles require an accounting of the flowthrough effects from the markets of the regulated firm into myriad other markets, then the analyst is little better off than if he ignored them; the required data and computational complexity would be overwhelming. Thus, any modifications to the pricing rules we have discussed in previous chapters should be simple ones. The efficient pricing theory which we have discussed thus far requires only that the regulator know the demands and costs for the products sold by the regulated firm. We call this level of required information the *myopic* level. In expanding our analysis to consider flowthrough effects we would like to preserve the myopic character of efficient pricing rules as far as possible.

Section 6.2 below analyzes efficient uniform pricing where prices are to set so as to maximize total surplus over utility's business and residence markets. Particular attention is paid to the question of when pricing rules are myopic in character, using a downstream industry model in which there is free entry and firms set prices assuming a constant conjectural variation.[1] In Section 6.3 we analyze the optimal nonuniform pricing rule where different downstream industries have different tastes for the utility's services. Because of the greatly increased complication of the nonuniform pricing problem we make very strong assumptions about downstream cost and supply structure. These assumptions are met in perfectly competitive markets and, under still further assumptions, by markets which are contestable. Section 6.4 contains conclusions for the practitioner of public utility pricing.

6.2 Efficient uniform prices and flowthrough

A. The simplest model

Initially we shall analyze flowthrough using a very simplified paradigm. The utility sells an amount X_R to residential customers and X_B to business customers, at prices P_R and P_B respectively. Consumers are identical to each other, as are firms. For further simplicity, we will assume that the utility's business customers all form a single industry which produces an output Q which is sold to the utility's residential

---

[1]

   As noted below, however if downstream firms have average cost curves with flat bottoms, the same results follow in perfectly contestable markets.

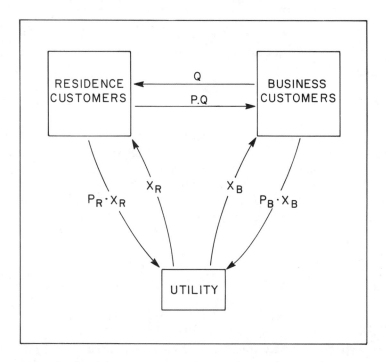

Figure 6.1

customers at a price P. Figure 6.1 depicts this arrangement schematically. (To allow the utility's business customers to comprise more than one industry would not change the character of the analysis or the results.)

Thus, consumers are buying three outputs: X_R, Q, and a third composite good so as to maximize consumer surplus:

$$\max_{\{X_R\, Q\}} \left[U(X_R, Q) - P_R X_R - PQ \right] \tag{1}$$

$$\frac{\partial U}{\partial X_R} = P_R \tag{2}$$

$$\frac{\partial U}{\partial Q} = P. \tag{3}$$

The solution of equations (2) and (3) leads straightforwardly to the demand functions $X_R(P_R, P)$ and $Q(P_R, P)$.

We describe behavior among firms producing Q by a conjectural variation model with free entry. Firms are assumed to be identical and number n. Thus, each firm picks an output q to maximize its own profit, π^Q, where

$$\pi^Q = P(Q) \cdot q - C(q, P_B, \omega) - H \tag{4}$$

where Q is industry output and q that of the individual firm. ω is the vector of prices for inputs other than X_B. $H \geq 0$ is a fixed cost. Profit maximization leads to

$$vqP' + P - C_q = 0, \frac{d^2\pi}{dq^2} < 0 \tag{5}$$

where v is the derivative of Q with respect to q.[2] v is termed the conjectural variation of industry output with respect to a change in the output of an individual firm (See Section 2.4 above). For $v = 0$ we have perfect competition, for $v=1$ the quantity-setting Cournot model and for $v=n$ the case of perfect collusion. The number of firms, n, adjusts so that $\pi^Q = 0$. Letting $Q = nq$, the free entry condition can be written as

$$P(nq) \cdot q - C(q, P_B, \omega) - H = 0. \tag{6}$$

In this model, a reduction in P_B will generate momentary excess profits, which will be dissipated by entry. However, because $P > C_q$ as long as $v > 0$, it may be that not all of the potential savings flow through to consumers in the form of price reductions.

The equilibrium price P in the downstream market is given by $P(nq)$, where n and q are given by solving (5) and (6). Clearly, the reduced form equilibrium price P will depend on P_B. However, P will also depend on P_R whenever the demands for X_R and Q are not independent. To calculate the effects of the utility's price P_B on the equilibrium price P is complex, and the derivation is relegated to the appendix to this chapter. For the purpose of our discussion, we will make simplifying assumptions regarding the business customers' variable cost function, $C(q, P_B, \omega)$: there exist locally constant marginal variable costs ($C_{qq} = 0$) and a unitary scale elasticity of demand for the input.[3] Using

---

2

As is well known, this class of models has the conceptual flaw that when firms are out of equilibrium their conjectures are rarely correct. On the other hand, the results of Perry [1982] suggest that "consistent" conjectures exist only under relatively special conditions when free entry is allowed. It seems best for our purpose, therefore, to retain the rough plausibility which the constant conjectural variation model possesses as a descriptor of a wide range of market structures, even though firms' conjectures will not be consistent in general.

3

The scale elasticity of demand is defined as $e = \dfrac{\partial X_B}{\partial q} \cdot \dfrac{q}{X_B}$ where χ_B represents the input of X_B by a typical firm. One way to have $C_{qq} = 0$ with $e = 1$ is to assume that the variable cost function C has locally constant returns. Because the fixed cost $H > 0$, average cost would decline with output.

these assumptions, we can write dP/dP_B in an extremely convenient form:

$$\frac{dP}{dP_B} = \frac{\chi_B}{q} \cdot \frac{1}{(1 + v\frac{M}{2n})} \tag{7}$$

where $\chi_B \equiv \dfrac{X_B}{n}$ is usage of X_B per firm and

$$M \equiv \frac{QP''}{P'}$$

$(P' \equiv \partial P/\partial Q, P'' \equiv \partial^2 P/\partial Q^2)$. Common sense requires that a rise in the input price P_B should increase P, so whatever the sign of M, we require $1 + vM/2n > 0$. As argued in the appendix this is guaranteed by assuming $P' - C_{qq} < 0$.[4] Two features of (7) are of interest. First, when the downstream industry is perfectly competitive $(v = 0)$, the flowthrough effect on the output price P is proportional to a typical firm's input of X per unit of output q:

$$dP = \frac{\chi_B}{q} \cdot dP_B. \tag{8}$$

Thus, if the production of q is quite intensive in X_B, the price rises by more than if q used only a small amount of the utility's product. Second, even when $v > 0$, if the downstream demand curve is linear so that $M = 0$, the flowthrough effect is the same; that is, although $v > 0$ drives a wedge between price and marginal cost, it does not distort the flowthrough effects of changes in input prices. Intuitively, v should only affect the setting of P_B to the extent that change in P_B improves or worsens the downstream distortion between price and marginal cost. This distortion, normalized by q, is given by

$$\frac{P - C_q}{q} = -vP'(Q). \tag{9}$$

When $M = 0$, changes in P_B leave $-vP'$ and, hence, the distortion, unchanged. Therefore v plays no role in the flowthrough effects. When P'' is different from zero, a change change in P_B can either increase the

----

4
Seade [1980] has shown that $P' - C_{qq} < 0$ is necessary for market equilibrium to be stable when n is fixed. We are not claiming that $P' - C_{qq} < 0$ is necessary for stability when n is variable. We are taking the stance that a reasonable model with variable n should be stable if n were fixed. Thus, we impose the restriction $P' - C_{qq} < 0$.

downstream distortion ($P'' > 0$) or decrease it ($P'' < 0$). Hence, when $M \neq 0$ the flowthrough effects of P_B may be either greater or less than one would estimate by ignoring the term $\nu M / 2n$.

We should note at this point that equation (8) also holds in a perfectly contestable market whenever (a) firms are producing at minimum average cost and (b) all demand is satisfied at a price equal to minimum average cost. To see this, if price is equal to average cost

$$P = \frac{C(q, P_B, z)}{q}$$

and

$$dP = \left[\frac{\partial(C/q)}{\partial q} \frac{\partial q}{\partial B} + \frac{1}{q} \frac{\partial C}{\partial P_B} \right] dP_B .$$

From (a), $\partial(C/q)/\partial q = 0$ and from Shepherd's Lemma $\partial C/\partial P_B = \chi_B$. Therefore

$$dP = \frac{\chi_B}{q} dP_B$$

which is equation (8). However, as Sharkey [1982] has shown, when cost curves follow the Vinerian U-shape contestable market equilibrium given (a) violates (b); i.e., some demand is left unsatisfied. Baumol, Panzar and Willig [1982, p.32-40] show that if downstream firms' average cost curves have flat bottoms over some finite range of output and if market demand is such that firms produce at minimum average cost then firms earn zero profits and meet market demand (see Baumol, Panzar and Willig [1982], Proposition 2D2).

B. Flowthrough and improvements in efficiency

In this section we address the first question posed in the introduction to this chapter: given arbitrary changes $dP_R > 0$ and $dP_B < 0$, when can we say that consumer surplus increases as a net effect of flowthrough? To provide a basis for comparison we will assume that the utility earns the same level of profit under both the new and the old prices.

Consumers benefit from flowthrough when P falls. Given small changes in P_R and P, the effect on consumer surplus is given by

$$- X_R \, dP_R - Q \, dP \tag{10}$$

through simple application of the envelope theorem to maximized consumer surplus. Assuming for the moment that the demands for X_R and Q are independent, we can apply (7) to this expression,

$$dCS = - X_R \, dP_R - \frac{X_B}{1 + \dfrac{vM}{2n}} \, dP_B. \tag{11}$$

Under perfect competition $(v = 0)$ this expression reduces to

$$dCS = - X_R \, dP_R - X_B \, dP_B \tag{12}$$

which is myopic, in the sense that the price-setter does not need to look beyond the market for X_B. The downstream industry producing Q is only a "veil" between consumers and the utility's business market. It is as if consumers bought X_B directly, so that (12) reduces to the simple differential of consumer surplus with respect to the prices which the consumer faces for the goods he buys. Although (11) is not a myopic formula, under certain conditions the term $vM/2n$ may be ignored. For example, as long as the changes $dP_R > 0$ and $dP_B < 0$ are small, the change dP will be "small," too; in such a case we may take $Q(P)$ as *locally* linear and set $P'' \sim 0$, so that $M \sim 0$. Alternatively, n may be large enough so that $M/2n \sim 0.$[5] Therefore, even when $v > 0$, and imperfect competition exists it may be appropriate to use the approximation

$$dCS \sim - X_R \, dP_R - X_B \, dP_B \tag{13}$$

which is myopic.

We can derive an expression for bounds on the error involved in using (13) instead of (11) when $vM/2n$ is non-zero. Let dCS^0 be the true change in consumer surplus resulting from given price changes dP_R and dP_B (equation (11)) and let dCS^1 be the estimate of dCS^0 obtained by ignoring $vM/2n$ and using equation (13). Then

$$\phi \equiv \frac{dCS^0 - dCS^1}{X_B dP_B} = \frac{vM/2n}{1 + vM/2n} \tag{14}$$

is the error, normalized by the change in business revenues. The absolute error[6] is

$$|\phi| = \frac{\dfrac{v|M|}{2n}}{1 + \dfrac{vM}{2n}}. \tag{15}$$

---

[5] If $Q(P) = P^{-b}$, then $M/2n = b + 1/2nb$. For b close to 1.0, $M/2n \sim 1/n$. If $v = 1$ (Cournot) then for $n \geq 20$, the error in ignoring this term and acting myopically is less than five percent of $X_B \, dP_B$.

[6] As noted above, to have $dP/dP_B > 0$ requires that $1 + vM/2n > 0$, so $|1 + vM/2n| = 1 + vM/2n$.

It can be shown that under reasonable conditions[7]

$$\frac{\partial |\phi|}{\partial v} = \frac{v|M|}{2n \cdot (1 + \frac{vM}{2n})^2} \geqq 0 .$$ (16)

Because $v \leqq n$, this yields an upper bound on $|\phi|$:

$$|\phi| \leqq \frac{|M|/2}{1 + M/2} .$$ (17)

As an error bound this expression is not completely satisfactory because M is not a myopic quantity. However, it does make more precise the suggestion in the preceeding discussion that when downstream demand curves are approximately linear, myopic pricing rates may be used. Thus, if one had a rough idea of M and no idea at all of v, (17) could be a useful error bound.

If the demands for X_R and Q are not independent, then the expression for dCS becomes more complicated:

$$dCS = - X_R dP_R - Q \cdot \left[\frac{\partial P}{\partial P_R} dP_R + \frac{\partial P}{\partial P_B} dP_B \right] .$$

In the appendix to this chapter it is shown that if (a) the downstream industry is perfectly competitive or (b) the demand function $Q(P, P_R)$ is linear, then $\partial P / \partial P_R = 0$. It is also true that under such conditions $dP/dP_B = \chi_B/q$. This leaves us with the formula

$$dCS = - X_R dP_R - X_B dP_B$$

which is myopic.

The same result will hold in perfectly contestable markets where firms produce the same outputs and have flat-bottomed average cost curves. This is true because equation (8) carries through, as noted above, and because shifts in the demand for Q cause no increase in price ($\partial P / \partial P_R = 0$).

C. Ramsey pricing with flowthrough

In this section we derive prices P_R and P_B which maximize total surplus while allowing the utility to break even and which take account of flowthrough effects. Initially we will present the analysis in such a way

---

[7]

To get this expression one must assume either that $M \geqq 0$ or that $|M|$ is small enough so that $M \cdot |M|$ is of second order importance and may be ignored. For small changes in P this is reasonable and, of course, weaker than assuming $M \sim 0$, as we did above.

as to clarify the role of efficient prices in correcting for pricing distortion in the downstream industry which arises because of imperfect competition $(v > 0)$. (As before, we will assume that entry into the downstream industry is free and costless.) After this is clear we will investigate the important issue of when these efficient pricing rules are myopic. We do not assume that the demands for Q and X_R are independent.

Total surplus TS is the sum of producer surplus for the utility, π^U, producer surplus downstream, π^Q and consumer surplus:

$$TS = \pi^U + \pi^Q + CS. \tag{18}$$

Because $\pi^Q \equiv 0$ due to our free entry assumption

$$TS = \pi^U + CS \tag{19}$$

$$= (P_R - C_R) X_R + (P_B - C_B) X_B - F$$

$$+ U(X_R(P_R, P), Q(P_R, P))$$

$$- P_R \cdot X_R(P_R, P) - P \cdot Q(P_R, P)$$

where $X_R(P_R, P)$ and $Q(P_R, P)$ are the demand functions for X_R and Q which maximize consumer surplus, given prices P_R and P. In (19) C_R and C_B are the constant marginal costs of production for the utility in the residential and business markets, respectively; $F > 0$ is a fixed cost of production for the utility. Thus, the efficient pricing problem is

$$\underset{\{P_R, P_B\}}{\text{maximize}} \ [\pi^U + CS] \tag{20}$$

subject to

$$\pi^U = 0 \tag{20a}$$

$$vqP' + P - C_q = 0 \tag{20b}$$

$$P(nq) \cdot q - C(q, P_B, z) = 0. \tag{20c}$$

We can replace the constraints on downstream industry behavior (20b) and (20c) by using the comparative static information contained in equation (7) above, which allows us to write the downstream equilibrium price as $P = P(P_B, P_R; v)$ with the correct properties. Substituting $P(P_B, P_R; v)$ into the demand functions for X_R, X_B and Q we see that we are now working with the *equilibrium* demand functions for these commodities, rather than those resulting from economic agents' individual surplus and profit maximization, which take all prices as given. This leaves us with (20a) which we account for in traditional fashion by setting up the following Lagrangian:

$$\mathscr{L} = U\{X_R(P_R, P), Q(P_R, P)\} - P_R \cdot X_R(P_R, P) - P \cdot Q(P_R, P) \quad (21)$$

$$+ \ (1+\mu) \cdot \{(P_R - C_R)X_R(P_R, P) + (P_B - C_B) \cdot X_B(P_B, P) - F\}$$

where μ is the Lagrange multiplier for the utility's profit constraint and where $P = P(P_R, P_B)$. As noted, $X_R(P_R, P)$ and $X_B(P_B, P)$ are the equilibrium demand functions for the utility's business and residential markets.

Maximizing $\mathscr{L}$ with respect to P_R, P_B and μ we obtain the first-order conditions:

$$\frac{\partial \mathscr{L}}{\partial P_R} = - X_R - Q \cdot \frac{\partial P}{\partial P_R} + (1+\mu) \frac{\partial \pi^U}{\partial P_R} = 0 \qquad (22a)$$

$$\frac{\partial \mathscr{L}}{\partial P_B} = - Q \cdot \frac{\partial P}{\partial P_B} + (1+\mu) \frac{\partial \pi^U}{\partial P_B} = 0 \qquad (22b)$$

$$\frac{\partial \mathscr{L}}{\partial \mu} = \pi^U = 0 \qquad (22c)$$

In general, these conditions differ from those of ordinary Ramsey pricing. Dividing (22a) by (22b)

$$\frac{\partial \pi^U}{\partial P_R} \cdot \frac{1}{(X_R + Q \frac{\partial P}{\partial P_R})} = \frac{\partial \pi^U}{\partial P_B} \cdot \frac{1}{Q \partial P / \partial P_B} . \qquad (22d)$$

This expression[8] invites comparison to Version I of Ramsey pricing in Baumol and Bradford [1970]. For any two services i and j of a multiproduct firm, Version I of Baumol and Bradford characterizes the Ramsey prices by

$$\frac{1}{1+\mu} = \frac{\partial \pi^U}{\partial P_i} \cdot \frac{1}{X_i} = \frac{\partial \pi^U}{\partial P_j} \cdot \frac{1}{X_j} .$$

Returning to (22d), in general

---

[8]
This expression (after suitable rearrangement) is also reminiscent of Brander and Spencer [1983] equation (13). Brander and Spencer assume barriers to entry, however, so that our equation (19) does not reduce to their equation (13). Robert Willig has obtained analogous results in a sophisticated analysis of an optimal tax problem with a much more complicated set of vertical relationships between different downstream industries than is contained herein. See Willig [1983]. Brander, Spencer and Willig all assume that the number of firms in each downstream industry is fixed, so that entry barriers are implicitly assumed, and use a model with a constant conjectural variation.

$$Q \cdot \frac{\partial P}{\partial P_B} \neq X_B$$

so that

$$\frac{\partial \pi^U}{\partial P_R} \cdot \frac{1}{X_R} \neq \frac{\partial \pi^U}{\partial P_B} \cdot \frac{1}{X_B}$$

and optimal pricing with flowthrough differs from Version I. However, if either $v = 0$ or the demand function $Q(P, P_R)$ is linear

$$\frac{\partial P}{\partial P_B} = \frac{\chi_B}{q} \quad \text{and} \quad \frac{\partial P}{\partial P_R} = 0$$

so that

$$Q \frac{\partial P}{\partial P_B} = \frac{Q}{q} \chi_B = X_B$$

and

$$\frac{1}{1 + \mu} = \frac{\partial \pi^U}{\partial P_R} \cdot \frac{1}{X_R} = \frac{\partial \pi^U}{\partial P_B} \cdot \frac{1}{X_B}. \tag{23}$$

This is equivalent to Baumol and Bradford's Version I, so that the usual Ramsey formulae hold true even with flowthrough. Furthermore, it is myopic, involving only the equilibrium demand functions for X_R and X_B, and not any knowledge of v or Q beyond the assumptions just stated.

If the market structure of the Q industry follows the perfectly contestable model with symmetric firms, rather than the conjectural variation model and if average cost curves are flat-bottomed, then the optimal pricing rule is also myopic, given by equation (23). The reasoning is familiar. From the fact that average cost is minimized, equation (8) holds true, so that in equation (22d)

$$Q \frac{\partial P}{\partial P_B} = \frac{Q \chi_B}{q} = X_B.$$

Because the industry supply curve is flat in such a model, $\partial P / \partial P_R = 0$. Therefore (22d) reduces to (23).

If demands are also independent we get inverse elasticity rules[9]:

---

[9]

Willig [1983] and Zajac [1979] have also obtained these results in the case of perfect competition ($v = 0$).

$$\frac{P_R - C_R}{P_R} = \frac{\mu}{1+\mu} \cdot \frac{1}{\epsilon_R} \tag{24}$$

$$\frac{P_B - C_B}{P_B} = \frac{\mu}{1+\mu} \cdot \frac{1}{\epsilon_B} \cdot \tag{25}$$

Once again, the price elasticities ϵ_R and ϵ_B must be calculated from the equilibrium demand curve $X_R(P_R, P_B)$ and $X_B(P_R, P_B)$.

Keeping the assumption that cross-elasticities between Q and X_R are zero we can gain some insight into the role of P_B in correcting downstream pricing distortions. With $v > 0$, equation (22b) can be rewritten to yield the following expression:

$$\frac{P_B - C_B}{P_B} = \frac{1}{\epsilon_B} \cdot \left[1 + \frac{n}{v \cdot (1+\mu)} \cdot \frac{Q \cdot (P - C_q)}{X_B P_B} \cdot \frac{d \ln Q}{d \ln P_B} \right] . \tag{26}$$

The term

$$\frac{d \ln Q}{d \ln P_B} < 0$$

is the elasticity of equilibrium output downstream with respect to P_B. Clearly, one of the functions of P_B is to correct for downstream pricing distortion; the term $Q \cdot (P - C_q)$ is an approximation to the loss in downstream consumer surplus due to imperfect competition. The larger is this consumer surplus shortfall relative to business revenues $X_B P_B$, the lower should be the markup of business price P_B over C_B. The more pronounced is the elasticity of downstream equilibrium output Q with respect to P_B, the lower the markup of P_B over marginal cost C_B.

Although this pricing condition gives an intuitive indication of how flowthrough effects can complicate the role of efficient pricing, it bodes ill for the practicality of efficient pricing with flowthrough because it seems to require detailed knowledge of the pricing distortions downstream and the equilibrium impact of P_B on P. Fortunately, if we can assume locally constant marginal variable costs and $e = 1$ in the Q industry, equation (8) comes to our aid again; substituting it into (16b) we obtain a far more manageable expression:

$$\frac{P_B - C_B}{P_B} = \frac{1}{\epsilon_B} \cdot \left[1 - \frac{1}{(1+\mu)(1+\frac{vM}{2n})} \right] . \tag{27}$$

To compute this expression exactly given knowledge of v, we only need to know the downstream demand curve $Q(P)$, so that M can be computed. This represents a great advance in simplicity over equation

(26). Furthermore, as argued above, $\nu M/2n$ may be small enough to ignore either if $P'' \sim 0$, n is large or both. In that case the efficient price P_B can be approximated by the simple Inverse Elasticity Rule

$$\frac{P_B - c_B}{P_B} \sim \frac{1}{\epsilon_B} \cdot \frac{\mu}{1+\mu} \,, \tag{28}$$

and the efficient pricing rule (27) can be approximated by the myopic rule (28).

On the other hand, equation (27) is more complicated than it looks. This is because if we were to go to Ramsey prices from some other set of prices, the changes in P_R, P_B and the induced change in P will not, in general, be "small." This means that we cannot regard just any nonlinear demand curve $Q(P)$ as locally linear and set $M \sim 0$. To calculate the correct Ramsey prices with flowthrough the myopic character of the traditional Ramsey pricing rules is lost, unless $Q(P)$ is linear.

D. Multiproduct effects

Thus far, our analysis has been confined to a highly simplified case in which the utility sells a single output in each of its two markets (residential, business). In this section we relax this assumption and assume N business services, indexed by k. The price of the kth service is P_{Bk}. As before, a main concern is to arrive at pricing rules which can be implemented without requiring the analyst to use more information than is available from the utility's cost function and equilibrium demand curves.

We retain the assumption that if downstream industries are imperfectly competitive, their behavior can be adequately described by the constant conjectural variation model with free entry. We will also assume that in each downstream industry j each firm has locally constant marginal costs and that $e = 1$. Finally, we assume that either (a) industry j is perfectly competitive ($\nu_j = 0$) and/or (b) the demand functions for the J downstream industries are all linear or (c) downstream markets are contestable with flat-bottomed cost curves. Under these assumptions, when the price of the utility's k^{th} business service, P_{Bk}, rises, the price P_j changes according to the formula:

$$\frac{\partial P_j}{\partial P_{0k}} = \frac{x_{k_j}}{q_j} \tag{29}$$

where X_k^j is the amount of the utility's k^{th} service used by a firm in industry j.

The N business services, $X_1, X_2, ..., X_N$ are used as inputs to produce J outputs by the utility's business customers. Consumer surplus for residential consumers includes consumption of these J outputs:

$$CS_R = U(X_R, Q_1, Q_2, ..., Q_J) - P_R X_R - \sum_{j=1}^{J} P_j Q_j .$$ (30)

It is not necessary that the residential customers of the utility consume all of each of the J outputs of the utility's business customers. They need only experience the changes in P_j effected by changes in the utility's business prices P_k.

As before, we begin by examining the effects of given changes in the utility's prices on consumer surplus of residential customers. (from our free entry assumption, downstream firms all earn identically zero profits). The change in the maximized value of (27) is given, via the envelope theorem, by

$$dCS_R = - X_R \, dP_R - \sum_{j=1}^{J} Q_j \, dP_j$$ (31)

where the P_j changes in response to changes in the utility's prices P_{Bk} according to (29). The resulting expression is

$$dCS_R = - X_R dP_R - \sum_{j=1}^{J} Q_j \cdot \sum_{k=1}^{N} \frac{\partial P_j}{\partial P_{Bk}} \, dP_{Bk} - \sum_{j=1}^{J} Q_j \frac{\partial P_j}{\partial P_R} \, dP_R$$

(32)

$$= - X_R dP_R - \sum_{j=1}^{J} \sum_{k=1}^{N} \frac{X_k^j}{T_j} \, dP_{Bk} - \sum_{j=1}^{J} Q_j \frac{\partial P_j}{\partial P_R} \, dP_R$$

where

X_k^j = amount of the kth product of the utility used by firms in industry $j, j = 1, 2, ..., J$.

$$T_j = \frac{1}{1 + \dfrac{v_j M_i}{2n_j}} .$$

The formula given in (32) should be recognizable as a straightforward extension of (11). When either $v_j = 0$ (perfect competition) or the demands Q_j are linear for all j, $T_j = 1$ and $\dfrac{\partial P_j}{\partial P_R} = 0$, so that the change in consumer surplus is even simpler:

$$dCS_R = -X_R \, dP_R - \sum_{k=1}^{N} X_k \, dP_{Bk}$$ (33)

which is the exact extension of (11). As we argued above, if the change dP_{Bk} is "small" then the myopic expression (32) will be a good approximation to the correct expression (31) even when $Q(\cdot)$ is not linear.

To compute Ramsey prices in this more complex framework we form the following Lagrangian

$$\mathscr{L} = U(X_R, Q_1, ..., Q_J) - P_R X_R - \sum_{j=1}^{J} P_j Q_j$$

$$(34)$$

$$+ (1 + \mu) \cdot \left\{ (P_R - C_R) X_R + \sum_{j=1}^{J} \sum_{k=1}^{N} X_k^j \cdot (P_{Bk} - C_k) - F \right\}$$

The fact that we have excluded downstream firms' profit from the social welfare function reflects our assumption that entry into all downstream industries is free and costless, so that profits are identically zero. In this expression, the demand functions X_k are the equilibrium demands $X_k^j \left(P_R, P_{B1}, P_{B2}, ..., P_{BN} \right)$.

We choose P_R, P_k and μ to maximize $\mathscr{L}$, obtaining the following first order conditions:

$$\frac{\partial \mathscr{L}}{\partial P_R} = - X_R - \sum_{j=1}^{j} Q_j \frac{\partial P_j}{\partial P_R} + (1 + \mu) \frac{\partial \pi^U}{\partial P_R} = 0 \qquad (35a)$$

$$\frac{\partial \mathscr{L}}{\partial P_{Bk}} = - \sum_{j=1}^{J} Q_j \frac{\partial P_j}{\partial P_{Bk}} + (1 + \mu) \cdot \frac{\partial \pi_U}{\partial P_R} = 0 \qquad (35b)$$

$$\frac{\partial \mathscr{L}}{\partial \mu} = \pi^U = 0 \qquad (35c)$$

These necessary conditions imply

$$\frac{1}{1 + \mu} = \frac{\partial \pi^U}{\partial P_R} \cdot \frac{1}{\left[X_R + \sum_{j=1}^{J} Q_j \cdot \frac{\partial P_j}{\partial P_R} \right]} = \frac{\partial \pi^U}{\partial P_{Bk}} \cdot \frac{1}{\sum_{j=1}^{J} Q_j \frac{\partial P_j}{\partial P_{Bk}}} . \qquad (36)$$

We show in the appendix to this chapter that if $v_j = 0$ and/or $Q_j (P_R, P_1, P_2, ..., P_J)$ is linear for all j, then

$$\frac{\partial P_j}{\partial P_R} = 0 = \frac{\partial P_j}{\partial P_i} , \quad i \neq j$$

$$(37)$$

$$\frac{\partial P_j}{\partial P_{Bk}} = \frac{x_k^j}{q_j}$$

where P_i is the output price in a downstream industry other than j. Under these assumptions we obtain the standard Ramsey rule:

$$\frac{1}{1 + \mu} = \frac{\partial \pi^U}{\partial P_R} \cdot \frac{1}{X_R} = \frac{\partial \pi^U}{\partial P_{Bk}} \cdot \frac{1}{X_k} \qquad (39)$$

where

$$X_k = \sum_{j=1}^{J} X_k^j$$

is total demand for X_k aggregated across all J downstream industries.

If the demands for inputs X_k are all independent of each other in equilibrium, than (39) reduces to the inverse elasticity rule. This expression is identical to equation (2a) in Baumol and Bradford [1970], expect that (39) is based on the equilibrium demand curves for the X_{Bk}. It should be repeated that the above results do not stand or fall on the assumption that the downstream firms all behave according to the conjectural variation model. Two features of downstream market equilibrium were needed: equation (37) and (38), from which the myopic pricing rule (39) follows at once. Both of these comparative static results hold true in a perfectly contestable market in which firms are identical and have flat-bottomed average cost curves, as long as changes in P_R and P_j still leave q_j in the region of minimum average cost. No linearity assumptions about demand are needed.

6.3 Nonuniform pricing for business customers

At this point we extend to nonuniform pricing our inquiry concerning the efficient pricing of business services. The analysis here is more complex than with uniform pricing; for this reason we will confine our attention to the case in which customer firms are all perfectly competitive.

There is a further modelling issue to be faced at the outset. The theory of nonuniform pricing is based on the incentive for the regulated firm to offer a heterogeneous population of consumers a single price schedule which will induce them to sort themselves according to their willingness to pay for the firm's services. When consumers are residential, this comes about because of some sort of taste or income variable which varies across the population. When customers are business firms it is less obvious where the heterogeneity should come from. Ordover and Panzar [1982] addressed this problem by assuming that the regulated firm is selling to a single industry whose firms are of varying degrees of efficiency and that the "taste" variable θ indicates a particular firm type. Low values of θ indicate less efficient firms with a smaller demand for the regulated firm's product. Whatever efficiency differences between firms are connoted by θ, it is assumed that they cannot be arbitraged away by trade among firms. Firms act as price takers. Efficient firms earn positive profits and the equilibrium market price in the downstream industry is equal to the average cost of the least efficient firm which is able to earn nonnegative profits. With this setup, Ordover and Panzar have shown that the regulated firm's surplus - maximizing nonuniform price schedule differs in an important way from the conventional case: the marginal price schedule does not decline to marginal cost for the final unit consumed by the largest consumer, which it must do in the usual case. In an earlier paper, Ordover and Panzar [1980] showed that the Willig Pareto dominance result need no longer hold true in such a framework.

We will take a different approach. We take each customer type to refer to a specific customer industry, within which all firms are identical and perfectly competitive. The motivation for our approach is that for a given industry, all firms generally have access to the same technology and that there are relatively few scarce inputs which are not traded. Given access to the same technology, it is a reasonable working assumption to treat firms as identical within each industry, at least over a planning horizon long enough for firms to alter their technologies. We will index industries by k, $k = 1, 2, ..., N$. In this framework, $k = 1$ might correspond to a steel firm's demand for telephone service, $k = 2$ that of a data processing firm, etc. The function g_k refers to the number of the regulated firm's customers that come from the kth industry. The maximum horizontal difference between the demand curves for X of typical firms in any two adjacent industries is denoted by Δ. Unlike traditional nonuniform pricing theory, g_k is not fixed and is not a probability density function. It will vary according to the equilibrium attained in industry k and will depend on the prices of all of the utility's services.

Figure 6.2 depicts the flowthrough paradigm which we are using. It considers both the vertical relationships going from the monopolist through its business customers to final consumers and the horizontal relationships between final product markets. This is not intended to be a general equilibrium model; there are other markets in the economy besides those considered here.

Given this framework, our procedure will be to compute the constrained surplus-maximizing N-part tariff for a discrete distribution of k, and then let the size of rate steps and Δ tend to zero; when Δ becomes small, the distribution of customer types is becoming continuous. In the limit we will obtain a nonuniform price schedule which is optimal for a continuous distribution of consumer types. The N-part tariff is represented by the following outlay function

$$R(X) = \hat{R}_k + (X - \hat{X}_k) \cdot \omega_k$$

$$\hat{X}_k \leqq X < \hat{X}_{k+1} . \tag{41}$$

$$\hat{R}_k \equiv \sum_{i=0}^{k-1} (\hat{X}_i - \hat{X}_{i-1}) \cdot \omega_i .$$

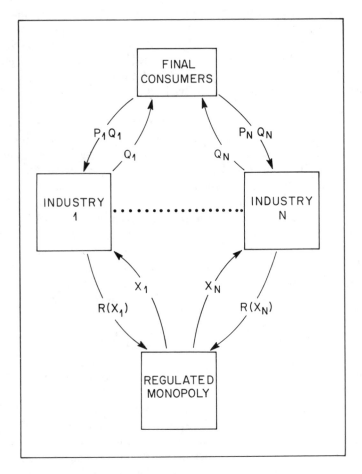

Figure 6.2

In this formulation $\hat{X}_{i+1} - \hat{X}_i \equiv \epsilon_i$ represents the size of the ith rate step; the (constant) marginal price in that rate step is ω_i, and $\hat{R}_i$ gives the total outlay up to that step. The slope of $R(X)$ is continuous from the right. The monopolist is assumed to have a constant marginal cost c and positive fixed cost ϕ.

In Section A below we will first discuss the properties of industry equilibrium in each of the output markets. In Section B we will characterize the optimal N-part tariff and then find the optimal tariff as Δ gets small.

A. Downstream industries

1. The individual firm. The profit of a representative firm in industry k is given by

$$\pi_k = P_k F^k(X, B_k) - C_k \,,\; C_k = \hat{R}_i + (X - \hat{X}_i) \cdot w_i + z_k' B_k \tag{42}$$

where z_k is the vector of unit input prices other than that of X and B_k is the vector of other inputs used in industry k. $F^k(X, B_k)$ is the firm's production function and $q_k = F^k(X, B_k)$ is the firm's output. For any output level q_k, the firm chooses X and B_k to minimize cost:

$$\frac{F_X^k}{F_B^k} = \frac{w_i}{z_k} . \tag{43}$$

Denote the cost-minimizing value of X by X_k^*. We will suppose that the firm's profit-maximizing choice of the input X puts it on the ith rate step with the marginal price w_i. The minimum cost function corresponding to a given output level is $C_k(q, w_0, w_1, ..., w_i, z_k)$; that is, the only marginal prices of X which are relevant are those going up to and including the ith rate step. Whatever the structure of $R(X)$, we will assume that marginal costs $\partial C_k / \partial q_k$ rise with q_k; i.e., $\partial^2 C_k / \partial q_k^2 > 0$, and that average costs are U-shaped.[10] For small changes in q_k only the marginal price w_i is relevant for input choices, so that

$$\frac{\partial C_k}{\partial q_k} \equiv c_k(q_k, w_i, z_k) . \tag{44}$$

To maximize profit each firm selects output q_k^* such that price is equal to marginal cost:

$$P_k = c_k(q_k^*, w_i, z_k) .$$

This allows us to write q_k^* as $q_k^*(P_k, w_i, z_k)$, with

---

10

Obviously, this amounts to assuming something about the nature of the solution we are seeking. In the traditional, nonuniform pricing literature this kind of assumption is often made and has as its justification the fact that one can find many examples where the assumption is not violated. Just how good an assumption it is to make in the flowthrough case is not altogether clear. It is not hard to imagine situations under which the average cost curve will be U-shaped whatever the shape of $R(x)$; for example, this will be true if the average cost of inputs other than X first falls in low ranges of output, but becomes infinite at some output high level. Alternatively, if $R(X)$ is a minor part of the firms' total costs, average costs could be U-shaped under less extreme assumptions about the average cost of inputs other than X.

$$\frac{\partial q_k^*}{\partial P_k} = \frac{1}{\partial^2 C_k / \partial q_k^2} > 0 \tag{45}$$

$$\frac{\partial q_k^*}{\partial w_i} = -\frac{\partial X_k^* / \partial q_k}{\partial^2 C_k / \partial q_k^2} < 0 \tag{46}$$

under the assumption that X is a normal input. The optimal value for X, X_k^*, is written as $X_k^*(q_k^*, w_i, z_k) = X_k^*(q^*(P_k, w_i, z_k), w_i, z_k)$ using the equation for the profit-maximizing output q^*.

2. Market equilibrium. The equilibrium condition is zero profit, so that the output price P_k is given by

$$P_k = \frac{\hat{R}_i + (X_k^*(q_k^*, w_i) - \hat{X}_i) \cdot w_i + z_k' B_k^*}{q_k^*} = c_k(q_k^*, w_i, z_k). \tag{47}$$

This defines the equilibrium price P_k as $P_k = P_k(\hat{R}_i, w_i, z_k)$. It is important to notice that when w_i changes and the industry reaches a new equilibrium, the change in price is

$$\frac{\partial P_k}{\partial w_i} = \frac{X_k^* - \hat{X}_i}{q_k^*}. \tag{48}$$

To see this, take the differential of π_k:

$$d\pi_k = (P_k - z_k \frac{\partial B_k^*}{\partial q_k} - w_i \frac{\partial X_k^*}{\partial q_k}) dq + q_k^* \, dP_k \tag{49}$$

$$- (X_k^* - \hat{X}_i) dw_i.$$

The first term in parentheses vanishes from profit maximization; from the zero profit condition $\pi_k \equiv 0$, so $d\pi_k = 0$ and we have the stated result. It is assumed that the input prices z_k are unchanged.

Demand at price P_k is given by the demand function $Q_k(P_k, \tilde{P}_{-k})$ where $\tilde{P}_{-k} = \{P_1, P_2, ..., P_{k-1}, P_{k+1}, ..., P_N\}$ is a vector of prices in other industries. Given $Q_k(P_k, \tilde{P}_{-k})$ and q_k^*, the equilibrium number of firms in industry k is given by the ratio of industry output to output per firm:

$$g_k \equiv \frac{Q_k}{q_k^*} \tag{50}$$

with

$$\frac{\partial g_k}{\partial P_k} = -\frac{Q_k}{(q_k^*)^2} \cdot \frac{\partial q_k^*}{\partial P_k} + \frac{1}{q_k^*} \cdot \frac{\partial Q_k}{\partial P_k} < 0 \qquad (51)$$

and

$$\frac{\partial g_k}{\partial P_{-k}} = \frac{1}{q_k^*} \frac{\partial Q_k(P_k, \tilde{P}_{-k})}{\partial P_{-k}}, \text{ where } P_{-k} \in \tilde{P}_{-k} . \qquad (52)$$

The sign of $\partial g_k / \partial P_{-k}$ is positive or negative depending on where the output of industry $j \neq k$ is a substitute or a complement to that of industry k. Because average costs are U-shaped, the industry supply curve is flat. Among other things, this means that although changes in price for some other industry $j \neq k$ will affect output and the number of firms in industry k, it will not affect the equilibrium price P_k. Finally, it is important to define a firm's equilibrium demand curve for X. Given the output price P_k in industry k, firms in that industry choose X so that $P_k = c_k$; the profit-maximizing $X_k^* = X_k^*(w_i, P_k)$. In equilibrium

$$P_k = c_k = \frac{\hat{R}_i + w_i \cdot (X_k^* - \hat{X}_i) + z_k' B_k^*}{q_k^*}$$

so that X_k^* depends on average cost and, hence, the inframarginal marginal prices $w_1, w_2, ..., w_{i-1}$ as well as w_i. Thus, the firm's equilibrium demand curve for X is given by

$$X_k^* = X_k^*(w_1, w_2, ..., w_i, z_k) .$$

and the industry equilibrium demand curve is $g_k \cdot X_k^*$. Schmallensee [1976] and Anderson [1976] have both shown that when there is a change in an input price w_i, the consumer surplus effects in competitive downstream output markets are correctly calculated by integrating under downstream firms' equilibrium input demand curves.

As noted in the appendix to this chapter, the optimal pricing results derived below also follow from the perfectly contestable model in the case where average cost curves are flat-bottomed. A difficulty here is how to reconcile flat average costs over a finite output range with the fact that $R(X)$ is nonuniform. One can reconcile this contradiction by regarding flat average costs as an approximation or by asserting that the scale elasticity of demand for X is locally zero.

B. *Optimal pricing*

In this section we will compute an optimal nonuniform price schedule for business customers serving N downstream final output markets. We will confine our attention to the special limiting case in which the demand functions for X of typical firms in any two downstream industries i and $i+1$, with input demand curves which are adjacent, are only infinitesimally different: i.e., $\Delta \to 0$. We will find that the optimal nonuniform price schedule in this case exhibits properties similar to those obtained in the previous literature.[11] In particular, marginal price converges to marginal cost for the last unit consumed by the highest demander.

This equivalence between the optimal price schedule in the present model and earlier results is due entirely to the fact that we are considering only the case where $\Delta \to 0$; i.e., the set of consumer tastes is continuous. ($\Delta \to 0$ also describes some cases in which the distribution of customer types is discrete with a countably infinite number of types.) In general, the presence of flowthrough effects complicates optimal pricing a great deal. In the traditional model, when the usage charge w_i for a given rate step ϵ_i is changed, the effects on consumption are confined to consumers who were in equilibrium on that rate step; in the terminology of Chapter 5, as $\epsilon_i \to 0$, the demands in different increment markets were independent. With flowthrough effects present as in our model, this independence is violated in two kinds of ways. First, when w_i is increased, $\hat{R}_{i+1}$, $\hat{R}_{i+2}$, ..., $\hat{R}_N$ are increased so that the output prices in all industries that equilibrate on rate step $i+1$ or higher are increased, too. When these output prices are increased, total demand for X in steps ϵ_{i+1}, ϵ_{i+2}, ..., ϵ_N is reduced because some firms in those industries go out of business. Second, when an output price in *any* industry increases due to a rise in w_i, the output demand curves shift in all other industries with whom its output is a substitute or a complement. This will change the equilibrium number of firms in those industries and, hence, the demand in each increment market, including that for ϵ_i. Because of these complications, optimal nonuniform prices will usually not resemble the traditional pricing rules if Δ is not small. However it turns out that in the special case where $\Delta \to 0$, so that the set of customer types is nearly continuous, these complicated effects going on *between* ϵ_i markets are of order Δ^2 and can be ignored. The

---

[11] The similarity, of course, will be qualitative, in that the marginal price will converge to marginal cost for the largest user. Because all of this involves the equilibrium demand functions for X, the actual prices would be different.

result is that the smooth optimal nonuniform price schedules which we obtain will look very much like the Ramsey pricing formulae for nonuniform pricing presented in Chapter 5.

We must begin by describing an analytical device which considerably simplifies the ensuing analysis: we confine our attention to "fully separating" tariffs. A fully separating tariff consists of usage charges $(w_1, w_2, ..., w_N)$ and rate steps $(\epsilon_1, \epsilon_2, ..., \epsilon_N)$ such that on each rate step ϵ_i only one firm type is in equilibrium. That is, on rate step i, industry i consumes X_i^* where $\hat{X}_i \leqq X_i^* \leqq \hat{X}_{i+1}$; for all $k \neq i$ $X_k^* > \hat{X}_{i+1}$ or $X_k^* < \hat{X}_i$. In other words, given N firm types we confine ourselves to N-part tariffs where only one firm type is in equilibrium on each rate step. Because we order industries by i, we can index rate steps and usage charges in the same way. Our use of fully separating tariffs is helpful analytically but actually involves no essential loss of generality. If it is optimal for firms in two adjacent industries i and $i+1$ to be paying the same marginal price — be on the same rate step, in other words — then the optimal values of w_i and w_{i+1} will be the same, and would be so in our analysis. The full separation construct implies the following inequality:

$$2\Delta \geqq \epsilon \geqq \epsilon_i , \epsilon \equiv \max_i \epsilon_i$$

from which we can deduce that for Δ sufficiently small $\epsilon = \epsilon_i = o(\Delta)$. Hence $\Delta \to 0$ ensures that $\epsilon_i \to 0$ without having to take two limits.

Two assumptions about the equilibrium behavior of the set of N downstream industries are important to the analysis. First we extend the strong monotonicity assumption used in Chapter 5 to the equilibrium demand curves of the customer firms. Specifically, let X_i and X_j be the equilibrium demand curves of representative firms in industries i and j. Facing a common marginal price w, if $X_i(w) > X_j(w)$ then for $w' \neq w$, $X_i(w') > X_j(w')$. The second assumption is that if $\epsilon_k^* \equiv X_k^* - \hat{X}_k$ is the consumption of a firm of industry k in the kth rate step and g_k the equilibrium number of firms, $\epsilon_k^* g_k$ is a decreasing function of marginal prices in lower rate blocks:

$$\frac{\partial \epsilon_k^* g_k}{\partial w_i} < 0 , \; i < k \tag{53}$$

This assumption is complicated, but reasonable. It says, in effect, that as w_i rises, both the number of firms and aggregate demand for X in industry k will fall. If w_i rises, average cost in industry k goes up, and with it the equilibrium output price P_k. Since $\partial g_k/\partial P_k < 0$ and since X_k^* is determined at the margin by w_k, $\epsilon_k^* g_k$ should fall; however, the rise in w_i also increases price in all other industries buying in rate steps $i+1, i+2, ..., N$. To the extent that one or more of these industries produces an output which is a substitute for X_k, this could counteract the fall in g_k. Thus, our assumption is that such effects do not outweigh the direct impact of P_k on Q_k.

After this lengthy development it will be useful to collect all of our important assumptions in one place:

1. In each industry, firms' average cost curves are U-shaped.
2. Industry supply curves are flat.
3. Tariffs are fully separating and marginal prices are continuous from the right.
4. For typical firms in different industries, equilibrium input demand curves satisfy the strong monotonicity (noncrossing) assumption.
5. For $i \le k$, $\dfrac{\partial[\epsilon_k^* g_k]}{\partial w_i} < 0$.
6. Let $\Delta \equiv \sup\limits_{\{i,\,w\}} |X_i^*(w) - X_{i+1}^*(w)|$. Δ exists and is finite.

The next step is to compute the consumer surplus (CS_k) and producer surplus (PS_k) generated in each rate step k and then obtain total consumer surplus (CS) and producer surplus (PS) by summing across k:

$$CS \equiv \sum_{k=1}^{N} CS_k \tag{54}$$

$$PS \equiv \sum_{k=1}^{N} PS_k . \tag{55}$$

To compute the welfare effects of a change in the price w_k on the kth rate step we make use of the results of Anderson [1976] and Schmallensee [1976] who showed that when the price of an input is changed which is used by a perfectly competitive industry, the effect on the consumer surplus of final consumers may be calculated by integrating under firms' input demand curves where output prices are varied to maintain equilibrium in downstream output markets.[12] In rate

---

[12]

This point requires further explication. The Anderson [1976] and Schmallensee [1976] results were derived for the case of a single input price change for an industry producing a single output. In our optimization problem we are interested in the effects of a change in w_k on consumer surplus in equilibrium in N rate step markets. Hence, it is not clear that the Anderson and Schmallensee results can be carried over to our case, although Just, Hueth and Schmitz [1982] argue that the procedure is likely to be adequately accurate in practice (see Just, Hueth and Schmitz, *ibid*, pp 192-196.) In our limiting case, though, the Anderson and Schmallensee results are applicable because the effects of w_k on other rate steps are $o(\Delta^2)$ and vanish as $\Delta \to 0$. Hence, in the limit we may regard demands in different rate steps as being approximately independent as $\Delta \to 0$. Furthermore, demands in a given rate step across industries in that rate step are independent, as well. With independence, we are back to the case considered by Anderson and Schmallensee.

step k, industry k earns consumer surplus equal to

$$\int_{\hat{X}_k}^{x_k^*} P_k F_x^k dx \; - \; w_k \cdot \epsilon_k^*. \tag{56}$$

Firms $j > k$ generate

$$\int_{\hat{X}_k}^{\hat{X}_{k+1}} P_j F_x^j dx \; - \; w_k \epsilon_k. \tag{57}$$

Total consumer surplus in the kth rate step is given by

$$CS_k = \left\{\int_{\hat{X}_k}^{x_k^*} P_k F_x^k dx - w_k \epsilon_k^*\right\} \cdot g_k + \sum_{j \geq k+1} \left\{\int_{\hat{X}_k}^{\hat{X}_{k+1}} P_j F_x^j dx - w_k \epsilon_k\right\} \cdot g_j.$$

Similarly, PS_k is given by

$$PS_k = (w_k - c) \cdot \left\{\epsilon_k^* g_k + \epsilon_k \cdot \sum_{j \geq k+1} g_j\right\}.$$

Given the expression for CS and PS, our aim is to choose a tariff $(w_1, w_2, ..., w_N)$, $(\epsilon_1, \epsilon_2, ..., \epsilon_N)$ so as to maximize total surplus subject to a nonegativity constraint on producer surplus. Our procedure is to follow Goldman, Leland and Sibley [1984] and treat the N rate steps as if they were markets. Accordingly, we solve the following problem:

$$\max_{\substack{\{w_1, w_2, \cdots, w_N\} \\ \{\epsilon_1, \epsilon_2, \cdots, \epsilon_N\}}} [CS + PS]$$

$$s.t. \quad PS - \phi \geq 0.$$

The Lagrangian corresponding to this problem is

$$\mathscr{L} = CS + (1+\lambda) \cdot PS. \tag{58}$$

The necessary conditions for a optimum are

$$\frac{\partial \mathscr{L}}{\partial w_i} = \frac{\partial CS}{\partial w_i} + (1 + \lambda) \cdot \frac{\partial PS}{\partial w_i} = 0 \;, \; i = 1, 2, ..., N \tag{59a}$$

$$\frac{\partial \mathscr{L}}{\partial \epsilon_i} = \frac{\partial CS}{\partial \epsilon_i} + (1 + \lambda) \cdot \frac{\partial PS}{\partial \epsilon_i} = 0 \tag{59b}$$

$$\frac{\partial \mathscr{L}}{\partial \lambda} = PS = 0 \tag{59c}$$

(In what follows we suppress the first-order conditions for $\{\epsilon_i\}$ because they are of little interest for our purpose.) In the appendix to this chapter it is shown that for small Δ

$$\frac{\partial \mathscr{L}}{\partial w_i} \cong \left[\frac{\partial CS_i}{\partial w_i} + (1 + \lambda) \cdot \frac{\partial PS_i}{\partial w_i} \right] \cong 0 \, , \, i = 1, 2, ..., N \tag{60a}$$

$$\frac{\partial \mathscr{L}}{\partial \lambda} = 0. \tag{60b}$$

This happens because all of the effects of changes in w_i on the consumer and producer surplus generated in other rate steps $k \neq i$ are $o(\Delta^2)$ and can be ignored for small Δ. At the optimal set of infinitesimal rate steps $\{\epsilon_i\}$ the following necessary conditions hold for $\{w_i\}$ and λ:

$$\lambda \cdot \left[\epsilon_i^* g_i + \epsilon_i \sum_{j \geq i+1} g_j \right] + (1 + \lambda) \cdot (w_i - c) \cdot \frac{\partial \epsilon_i^*}{\partial w_i} \cdot g_i = 0 \tag{61a}$$

$$\sum_{i=1}^{N} (w_i - c) \cdot \left[\epsilon_i^* g_i + \epsilon \sum_{j \geq i+1} g_j \right] - \phi = 0. \tag{61b}$$

These conditions imply pricing rules which are close counterparts of the rules obtained by Goldman, Leland and Sibley [1984], Mirman and Sibley [1980], Spence [1976], et al. First, the Ramsey interpretation of the nonuniform rule still obtains. To see this define

$$\chi_i^* \equiv \epsilon_i^* g_i + \epsilon_i \sum_{j \geq i+1} g_j \tag{62}$$

as aggregate consumption in the ith rate step. Because the first-order effect of w_i on χ_i^* is

$$\frac{\partial \chi_i^*}{\partial w_i} = \left[g_i \frac{\partial \epsilon_i^*}{\partial w_i} + o(\Delta^2) \right] \cong g_i \frac{\partial \epsilon_i^*}{\partial w_i} \tag{63}$$

we can write

$$\frac{w_i - c}{w_i} \cong \frac{\lambda}{1 + \lambda} \cdot \frac{1}{\dfrac{\partial \ln \chi_i^*}{\partial \ln w_i}} \tag{64}$$

so that the Inverse Elasticity Rule for the marginal prices of an optimal nonuniform schedule holds true even in multimarket equilibrium. Second, it is true in this model that marginal price converges to marginal cost for the marginal unit of the highest user. To see this, write the first-order condition $\partial \mathscr{L}/\partial w_N = 0$:

$$\lambda \epsilon_N^* g_N + (1 + \lambda)(w_N - c) \cdot g_N \, \frac{\partial \epsilon_N^*}{\partial w_N} \cong 0 \qquad (65)$$

or

$$\lambda \epsilon_N^* + (1 + \lambda) \cdot (w_N - c) \, \frac{\partial X_N^*}{\partial w_N} = 0 \qquad (66)$$

Because $\epsilon_N^* \leqq \epsilon_N = o(\Delta)$, for small Δ

$$(w_N - c) \cong 0 . \qquad (67)$$

This result contrasts to that obtained by Ordover and Panzar. The Ordover-Panzar model is of a monopolist utility selling to a single downstream industry in which firms differ according to their cost structure but act as price takers; a parameter θ indexes costs. Firms with small θ are high cost and firms with large θ are low cost. In equilibrium there is a particular θ_0 which just breaks even. Firms with $\theta < \theta_0$ produce nothing and firms with $\theta > \theta_0$ make positive profit. In such a model $w > c$ even for the final unit consumed by the largest producer because to lower w to c for this unit of consumption lowers the downstream market equilibrium price and reduces demand by small-θ firms "too much." The contrast between our limiting price schedule and that of Ordover and Panzar points up the importance of differences in assumed downstream industry structure in determining the character of optimal nonuniform pricing rules.

6.4 Conclusion

In this chapter we have tried to analyze the pricing complications which come about when we take account of the flowthrough effects of the utility's pricing policies. In doing so we have concentrated on isolating conditions under which the efficient pricing roles can be implemented myopically. Flowthrough effects can mitigate the unpleasant equity choices which appear to arise when price changes which increase total surplus do so to the benefit of business customers at the expense of residential customers. Indeed, if there is free entry into downstream industries there is no need for such a choice at all: price changes which increase total surplus will automatically increase consumer surplus, too.

This observation is of little practical use, however, unless we can test the effects of price changes without going to non-myopic tests. Fortunately, as equation (13) shows, when downstream industries behave according to the conjectural variation model with free entry a simple myopic test is available to see whether or not arbitrary (small) price changes leave residential consumers better off. Similarly, Ramsey pricing rules, to be useful, should be myopic. The case for myopic

Ramsey prices is not as strong, but equation (23) suggests that when downstream demand curves are approximately linear or when the conjectural variation is zero, then ordinary Ramsey pricing rules may be used. In all cases, price elasticities must be calculated from the equilibrium demand curves facing the utility.

If the model of perfect contestability applies, then these results follow without any linearity assumptions on demand. On the cost side, symmetric firm and flat-bottomed average costs are needed for the myopic pricing results to go through.

Optimal nonuniform pricing was analyzed using a paradigm with both vertical and horizontal relationships. In general, the computation of an N-part tariff is far more complex than in the conventional situation where the regulated monopolist is assumed to be selling to final consumers. This increased complication occurs because a change in a marginal price at a point along a nonuniform price schedule not only affects the firms in industries buying in that rate block, but has multimarket equilibrium effects on the demands for the utility's output by other firms buying in other rate blocks. Fortunately, as the distribution of firm types becomes continuous, these multimarket equilibrium effects turn out to be of second-order importance. The optimal nonuniform pricing rule takes on a form similar to the usual nonuniform pricing rules as contained in Goldman-Leland-Sibley and Mirman-Sibley, except that the number of firms in each industry is endogenous to the monopolist's tariff.

From a computational point of view, this may be a serious difference; to calculate the effects on g_i of a perturbation in the marginal price w_i adds greatly to the complexity of optimal nonuniform pricing. Two routes are left open to the analyst who wishes to investigate the properties of nonuniform pricing on business customers. First, depending on the case at issue, one may be able to assume that the effects of tariff changes on the number of firms in each downstream industry are small enough to ignore, in which case the optimal pricing formula is the same as that presented in Chapter 5 except that the equilibrium demand curves for all customer firms must be used. In the absence of equilibrium demand curves, the analyst may have to apply the conventional pricing formula to ordinary demand curves and interpret resulting surplus changes as short-run changes which occur before output prices in downstream industries have time to adjust. This raises the question of how one would interpret the resulting the welfare gain. It is not hard to see that the gain that one will compute is a lower bound on the true equilibrium welfare gain. To see why, suppose that a variation in the utility's outlay schedule $R(x)$ leaves downstream industry k with momentary excess profits before either output price or the number of firms has had time to adjust. This is the effect that will be picked up when the analyst employs a fixed distribution of customer types and usual value of marginal product input demand curves. Given this excess profit, entry will occur and price will fall so consumer surplus in the final output market k will rise not only by the amount of the initial excess profit but also by the welfare triangle associated with increased output. Thus, the short-run increase in consumer surplus is less than the long-run increase. Similarly, if the variation in $R(x)$ were such that an industry were momentarily losing money as a result, firms would exit the industry, and industry output would fall. The resulting long-run reduction in total surplus would be less than the short-run reduction by the Harberger triangle above the output demand curve in market k. Because the short-run impacts understate long-run gains and overstate long-run losses, the analysis which holds g_i fixed and uses ordinary input demand curves fox will be understating any efficiency gains which would result from a particular set of price changes.

CHAPTER 7

Efficient pricing for policy analysis

7.1 Introduction

In this chapter we will apply efficient pricing theory to policy questions
relying heavily on a special, but important, case study: the market for
message service on AT&T's public switched network. The particular
interest of using this market is that the relative merits of FDC pricing,
Ramsey pricing, and nonuniform pricing in this market were vigorously
debated for years, with few clearcut results. Although our analysis will
probably raise more questions than it settles, it will bring a useful
perspective to that debate.

For some years, AT&T and the Federal Communications
Commission (FCC) debated the rationale for offering Wide Area
Telephone Service (WATS) as a service distinct from ordinary Message
Toll Service (MTS); the latter is sold under a predominately uniform
price tariff[1] and the former under a tariff displaying quantity discounts.
AT&T argued that WATS is fundamentally a different service from
MTS, so that it can be offered under a different tariff. The FCC took
the view that WATS and MTS had so much in common that they
should be regarded as the same service in all functional aspects and that
any tariff differences between the two should be due only to cost
differences. The FCC argued that, absent such cost differences, the
existence of WATS as a separate service with a bulk discount tariff
constituted price discrimination against small users, who bought on the
MTS tariff, which has a higher usage charge. By this analysis, to
abolish WATS or to require AT&T to allow resale from WATS tariffs,

---

[1] Usually the first minute (or three minute) charge for duration of an MTS
call is higher than the charge for additional minutes. However, this quantity
discount is not numerically large and the MTS tariff is best described as a
uniform price tariff.

would eliminate the alleged cross subsidy in favor of large users, therefore lowering the price small users face. By contrast, a simple application of the theory of nonuniform pricing as described in preceding chapters will show that even if MTS and WATS were functionally equivalent services, the FCC's price discrimination analysis was flawed and could easily lead to results the opposite of those intended. That is, the price that small users face could rise, not fall, as the result of resale of abolition of WATS.

It should be noted that the same issues have arisen in connection with resale of toll services now provided by local exchange carriers since the breakup of AT&T.

Next, using publicly available data sources, we compute the efficiency gains achieved by Ramsey pricing and optimal nonuniform pricing relative to FDC pricing. (Once again, the analysis concerns AT&T's message service market.) Our aim is simply to get a feel for how efficient prices would look, especially the optimal nonuniform prices, which have not been studied from a quantitative standpoint. Too, we will try to get a rough idea of whether the efficiency gains resulting from Ramsey and optimal nonuniform pricing appear to be large enough to justify their increased complication. A main source of the increased complication involved with efficient pricing in the fact that much more information is required to compute efficient prices than to compute FDC prices. Briefly, the results of our pricing simulations are:

- Given perfect information, optimal nonuniform pricing — under a wide variety of assumptions regarding underlying parameter values — leads to a gain in total surplus in the range of 9 to 15 percent of average billing under FDC pricing.
- The surplus gains resulting from Ramsey prices are not particularly large — on the order of 2 to 3 percent of average billing for most sets of parameter values.
- For the purpose of nonuniform pricing, the most important underlying relationship to measure accurately is curvature of the demand curve of the individual consumer at prices high enough to reduce consumption to near-zero levels. Errors in the estimation of other parameters and relationships have far less serious consequences.

The chapter concludes with a discussion of lifeline tariffs. In many cases, the regulator is concerned that certain poor users not be forced to discontinue use of the public utility's service. Hence special lifeline rates are sometimes introduced with the goal of making it possible to buy small to moderate amounts at a reduced rate. We show that it is sometimes possible to introduce such rates without having to raise prices paid by non-lifeline users. In general, optional tariff theory suggests how lifeline concerns can be met with minimal loss to the general body of consumers; it may even be possible to offer lifeline tariffs which are profitable.

The chapter is organized into five sections. Section 2 summarizes the MTS-WATS price discrimination debate. Section 3 considers the magnitude of efficiency gains from different pricing schemes using AT&T data, and Section 4 contains the discussion of lifeline tariffs. Section 5 presents conclusions.

7.2 Nonuniform pricing and price discrimination — MTS and WATS

In both electricity and telecommunications it has been argued that nonuniform pricing structures amount to unjustifiable price discrimination and that they induce cross subsidy between consumer groups. Indeed, as we noted in Chapter 5, this view is enshrined in recent legislation.[2] The debate has been particularly interesting in telecommunications and we will motivate the analysis by reviewing the long-running debate between the FCC and AT&T concerning the legality of AT&T's MTS and WATS tariffs.

MTS service is sold under a largely uniform price tariff with a relatively high usage charge. WATS service consists of two subdivisions: Measured Time WATS (MT) and Full Business Day WATS (FBD). Both are bulk discounts, FBD more so than MT. In 1977 the FCC instituted an inquiry[3] as to whether or not MTS and WATS were "like" services within the meaning of Section 202(a) of the Communications Act of 1934 (47 USC 202(a)). This section says in part:

> It shall be unlawful for any common carrier to make unjust or unreasonable discrimination in charges, practices, classifications, regulations, facilities or services for or in connection with like communications services.

The FCC defined "like" to mean "functionally equivalent."[4]

AT&T presented evidence that the two services were unlike. Summarizing briefly a large volume of evidence submitted, proponents of the "unlike" view of the two services pointed out the following differences in cost and service quality between MTS and WATS.[5]

---

[2] See the Public Utility Regulatory Pricing Act (PURPA) of 1978.

[3] 66 FCC 2nd at 224 [1977] (*Notice*)

[4] 78 FCC 2nd at 604 (*Order*)

[5] These differences pertain to MTS and WATS as they were tariffed in the years going up to early 1982, when WATS tariffs were restructured in a number of ways.

MTS	*WATS*
1. Provides itemized billing	1. Only provides itemized billing for usage in excess of 240 hours per month for each FBD line and 10 hours per month for each MT line.
2. Two-directional access to network.	2. WATS tariffs only apply to calls going from the WATS customer (Outward WATS) or to the WATS customer (Inward WATS).
3. Uses common central office facilities.	3. Has some dedicated central office equipment.
4. Caller can place calls at any time of day.	4. Peak-hour congestion in the WATS line forces callers to off-peak periods.

The FCC, however, ruled that MTS and WATS were functionally equivalent[6] apart from differences in their tariffs. Therefore, it concluded that the differences in pricing between the two services were no more than price discrimination.

Given this factual finding, the FCC presented a simple and appealing economic analysis of the economic effects of the existing MTS-WATS combination.

> In order for price discrimination to be effective there must be some basis developed for classifying and hence separating customers or products. In telecommunications, customer classification is usually based on usage or volume. The resulting bulk discounts may reflect differing price elasticities of demand between large users who may have alternative sources of supply (and hence more elastic demand) and small users who have relatively fewer sources of supply (and presumably lower elasticities of demand). Thus a large customer may be able to command a lower price than a small one.[7]

In the absence of such price discrimination the FCC argued that prices

---

[6] 70 FCC 2nd [1979] at 614.

[7] *Supra* at 605-606.

would tend to cost, benefiting current MTS users and, perhaps, hurting large WATS users. In this decision the FCC said that AT&T could refile tariffs which were consistent with demonstrable cost differences. Subsequently, the FCC required AT&T (and other common carriers) to allow resale from its switched services.[8] By allowing resellers to buy from WATS and resell to small customers who would normally be MTS users, this would put market pressure on AT&T to erase any tariff differences not due to cost.

The extent of this pressure will depend on the costs of resale. If resale costs are high, then substantial quantity discounts may be sustainable by AT&T. If not, then any quantity discount will be negated by resellers. In the discussion that follows we will make the extreme assumption that resale is perfectly costless, since this will serve to illuminate the issues involved.

Unfortunately, the FCC's analysis, though appealing, is flawed in important ways. The simple principles of nonuniform pricing theory make this clear. To show this we will abstract from the specifics of the MTS-WATS controversy and consider the case of two services which are exactly the same in cost and attributes and differ only in the tariffs under which they are sold; again, this is how the FCC viewed MTS and WATS. Service 1 is sold at a uniform price P_1 and Service 2 at a two-part tariff with entry fee E and usage charge P_2, where $P_2 < P_1$. The amount of E does not exceed area "a" plus area "e" plus area "f" in Figure 7.1.

Figure 7.1 reflects the initial situation. There are two consumers, one large and one small. The small consumer chooses to buy Service 1 and consumes Q_1. The large consumer buys Service 2 and consumes Q_2 because the fact that $P_2 < P_1$ compensates for having to pay the entry fee E. The firm's marginal cost for both services is mc, there is a fixed cost F and $P_2 > mc$. The fixed cost F could arise either through the technology of the firm or because sales of Q must provide a prescribed dollar subsidy to some other service; for example interstate separation payments to local telephone companies acted as a fixed cost on interstate services. The firm earns profit from the two customers which is equal to area "a" + "b" from the first customer plus "b" + "c" + "d" + E from the second customer minus the fixed cost F, and we will suppose that the firm is regulated, so that profit is equal to zero.

Under the FCC analysis this situation is one of price discrimination and should be rectified, either by forcing the carrier to refile "cost-based" tariffs or by allowed resale. In either case the result would be

[8] 83 FCC 2nd [1981]

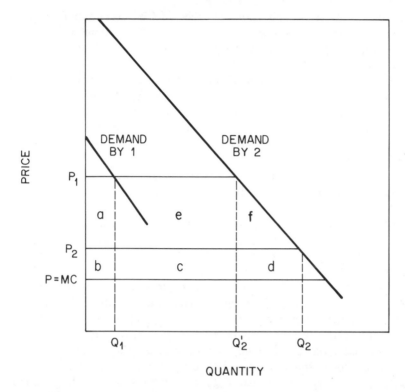

Figure 7.1

that both consumers would be faced with a single uniform price $\bar{P}$ at average cost. However, it may turn out that $\bar{P}$ is higher than both P_1 and P_2, so that the small consumer as well as the large one will pay a *higher* price instead of a lower one, as implied by the FCC analysis.

To see this, imagine that Service 2 is withdrawn and that, initially, the price of Service 1 is held at the level P_1. The small customer has no incentive to change his behavior, but the large consumer cuts his consumption back to Q'_2. There are two countervailing effects on profits. To the extent that the large consumer's first Q'_2 units are purchased at a higher price than before, profit goes up by area "e" plus area "a". However, the firm loses the entry fee E that it had been earning on the large consumer. Furthermore, because $P_2 > c$ the firm had been earning profit equal to "d" on the $Q_2 - Q'_2$ units by which the large consumer now cuts back now that the quantity discount has disappeared. The net effect on profit is ("a" + "e") − ("d" + "E"). This can be either positive or negative. If it is negative, then the carrier is making a loss at the price P_1 and will have to obtain a higher price $\bar{P}$ which will cover its total costs. In this example, then, it is entirely possible that the application of the FCC's over-simplified price discrimination analysis would lead to the opposite of its intended result. *Both* consumers would be worse off as the result of eliminating the bulk tariff.

Given that the elimination of the bulk discounted service will drive the regulated firm to simple average cost pricing, another point can be made. From Willig's Pareto dominance result (see Chapter 4) we know that it is always possible to devise an optional two-part tariff which, if offered along with an initial uniform price, would allow *all* customers to be made better off than under any single uniform price which exceeds marginal cost. Since the FCC's analysis makes such an optional tariff illegal or nugatory (by requiring resale), any possibility of such a gain is foreclosed.

There is a second, less obvious, adverse effect of resale. As argued in Chapters 2 and 6, an increase in the consumer surplus measured from the equilibrium demand curves of the regulated firm's immediate business customers is transmitted dollar for dollar to final consumers (as long as there is free entry into and perfect competition in the downstream industries). By requiring resale, a regulator is limiting the size of welfare gains achievable through the regulated firm's pricing structure. The adverse effects on final consumers of "protecting" small business users via resale would seem to undercut the presumed fairness of resale. For example, suppose that dry cleaning firms are small users of telephone service and that data processing firms are large users. Initially, both types of users buy under a quantity discount tariff which we will assume, *arguendo*, maximizes total surplus while allowing the telephone company to cover its costs. With costless resale, telephone service would be sold at a uniform price. We will assume that the FCC conclusion is correct, and that dry cleaning firms benefit and data processing firms are hurt relative to the initial situation. However, by definition, total surplus has been reduced, so that a final consumer who does both data processing and sends his suits out to be cleaned is worse off than before, not better. This point calls into question the asserted fairness of resale.

It is possible to find types of nonuniform price schedules which can achieve significantly greater pricing efficiency than uniform prices but which may still be unobjectionable under the price discrimination/cross subsidy argument. For example, the regulated utility could offer a nonuniform price schedule as an *option* to a single uniform price which itself may be cost-based by whatever criteria are deemed relevant by the regulator. In our single market example, the regulator would set an initial price equal to what the firm's average cost *would* be if everyone bought at that price. By any *cost-based* criterion this price should be acceptable. If the firm has any positive fixed cost, then the average cost price will exceed marginal cost. This being the case, as the Willig result shows, one can always find an optional two-part tariff which can make all customers — large and small — as well as the firm better off. The undominated combination of the cost-based uniform price and the optional two-part tariff constitute a single nonuniform price schedule with a quantity discount. This type of nonuniform price schedule should be acceptable even under the "price discrimination" view and could still lead to important welfare gains which could, potentially, benefit all consumers as well as the regulated firm. One can view the numerical examples of PDIC tariffs in Chapter 4 as illustrating this possibility.

7.3 The gains from efficient pricing

At this point we move from qualitative analysis of the efficiency gains of different pricing structures to numerical simulations of their effects. We will do so using publicly available data from AT&T's message services to compare total surplus under FDC pricing, Ramsey pricing, and optimal nonuniform pricing. As we make clear in the discussion below, the different price structures which we compute are for a hypothetical "message service" with baseline quantities, prices and parameters taken from MTS and WATS, but which is not meant to correspond to these or any other actual service offerings.

A. Data for efficient pricing of message service

We begin with some further background information on message services. Calls on MTS and WATS go through AT&T's public switched network, unlike private line services, which have dedicated circuits. As pointed out above, MTS and WATS differ in tariffs, billing detail and service quality. Other common carriers (OCC's) offer switched message service, too, both on their own networks and on lines leased from AT&T. However, since these firms account only for about 5 percent of total message revenues, it seems safe to ignore them.

We will use MTS and WATS data in what follows, but only in order to calibrate a single hypothetical market for message services, in which customers purchase from a single unified tariff with no explicit MTS-WATS distinctions. Thus, the prices we compute should not be interpreted as MTS prices or WATS prices, but simply as prices for *message service*. This service will be assumed to have the same quality and billing detail as MTS, except that billing is based on total monthly minutes of usage, and not on the number of calls.

Markets for switched service can vary both by distance and by time of day. A recent study by AT&T setting forth the AT&T Telecommunications Policy Model (TELPOL) aggregates all distances and divides the message market into Day and Non-Day. The reason for this particular aggregation is that costs in message services vary much more by time of day than by distance. We will adopt the same market definition so as to make use of the information contained in the AT&T study.[9] It will become important below to note that the Day message market is largely a business market (78 percent of Day revenue in 1978 came from business customers) and that the Non-Day market is almost entirely residential (92 percent of Non-Day revenue in 1978). The system peak occurs during the day.

We will evaluate the effects of Ramsey pricing, optimal nonuniform pricing and FDC pricing using a common framework for consumer demands and cost. This means that we must use the model of consumer behavior and costs which we presented in the previous chapters. To do this we need the following information:

1. individual demand functions indexed by a taste parameter θ;
2. the distribution of θ across the population of actual and potential consumers;
3. marginal costs of Day and Non-Day service;
4. a required level of contribution over and above operating costs.

We will discuss each of these items in turn.

1. Demand functions. One difficulty with arriving at individual demand functions is that econometric work on the demand for message service has not focussed on the issue of estimating individuals' demand functions but has, instead, tried to estimate either aggregate demand or average demand.[10] Therefore, our procedure will be to assign the average customer in our population of consumers the average prices and quantities observed in Day and Non-Day demand and the price elasticities of demand arrived at in studies of aggregate and per capita

[9]
"Telecommunications Policy Model Evaluating Changes in Telecommunications Policies: Whose Ox will be Gored," by E. P. Marfisi, K. J. Murphy, M. M. Murphy, J. H. Rohlf and D. Silverstein, American Telephone and Telegraph Company, December, 1981.

[10]
See, however, Klein and Willig [1978] which sets out a methodology for estimating demand functions which are disaggregated to the customer level. See also the documentation of AT&T's RES model of MTS demand in *The General Rate Increase Filing, March 3, 1980, Volume 14: MTS Demand and Rate Change Evaluation.* This model breaks down MTS demand by day, evening, night and weekend, by distance and by customer class (business, residence). See also J. H. Rohlfs, *Economically Efficient Bell System Pricing,* Bell Laboratories discussion paper #138, January, 1979 for a survey of econometric work on telecommunications demand.

demand. Other customers differ from this average demand curve only in their values of θ.

We assume two alternative functional forms for demand. The first is linear:

$$Q_D = a_D + b_D P_D + \theta \tag{1}$$

$$Q_N = a_N + b_N P_N + \theta . \tag{2}$$

The second demand function we employ is a modified isoelastic form:

$$Q_D = a_D \, \theta \, P_D^{-\epsilon_D} \tag{3}$$

$$Q_N = a_N \, \theta \, P_N^{-\epsilon_N} \tag{4}$$

for $Q_D \geqslant 1$ and $Q_N \geqslant 1$. For quantities less than one minute, demand is a vertical line for each consumer type. This means that we are assuming that diminishing marginal utility of usage only sets in after one minute per month. This truncation at one minute will result in tariffs with a one minute minimum billing period; given that a call is placed, the consumer is assumed to talk for the full minute, since his outlay is not reduced if he speaks for less than one minute.[11]

To calibrate these two functional forms for individuals' demand functions, we need average prices, average quantities and price elasticities of demand. In Table 7.1 we present average prices and quantities. The reader should be cautioned against comparing the prices too closely to any actual tariffs. The prices of 32¢ and 22¢ per minute represent average revenue for Day and Non-Day, where each category includes MTS and WATS users; the latter were served under highly nonlinear tariffs, so that our average revenue figures may not correspond closely to any of the marginal prices actually paid by users. Once again, it should be realized that our aim is not to simulate the effects of any actual tariffs. Rather, it is to compare hypothetical pricing structures using parameter values which are very roughly representative of the marketplace in 1978. Representative price elasticities are given in Table 7.2. These are taken from the TELPOL report and represent elasticities typical of many studies. We will assume that they hold for the average consumer in our population of consumers who differ by the taste parameter θ.

---

[11]
The truncation also ensures that our surplus integrals exist, which would not be the case otherwise with price elasticities of demand less than unity in this isoelastic case.

Table 7.1 Average Prices and Quantities for Business Customers[†]

	Price ($/min)	Quantity (mins/month)
Day	.32	111
Non-Day	.22	28

† Business prices and quantities include business MTS, MT
WATS and FBD WATS. See the appendix to this chapter
for details.

Using this information, as well as other information presented below,
we want to calculate the parameters of these demand functions. The
parameter estimates are contained in Table 7.3. The precise procedures
used to arrive at these estimates are described in the appendix to this
chapter.

Because the linear and isoelastic demand functions are calibrated to
the same average price $\bar{P}$, quantity $\bar{Q}$ and price elasticity, they must be
tangent at $(\bar{P}, \bar{Q})$. This is shown in Figure 7.2. To forshadow a point
which we will bring out below, the analyst is not usually able to
discriminate between these two demand functions because he only has
price and quantity information in the region of average price and
average demand. If Ramsey prices or nonuniform prices differ
significantly depending on which functional form is correct for
describing behavior away from $(\bar{P}, \bar{Q})$, then additional empirical work is
urgently needed in order to implement these price structures.

Table 7.2 Price Elasticities of Demand

	Business	
	Day	Non-Day
Day	−.534	.037
Non-Day	.165	−.77

Source: Marfisi *et al.* [1981] pp. 54-55.

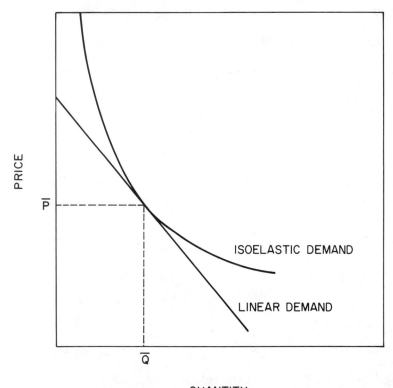

Figure 7.2

Table 7.3 Demand Functions

Linear:	$Q_D = -77.78 - 246.21\, P_D + .8\,\theta$
	$Q_N = -28.31 - 128.8\, P_N + .2\,\theta$
Isoelastic:	$Q_D = .3257\,\theta\, P_D^{-.534}$
	$Q_N = .04705\,\theta\, P_N^{-.77}$

2. Distribution of customers' tastes. To obtain a distribution of consumers by taste, we start with some evidence on the distribution of billing. Table 7.4 gives the frequency distribution of monthly expenditures on long distance interstate calling for business customers.

Table 7.4 Distribution of Interstate Long Distance Business Billing

Average Monthly Billing	% of Total Customers	% of Total Revenues	Cumulative % of Revenues
0.00	14.1	.0	.0
2.00	28.5	.6	.6
4.00	10.8	.8	1.4
7.00	8.7	1.2	2.5
10.00	5.3	1.1	3.7
15.00	6.1	1.9	5.6
20.00	3.7	1.7	7.2
30.00	4.7	2.9	10.2
50.00	5.3	5.2	15.4
100.00	5.2	9.4	24.8
200.00	3.7	13.5	38.3
200.00+	3.9	61.7	100.0

Excludes Centrex customers and federal government.

Source: *The Dilemma of Telecommunications Policy*,
         Exhibit 8, Table 4.

Day and Non-Day expenditures are aggregated in these tables. In terms of our analysis, these distributions of billing are assumed to be generated from our assumed demand functions. Thus, in the linear case if we assume independent demands between Day and Non-Day the observed distribution of revenue is generated by

$$R = P_D \cdot (a_D - b_D P_D + \theta) + P_N \cdot (a_N - b_N P_N + \theta)$$

so that

$$\theta = \frac{R}{P_D + P_N} + \alpha$$

where

$$\alpha = \frac{-P_D \cdot (a_D - b_D P_D) - P_N \cdot (a_N - b_N P_N)}{P_D + P_N}.$$

We will assume that θ is distributed lognormally with logarithmic mean μ and variance σ^2. Also, the parameter α is estimated so that percentages of potential consumers who are priced out of the market at the average prices given in Table 7.1 correspond to the levels given in Table 7.4, 14.1 percent of business customers. Our estimated distributions of θ will depend, of course, on the precise demand functions used to generate them. Our estimates of μ and σ^2 are: $\mu = 2.53$, $\sigma^2 = 5.38$. (See the appendix to this chapter for details.)

3. Marginal costs. The TELPOL study gives marginal costs broken down by four categories of message service:

	MTS Day	MTS Non-Day	FBD WATS	MT WATS
Marginal Cost ($/min)	.13	.06	.08	.11

Clearly, this gives some latitude in the choice of marginal costs for Day and Non-Day service in our simulations. Recalling, however, that our stylized message service is to have the same service quality as MTS, it seems most appropriate to use the marginal costs of Day and Non-Day MTS. The marginal costs for FBD WATS and MT WATS presumably are affected by the lack of billing detail inherent in WATS service, differences in central office equipment, and the fact that peak and off-peak demands for WATS are heavily influenced by peak hour congestion in WATS lines. For this reason, we will employ a marginal cost of $.13 per minute for Day message service and $.06 per minute for Non-Day.

4. Required level of contribution. To get the target level of contribution for use with the various pricing structures, we simulate the effects of the current prices given in Table 7.1 on the population of consumers which we have described. To see how this is done, consider the business market when we assume that individuals' demand functions are isoelastic. Each consumer buys according to his demand function. For example, a business consumer with a taste index $\theta = 10$ buys according to the following demand functions for Day and Non-Day service:

$$Q_D = 32.57 \ P_D^{-.534} = 5.99 \text{ mins/month}$$
$$\text{at price } P_D = \$.32$$

$$Q_N = 4.705 \ P_N^{-.77} = 1.51 \text{ mins/month}$$
$$\text{at price } P_N = \$.22$$

Since it costs $.13 per minute in the Day and $.06 per minute in the Non-Day to supply the consumer, the firm earns

$$(\$.32 - \$.13) \times 5.99 + (\$.22 - \$.06) \times 1.51 = \$1.38.$$

With a θ value of 10 and a lognormal distribution of θ over the entire population with logarithmic mean 2.53 and variance of 5.38, the density of $\theta = 10$ customers in the population is equal to .397, so the weighted contribution of the $\theta = 10$ group is .397 × $1.38 = $.55. For each θ group we go through the same procedure. Summing the weighted contributions over all business customers who make any calls we get a contribution per head of $24.35. We will treat this level of contribution as our target levels in the simulations reported below.

We have now computed all of the inputs necessary to simulate the effects of the different pricing structures which we have studied. They constitute a base case for pricing simulations. We will test the results of the base case simulations by running further simulations in which the values of parameters are varied from their base case level.

B. Simulation procedure

The appendix to this chapter contains the mathematics which define FDC prices, Ramsey prices and optimal nonuniform prices within the context of the framework which we have set up in this chapter. Computational procedures are also described for the technical reader.

For the non-technical reader, the simulation procedure takes place in four stages. First, prices are determined by the formulae for FDC, Ramsey and nonuniform pricing which we described in Chapters 3, 4, and 5. Next, each consumer type θ in our population of consumers looks at the price structure with which he is faced — be it Ramsey, FDC or an entire nonuniform price schedule — and selects the quantity to consume which maximizes his consumer surplus. Third, the resulting consumer surpluses and contributions from each of the θ groups are weighted by the densities of the θ groups and then summed over all θ's which buy positive amounts. Fourth, we check to see if the firm's profit constraint is met. If it is, then we have found the set of prices we seek. If it is not, then we go back to the first step, adjust our prices to earn profit closer to the target level and try again.

C. Simulation results

As a prelude to presenting the simulation results for business customers, recall again the meaning which we will assign to maximization of business customers' surplus. Each level of θ represents the taste for message service of a particular industry which consists of identical firms which are perfect competitors. We interpret business demand curves — or, rather, their inverses — as value of marginal product curves for message service in each industry. In computing surplus from these demand curves we are computing short-run producers' surplus for these customer firms. When output prices adjust to eliminate short-run profits in these industries, this producer surplus is transferred to final consumers. As argued in Chapter 6, when aggregate short-run producer surplus of message service business customers goes up, this is an *underestimate* of the increase in consumer surplus which will be obtained by the final consumers of the products produced by the various θ-industries, using message service as an input, equilibrium adjustments have taken place.

The benchmark against which to compare efficient pricing is FDC pricing. We use the isoelastic demand formulation. The FDC results are depicted in Table 7.5 and in Figures 7.3 and 7.4. The Day price is 31.6¢ and the Non-Day price 24.6¢. (Notice that the difference between the two prices, 7¢, is equal to the difference between marginal costs in the two markets. This is what we would expect from the definition of FDC prices given in Chapter 3, where it is shown that FDC prices in each period are equal to the sum of marginal cost in that period and the average fixed cost over all periods; the difference in the prices of any two periods is simply the difference in their marginal costs.) These prices exclude about 19.1 percent of potential consumers from Day market and 41 percent from the Non-Day market. Average consumption over the two markets is 130.83 minutes per month. These

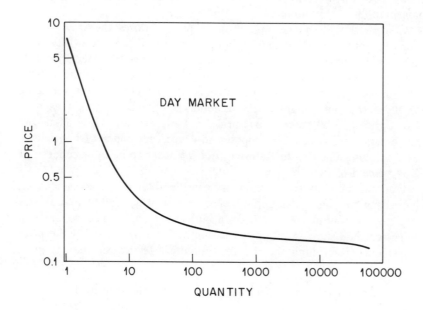

Figure 7.3

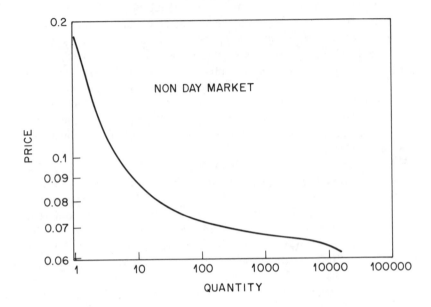

Figure 7.4

results square fairly well with the effects of the current prices, which excluded 19.1 percent from the Day market and lead to average consumption of 139 minutes.

Compared to FDC pricing, Ramsey pricing raises the Day price a fair amount, from 31.6¢ to 35¢, but lowers the off-peak Non-Day price drastically, from 24.6¢ to 10.6¢. Because of the off-peak price cut, average consumption increases in the Non-Day period, raising total consumption from 130.83 minutes to 147.62 minutes. Ramsey pricing excludes the same number of consumers in the Day market as does FDC pricing, 19.9 percent, but prices out substantially fewer Non-Day customers (30.3 percent, as opposed to 41 percent under FDC pricing). The surplus gains due to Ramsey pricing appear to be quite modest, at 2.67 percent of FDC revenue.

Optimal nonuniform pricing is considerably more efficacious at increasing surplus.[12] The price schedules for Day and Non-Day are depicted in Figures 7.3 and 7.4. In both cases the optimal nonuniform price schedule shows a quantity discount. In the Day market the price starts out rather high for the first minute. Thereafter the marginal

[12] See the appendix to this chapter for details on the algorithms used.

Table 7.5 Base Case Results

	FDC	Ramsey	Non-Uniform
1. Day Price ($)	.316	.350	10.745†
2. Non-Day Price ($)	.246	.106	.268†
3. Percent priced out of Day market	19.9	19.9	47.7
4. Percent priced out of Non-Day market	41.0	30.3	41.8
5. Average Consumption†† (total mins/month)	130.83	147.62	197.6
6. Surplus gain over FDC as percentage of revenue	—	2.67	10.62

† These are the marginal prices at zero consumption. The entire optimal nonuniform prices schedules one depicted in Figures 7.3 and 7.4.

†† Recall that all parameters have been calibrated to an average total consumption of 139 mins. based on a 1978 Day price of 32¢/min. and a Non-Day price of 22¢/min.

price declines sharply, so that for consumers buying more than about 70 minutes per month, the marginal price is lower than under either FDC or Ramsey pricing. The high initial marginal price forces 41.8 percent of potential business customers out of the market. In the Non-Day market the initial marginal price is 26.8¢, which excludes 34 percent from the Non-Day market. The quantity discounts displayed by the nonuniform price schedules stimulate the consumption of medium and large users to the point that average consumption rises to 197.6 minutes, far above average consumption under Ramsey or FDC pricing. Total surplus rises by 10.62 percent of revenues.

It is instructive to undertake a sensitivity analysis of these results. As a first step in that direction we simulated the effects of varying the price elasticity of demand for the Day and Non-Day markets. When these parameters are varied, concomitant changes in a_D and a_N are required in order to ensure that this altered population of consumers, when facing current prices, generates the same average consumption in each market and prices the same number of consumers out of the market as are actually observed. Namely,

$$\bar{Q}_D \quad = \quad 111 \text{ mins/month}$$

$$\bar{Q}_N \quad = \quad 28 \text{ mins/month}$$

14.1% of potential customers buy nothing.

We analyze five different cases:

	ϵ_D	ϵ_N	μ	σ
Case 1:	.534	.77	2.52	2.32
Case 2:	.75	.77	2.52	2.32
Case 3:	.534	1.08	2.52	2.32
Case 4:	.534	.77	1.16	2.9
Case 5:	.534	.77	3.65	1.75

Case 1 is simply the base case. In Case 2 we increase ϵ_D by 40 percent and in Case 3 we raise ϵ_N by that amount. Case 4 was generated by increasing the logarithmic standard deviation σ by 25 percent and then setting the logarithmic mean μ at the level which was consistent with a total business consumption of 139 minutes at the prices which are given in Table 7.1. In Case 5 σ is reduced by 25 percent and μ is chosen in the same way as in Case 4.

Table 7.6 contains the results of the simulations of Cases 1-3. Let us start with the effects of changing the price elasticities ϵ_D and ϵ_N. The effect of increasing ϵ_D from .534 to .75 (Case 2) is to lower the Ramsey Day price from 35¢ to 33.8¢; the Non-Day price must rise from 10.6¢ to 14.9¢ so as to meet the $24.35 revenue requirement. For nonuniform pricing, the Day marginal price schedule shifts downwards and the Non-Day price schedule rises. To indicate this we give the marginal prices at zero consumption in Table 7.6; the Day marginal price $P_D(0)$ falls from $10.745 to $6.475 and the Non-Day marginal price $P_N(0)$ rises from 26.8¢ to 78.4¢. When the Non-Day price elasticity ϵ_N is increased from .77 to 1.08, the Ramsey Non-Day price falls to 8.7¢, while the Day price rises slightly, to 35.3¢. For the nonuniform case, the Non-Day marginal price at zero consumption falls from 26.8¢ to 17.3¢. Evidently, the fact that ϵ_D exceeds unity in this case allows the price reduction in the Non-Day market to increase Non-Day contribution, because the Day marginal price at zero actually falls, from $10.745 to $10.386.

Efficiency gains to Ramsey pricing appear to be rather small, on the order of one to seven percent of the average billing under FDC pricing. Optimal nonuniform pricing does a lot better, increasing total surplus by a dollar amount on the order of ten to fifteen percent of FDC revenue. It should be noted that in simulations (not reported herein) in which the linear demand specification was used, both Ramsey and optimal nonuniform prices got about the same efficiency gains as in the isoelastic case.

Table 7.6 Sensitivity Analysis of Efficient Pricing

1. Prices ($/min)

	Nonuniform Pricing		Ramsey Pricing		FDC Pricing	
	$P_D(0)$	$P_N(0)$	P_D	P_N	P_D	P_N
Case 1	10.745	.268	.350	.106	.316	.246
Case 2	6.475	.784	.338	.149	.315	.245
Case 3	10.386	.173	.353	.087	.318	.248

2. Surplus Gains Over FDC Pricing
(as percent of FDC Revenue)

	Ramsey Pricing	Nonuniform Pricing
Case 1	2.67	10.62
Case 2	1.03	11.99
Case 3	6.70	14.92

Table 7.7 contains the results of the Case 4 and Case 5 simulations. In all types of pricing changing μ and σ has pronounced effects. This is particularly true of the percentage of customers who buy nothing. In Case 4, σ is high (2.9) and μ is low (1.16) which increases the proportion of low-θ customers, who can be easily priced out of the market. As a result, with all three price structures high proportions are priced out of the market. In the Day market, for example, the optimal nonuniform price schedule excludes 76 percent of consumers, Ramsey pricing excluding 41.8 percent and FDC pricing 41 percent. When μ is increased to 3.65 and σ reduced to 1.75 (Case 5), the percent excluded drops dramatically; to 22 percent for nonuniform pricing, 3.19 percent for Ramsey pricing and 3.6 percent for FDC pricing.

Table 7.7 Variations in μ and σ^2

1. Prices ($/min)

	Nonuniform Pricing		Ramsey Pricing		FDC Pricing	
	$P_D(0)$	$P_N(0)$	P_D	P_N	P_D	P_N
Case 4	12.75	.256	.351	.106	.315	.245
Case 5	9.99	.297	.352	.107	.318	.248

2. Percentage Consuming Nothing

	Nonuniform Pricing		Ramsey Pricing		FDC Pricing	
	Day	Non-Day	Day	Non-Day	Day	Non-Day
Case 4	76.0	61.5	41.8	52.3	41.0	61.1
Case 5	22.0	47.2	3.19	9.2	3.6	17.0

3. Surplus Gain as a Percentage of FDC Revenue

	Nonuniform Pricing	Ramsey Pricing
Case 4	9.08	2.77
Case 5	13.83	2.73

Concerning prices, neither the Ramsey prices nor the FDC prices change much between Case 4 and Case 5. The nonuniform price (at zero consumption) falls from $12.75 to $9.99 in the Day market, but rises in the Non-Day market. The magnitude of these changes as compared with FDC and Ramsey pricing suggest that optimal nonuniform pricing requires the analyst to have more information and more accurate information than do the other two approaches. It should be noted, however, that the nonuniform price schedules still display quantity discounts throughout the entire range of consumption.

In Cases 4 and 5 nonuniform pricing continues to increase surplus considerably more than does Ramsey pricing. Gains from Ramsey pricing are under three percent whereas nonuniform pricing leads to a gain of 9.08 percent in Case 4 and 13.83 percent in Case 5. Comparing the nonuniform pricing results in the two cases, it is apparent that an increase in σ reduces the surplus gain due to optimal nonuniform pricing. The basic aim of nonuniform pricing is to balance off efficient consumption levels by consumers who buy positive amounts against the need to avoid excluding too many customers from the market. With the isoelastic demand curve, which generates quantity discounts, this means that if $P_D(0)$ must be kept from rising, in order not to price consumers out, then $P_D(Q_D)$ for positive consumption cannot approach marginal cost as closely as it would otherwise. The effect of increasing σ^2 is to constrain $P_D(0)$. Therefore those who buy positive amounts do so at higher marginal prices and the surplus gain relative to FDC pricing will be less than with higher σ.

We should note at this point that the simulation results for the linear demand specification were the same in all but one respect. The FDC and Ramsey prices with linear demands differ only minutely from the loglinear case as do the efficiency gains to Ramsey pricing. The shapes of the optimal nonuniform price schedules are much different, as we will see shortly. However, the surplus gain to nonuniform pricing in the linear is on the same order as in the loglinear case, about 8 to 12 percent of FDC revenue.

Finally, it is necessary to vary the shape of the individual consumer's demand curve. The reason for this is that the sort of demand data usually available do not generally permit us to more than estimate the shape of an aggregate or per capita demand curve in the region of observed price and quantity. In other words, at best we have some knowledge of the behavior of the *average* consumer within a fairly narrow range of variation of price and quantity. The linear and isoelastic demand curves which are set out in Table 7.3 were specially calibrated to fit the same data on average consumption, price elasticity and to correspond fairly well on the percentage of customers excluded from the market by our estimated current prices. Therefore, most sets of data would not tell us which type of demand curve was more appropriate. Figure 7.5 shows that the shape of the demand away from the region of price and quantity for which we have data makes a startling difference in the shape of the optimal price schedule. Setting all parameters at their base case levels, the isoelastic demand assumption generates an optimal marginal price schedule which starts out high — $10.745 for the first minute — and then declines sharply in a quantity discount. With a linear demand assumption, however, the optimal marginal price starts out low, at $.324 and declines very close to marginal cost in the range of consumption chosen by most consumers. The very large consumers face a steep quantity premium before marginal price plunges down to marginal cost. Figure 7.5

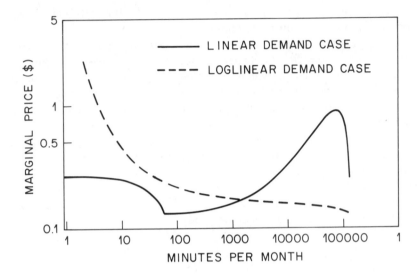

Figure 7.5

depicts this with marginal price schedules chosen for the entire business market, Day and Non-Day aggregated together.

In effect, the surplus-raising strategies are polar opposites in the two cases. With isoelastic demands, surplus is maximized by pricing many consumers out of the market and inducing medium and large users to buy large quantities at marginal prices much closer to marginal cost than under an FDC price. With linear demands nearly all consumers buy a positive amount, and small and medium users buy at prices close to marginal cost, while the contribution requirement is made up on the quantity premium for the very largest users.

At this point, certain questions of practicality arise. Relative to Ramsey pricing, optimal nonuniform pricing is substantially more efficient. However, in order to do Ramsey pricing, the analyst need only have a reliable estimate of the aggregate demand curve in each market. For nonuniform pricing, a demand curve must be estimated for each consumer type in each market and it is especially important that the estimates be accurate at very low levels of consumption, for which there may be no historical data. As we have just seen, whether individual demand curves are linear or isoelastic near the origin seems to determine whether the optimal price schedule shows a quantity discount or a quantity premium. Therefore, it is important that careful econometric work on individual demands precede any attempt to use optimal nonuniform pricing in an actual regulated market. The optimal

PDIC nonuniform price schedules discussed in Chapter 4 may represent a compromise. They only require the analyst to estimate the individual demand curves at prices lower than a tariff which is already in place, so that the data problem is not as severe.

D. Dollar magnitudes of welfare gains

It is of some interest to estimate the dollar gains in efficiency that are implied by these simulation results. In 1978, AT&T revenues for its interstate message services were nearly $11 billion.[13] A rough average of our Ramsey pricing simulations suggests an efficiency gain of about $300 million. Willig and Bailey [1977] study the effects of Ramsey pricing on MTS services in 1973. MTS revenue in 1978 was 79 percent of total message service, so it is of some interest that their range of estimated welfare gains, $69 million to $249 million, is not too unlike ours. In sum, it seems reasonable to project (loosely) that in 1978 dollars, Ramsey pricing would lead to a welfare gain of $300 million or less. Nonuniform pricing would lead to a gain exceeding $1 billion.[14]

7.4 Efficient pricing and the regulatory safety net

In the practical world of regulation, economic efficiency is only one concern of regulators. Frequently, a much more pressing concern is that regulatory policies should not have the effect of reducing any consumer's welfare below some minimal level. In the 1970's regulators, faced with rising electricity costs, frequently set up lifeline rates for customers, whose electricity bills would otherwise consume an unacceptably large fraction of their incomes. Following the divestiture of local telephone operating companies by AT&T in 1984, the public debate on the issue of access charges was driven in large part by concerns that small business and residential subscribers would suffer excessively if they had to pay the full costs of service. The term "regulatory safety net" was coined to describe measures taken by regulatory authorities to ensure that no consumers would suffer excessively from the joint impacts of Administration changes in social spending, the deregulation of several formerly regulated industries and

---

[13] See Marfisi, *et al.*, Table 2.3. The revenue figures therein for Day message, Non-Day message, FBD WATS and MT WATS are summed to get $10.9 billion.

[14] Most of our simulations show a 10-15 percent gain to nonuniform pricing. Using the a 10 percent figure we get an annual dollar gain of $1.1 billion and using the 15 percent figure $1.65 billion.

the changes in the structure and regulation of the telecommunication industry.

Economists have no special expertise to decide what the regulatory safety net should be. Whether poor or elderly customers should be given a lifeline rate for electricity is an ethical decision. However, there are important questions of implementation which arise once that ethical decision is made, and efficient pricing theory, together with common sense, can play an important role in responding to them.

For the purpose of convenient usage, we will assume that regulators are concerned with the impact of their policies on the poor, and we will divide customers into the poor and non-poor, assuming that the political/regulatory process has arrived at working definitions of these groups. (It is hardly necessary to point out that safety net policies are actually responsive to the needs of diverse groups who may not easily be categorized in this way.) How should policymakers proceed if they are concerned both with the well being of poor consumers and with economic efficiency?

To address this issue one must first decide whether or not the conflict between safety net — more generally, income distribution — concerns and efficiency should be resolved by the rate structures of regulated goods and services, or whether explicit subsidies funded from general tax revenues should be used. Given an answer to this question, another arises. Should the policymaker try to weigh the welfare levels of different consumers according to his or her social welfare notions, or should the policymaker instead specify some "entitlement" to basic services which then represents the right of every citizen?

By and large, theoretical research in economics has involved the use of a social welfare function. A social welfare function gives a public decisionmaker's preferences concerning the utility levels attained by different consumers. Papers by Mirrlees [1971, 1976], Feldstein [1972], Stern [1976], Spence [1977] and many others have used convenient mathematical forms of social welfare functions to compute taxes or prices that have the effect of maximizing these definitions of welfare. Generally, social welfare functions assume that individuals differ according to income, race or some other demographic characteristics over which the planner has some kind of ethical preference. Each type of consumer has his or her own utility function and the planner aims to design policies which maximize some kind of weighted sum of all consumers' utilities. Typically these weights are chosen to provide progressivity, that is to say they assume that the marginal social benefit of a dollar given to a poor consumer is higher than that given to a rich customer. As one might expect, the taxation or pricing schemes which maximize such a social welfare function can have one of a large variety of forms, depending on the precise weighting given to different consumers. However, there is one unifying result: with costless tax collection the optimal nonlinear tax schedule has the characteristic that the marginal tax rate on the last dollar earned by the richest customer is equal to the marginal collection cost, usually taken to be zero. This result parallels an important feature of optimal nonuniform pricing: the marginal price equals marginal cost for the last unit consumed by the largest user.

From the standpoint of the policymaker the main problems with such an approach are rather obvious. First, how is society to agree on an acceptable social welfare function? Absent such an agreement, many citizens would probably regard the resulting policies as arbitrary. In addition, it seems unlikely that many people have social preferences which are complete and internally consistent enough to construct a complete social welfare function.

Policymakers have tended to handle safety net concerns with the entitlement approach. Sometimes this is done through general tax revenues, examples being food stamps in the United States and the National Health Service, in Great Britain. In the case of services provided by regulated industries, the tendency in the United States has been to delegate safety net concerns to local and federal regulatory bodies, and not to handle them through general tax revenues.

Typically, the safety net problem takes the form of ensuring that each consumer can consume some minimal level of the regulated service or services. Unavoidably, this entails a certain degree of cross subsidy within the firm's rate structure. Sometimes, the entitlement is for only one service out of a number that the firm provides; for example, the Bell System, prior to divestiture, provided a number of voice and data services at all levels of jurisdiction, but the universal service goal applied only to local telephone service. To fulfill that goal, a procedure called the separations process existed to tax interstate revenues in order to help cover part of the non-traffic sensitive costs of local service. In other examples, the safety net applies to all services; a lifeline rate electricity user, for example, is usually thought to be entitled to both peak and off peak service. In such cases the subsidy flows, not from one group of services to another, but from one group of customers (the non-poor, for example) to another (the poor).

Thus, under the entitlement approach safety net issues are handled by defining a limited group of customers as deserving preferential treatment and presenting them with tariffs which make only a small or, even, a negative contribution to the overhead of the firm. Putting the issue in this way, it is easily combined with efficient pricing theory as it has been presented in this book. Efficiency considerations impinge in two ways. First, once the desirable level of contribution for safety net customers has been set on social welfare grounds, remaining services and customers should be priced on efficiency based criteria. Second, efficiency considerations can be used to advantage to provide a regulatory safety net at the least deadweight loss to the economy.

Our simulations of efficient prices for interstate message service are actually an example of maximizing total surplus of one group of customers subject to safety net constraints applying to another. To recall, the required level of contribution used in those simulations, $24.35, was obtained by simulating the contribution levels generated by uniform prices equal to 1978 average interstate revenue per minute for Day and Non-Day. Those average revenue numbers included separation payments to local service, as well as contributions to the overhead of interstate service. In 1978, it was felt that every American household and business should subscribe to local exchange service as a matter of social policy. Therefore, our efficient pricing analysis represents an effort to maximize interstate total surplus subject to that social policy.

Given the social goal of requiring no more than a low level of contribution from a particular group of poor customers, it still makes sense to try to do that at minimum deadweight loss. For example, suppose that social policy dictates that a poor customer be served at a lifeline rate less than marginal cost. From our discussion in Chapter 3 we know that we could replace this tariff by a price equal to marginal cost together with a required transfer payment which would compensate the poor customer for the higher price but still leave the firm — and, potentially, the non-poor customers — better off. For example, suppose that marginal cost is 10¢ per unit and that a poor consumer is only charged 5¢, at which price he consumes 100 units. If prices were raised to 10¢, the poor consumer's consumption would fall to 80 and his welfare would fall by the drop in his consumer surplus:

$$\Delta \text{ consumer surplus} = -80 \times (10\text{¢} - 5\text{¢}) - \frac{1}{2} (100-80) \times (10\text{¢} - 5\text{¢})$$

$$= -\$4.50.$$

The firm, however, had been losing $5 on this customer at the lifeline rate. Therefore, if it wrote the consumer a refund in a lump sum of $4.50 the poor consumer would be left no worse off than before and non-poor consumers would have to cover 50¢ less than initially.

In this example the poor customer was identified as poor and separated from other consumers for pricing purposes. This can be done in practice by requiring poor customers' to submit evidence as to their income and assets before admittance to a lifeline program. In some cases it is not possible to do this, so that safety net problems must be handled within the context of a rate structure which is available to all consumers, poor or non-poor. In such a case, the theory of self-selecting tariffs can be usefully employed. We give two examples of how this can be done.

We begin by positing a flat rate E_0 at which the firm is breaking even.[15] N_0 customers subscribe at this flat rate, and they consume an aggregate amount X_0. The break-even condition is thus expressed as

$$N_0 E_0 - F - c X_0 = 0$$

where F is the fixed cost of local service and c is the marginal usage cost; for simplicity, we ignore the marginal subscriber costs. Let x_m^0 be the consumption under the flat rate of smallest individual subscriber at the flat rate. As our discussion of the theory of the consumer showed, the smallest subscriber under a flat rate must consume a strictly positive amount: $x_m^0 > 0$. Now give consumers the following optional two-part tariff:

P_1 = usage charge = c

E_1 = entry fee = $E_0 - c x_m^0$.

We first analyze the reactions of consumers to this tariff option and then compute its effect on the profitability of the firm. Before doing so, note that we need very little information to compute this optional tariff. In contrast to the optimal two-part tariff and the optimal nonuniform price schedule, one does not need to know the distribution and form of individual demand curves to set up this optional tariff.

If any new customers subscribe as a result of the new tariff option then, by definition, they are strictly better off than before; let N_n be the number of new subscribers. From our discussion of consumer behavior above, if the subscription rate was not 100 percent under the flat rate, then it is likely that a lowering of the entry fee will cause more users to subscribe: $N_n > 0$. Consider next the consumer who made x_m^0 calls on the flat rate. His demand curve D_m is pictured in Fig. 7.6. He will find it strictly in his interest to select the new tariff option because the reduction in his fixed charge (area "a" + "b" + "c") is greater than the consumer surplus he loses by having a positive usage charge (area "a")

---

[15] This analysis is taken from Panzar [1979].

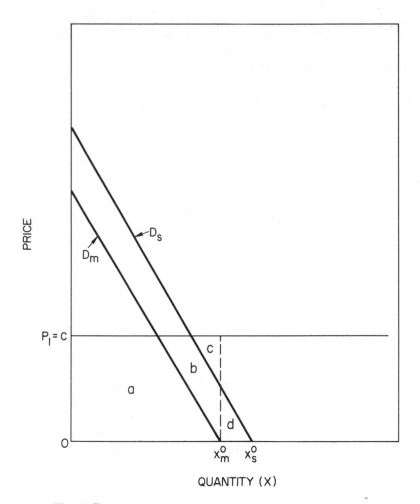

Figure 7.6

Source: Panzar [1979].

by an amount equal to "b" + "c". Now imagine a continuum of consumer types with demand curves lying either above or below D_m. There must exist a particular consumer type s which is just indifferent between switching to the new tariff option and staying on the flat rate tariff. Denote his consumption under the flat rate by x_s^0; the curve is drawn so that the two triangles "c" and "d" are equal. For type s consumers, the reduction in entry fee (area "a" + "b" + "c" in Fig. 7.6) just equals the loss in consumer surplus (triangle "a" + "b" +

"c") from facing the positive usage charge. Any consumer with a demand curve higher than D_s will find switching unprofitable, and will stay on the flat rate. Therefore, all consumers with demand curves below D_s are select the new option and are strictly better off; those with demand curves above D_s stay on the flat rate, with unchanged welfare.

We should note at this point for consumption less than or equal to x_m^0, the usage sensitive tarriff is cheaper; for greater consumption the flat rate is cheaper. Therefore the combination of the original flat rate and the new optional tariff is equivalent to a single declining block tariff with usage charge c for consumption up to x_m^1 and zero thereafter.

Now consider the effect on the firm. Let π denote profits. Under the flat rate it earns π_0, where

$$\pi_0 = N_0 E_0 - cX_0 - F$$

and with the optional tariff in place it earns π_1:

$$\pi_1 = E_1 \cdot (N_n + N_s) + E_0 \cdot (N_0 - N_s) + P_1 \cdot (X_n + X_s^1)$$

$$- c \cdot (X_n + X_s^1 + X_0 - X_s^0) - F \ .$$

where

X_s^1 = Total consumption of all switching consumers under the new optional tariff

X_s^0 = Total consumption of switching consumers when they were buying on the flat rate.

Subtraction yields

$$\Delta\pi \equiv \pi^1 - \pi^0 = E_1 \cdot N_n + c \cdot N_s \cdot (\bar{x}_s^0 - x_m)$$

where

$\bar{x}_s^0$ = average consumption of switching consumers when they were buying on the flat rate .

All consumers who switched bought x_m^0 or more under the flat rate. Therefore, their average flat rate consumption, x_s^0, must exceed x_m^0. This means that $\Delta\pi$ is positive.

The availability of the new tariff option has benefited all consumers with demand curves less than D_s and also allows the firm to increase its profit. Equivalently, the firm could accommodate an increase in total costs equal to $\Delta\pi$ while preserving the strict gain in consumer welfare.

Rough calculations based on Mitchell's model of local telephone service suggest that this particular optional tariff would allow about a two or three percent increase in revenue requirement without hurting any consumer.

This discussion has assumed that all customers must be given the option of buying under a pre-existing flat rate tariff. In current policy discussions, it is usually assumed that small users should have the option of buying under a usage sensitive tariff with a low entry fee. If *all* users faced such a tariff total contribution might fall to an unacceptably low level. Therefore, it is of interest to ask how to preserve the option of a particular usage sensitive lifeline tariff but to increase contribution by designing a service option that appeals more to medium and large users.

For simplicity, suppose that there are two consumer types, Big and Little. Big's demand $X^B(P)$ exceeds Little's demand $X^L(P)$ at any usage charge P. Initially, both face a two-part tariff with entry fee E_0 and usage charge P_0; $P_0 > c$. The firm earns

$$\pi_0 = (P_0 - c) \cdot (X^B(P_0) + X^L(P_0)) + 2E_0 - F.$$

Now suppose that costs rise. Is there any way to meet this cost increase without hurting Little?

We proceed much as in Chapter 4. Given them each a choice between the two-part tariff (E_0, P_0) and a new two-part tariff (E_1, P_1) constructed as follows:

$$P_0 > P_1 > c$$

$$E_1 = X^B(P_0) \cdot (P_0 - P_1) + E_0$$

Figure 7.7 depicts the situation. In the initial situation Little gets consumer surplus equal to the triangle "a" less the entry fee E_0; Big gets the triangle "a" + "b" minus E_0.

Little will not select the new tariff option because the increase $X^B(P_0) \cdot (P_0 - P_1)$ in the entry fee outweighs the benefit of buying at a lower usage charge. In terms of Fig. 7.7 the increase in entry fee is the rectangle "c" + "d" and exceeds the increase in consumer surplus, given by the trapezoid "c". Big will select the new tariff because the increase in consumer surplus due to the lower usage charge (trapezoid "c" + "d" + "e") outweighs the increase in the entry fee (rectangle "c" + "d") by the area "e".

As for the firm, it gets the same contribution as before from Little and more from Big. The increase in the entry fee compensates the firm

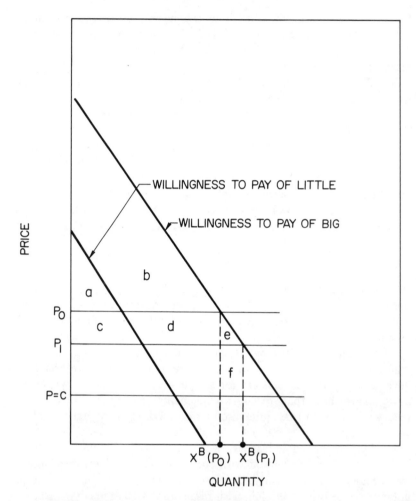

Figure 7.7

for the fact that the amount Big's initial consumption, $X^B(P_0)$, is being sold at a lower usage charge than before. The increase in profit arises from the fact that Big's increased consumption $X^B(P_1) - X^B(P_0)$ takes place at a usage charge P_1 which (by assumption) exceeds marginal cost. The profit increase is given by the rectangle "f" in Fig. 7.7 and is equal to

$$(X^B(P_1) - X^B(P_0)) \cdot (P_1 - c).$$

Therefore, if the revenue requirement applying to these two customers were to rise by an amount less than or equal to "f", the availability of the new tariff option would allow the increased cost to be covered without hurting any consumer; indeed Big would actually be better off. Thus, lifeline requirements may be met even in an environment of increased cost burden.

Two further points made in Chapter 4 should be noted. First, for low usage the original two-part tariff is cheaper, and for high usage the new one is cheaper. At some level $\hat{X}$ they are equally costly. Therefore, the combination of the original two-part tariff and the new optional tariff are equivalent to a single declining block tariff with a usage charge of P_0 up to a consumption level of $\hat{X}$ and P_1 thereafter. Second, the data requirements to construct the optimal tariff are minimal; we need know only the initial usage levels of each consumer. We do not need to know their demand function or the distribution of consumer types; both types of information were necessary to compute optimal two-part tariffs and general nonuniform prices.

7.5 Conclusions

In this chapter we have tried to show that efficient pricing theory can be usefully applied to policy issues in public utility pricing. We have conducted three analyses: (1) the possible implications of resale, in light of nonuniform pricing theory; (2) the efficiency gains to Ramsey and optimal nonuniform pricing as compared to FDC pricing; (3) safety issues and efficient pricing. In none of these analyses do we pretend to have provided firm conclusions for the policymaker. Rather, we hope to have shown him that recent developments in public utility pricing theory are likely to be quite useful in analyzing these issues and are worth learning.

In many regulated industries, even where declining block tariffs are widely used they are viewed with some suspicion and justified only on cost grounds. Consequently, they are sometimes viewed as constituting unlawful price discrimination, with resale an obvious remedy which, it is argued, will increase overall economic efficiency and certainly benefit small users who cannot take advantage of the discounts. Our analysis suggests that when marginal cost pricing will not generate adequate revenue, these conclusions are seriously flawed. First, total surplus may go down, not up. Second, small users may actually be hurt, not helped. The key to the difference in the analysis lies in viewing a declining block tariffs as equivalent to a set of self-selecting two-part tariffs which is being offered to a diverse consumer population. With costless resale, the effect is to pool all consumers onto a single contract; namely, a uniform price equal to average cost. In the absence of a choice from a well-designed set of two-part tariffs, it should not be surprising that consumers may be left worse off.

Moving to our simulations of different pricing schemes, one conclusion emerges: using interstate telephone data, Ramsey pricing displays efficiency gains over FDC pricing which are modest, at best. Typically, the gain in total surplus is less than seven percent of FDC revenue and is frequently less than three percent. This result is similar to that obtained by Bailey and Willig [1976]. Optimal nonuniform prices does considerably better, with gains in the range of 9 to 15 percent. However, as we pointed out, the precise shape of the marginal price schedule differed drastically depending on the precise shape of the individual demand curves. To get a reasonable feel for what these curves should look like in the crucial range around zero consumption, detailed knowledge of the price elasticity of participation in the market is probably necessary.

In our discussion of safety net problems, the main conclusion was a methodological one: since the welfare of poor consumers is usually protected by requiring only a modest, or negative, contribution from them, it is natural simply to treat such a cross-subsidy requirement as a fixed cost to be covered by other consumers. From this standpoint, efficient pricing is important in two ways. First, efficient design of lifeline tariffs can minimize the cost to the subsidizing customers of maintaining the safety net. Second, efficient pricing of the subsidizing customers will maximize economic efficiency without violating the social goal of maintaining a regulatory safety net. A key to both goals is the theory of optimal nonuniform pricing, particularly in its insight that by correctly designing tariffs, one group can benefit without hurting others.

Mathematical derivation of efficient prices

In this appendix we will quickly confirm the efficiency of marginal cost pricing when we allow for cross-elasticities of demand between the firm's services and for non-constant marginal costs. We will continue to assume that the conditions are met which guarantee that consumer surplus is a useful way to measure the impact of changes in the prices of the regulated firm on the welfare of consumers. Subsequently, we derive Ramsey prices mathematically.

The consumer surplus achievable at a given set of prices $P = (P_1, P_2, ..., P_M)$ can be written as the line integral

$$CS = \int_P^\infty \sum_{i=1}^M Q_i(P_1, P_2, ..., P_i, ..., P_M) dP_i$$

$$= U(Q_1, Q, ..., Q_M) - \sum_{i=1}^M P_i Q_i$$

We write producer's surplus as

$$PS(P) = \sum_{i=1}^M P_i Q_i(P_1, P_2, ..., P_i, ..., P_M)$$

$$- C(Q_1(\cdot), Q_2(\cdot), ..., Q_M(\cdot))$$

where $C(Q_1, Q_2, ..., Q_M)$ is the joint cost function of the firm. Therefore, total surplus $CS + PS$ is given by

$$CS + PS = \int_P^\infty \sum_{i=1}^M Q_i(P_1, P_2, ..., P_i, ..., P_M) dP_i + \sum_{i=1}^M P_i Q_i(P_1, P_2, ..., P_i, ..., P_M)$$

$$- C(Q_1(\cdot), Q_2(\cdot), ..., Q_M(\cdot)).$$

To obtain efficient prices we maximize total surplus $CS + PS$ with respect to the prices $P = (P_1, P_2, ..., P_M)$. We assume that the maximum is unique, so that the efficient prices $P^* = (P_1^*, P_2^*, ..., P_M^*)$

are given by the following first-order conditions:

$$\frac{\partial(CS+PS)}{\partial P_i}\Bigg|_{P=P^*} - \sum_{j=1}^{M}\left[P_j - \frac{\partial C}{\partial Q_j}\right]\frac{\partial Q_j}{\partial P_i}\Bigg|_{P=P^*} = 0$$

or, by the assumption of a unique maximum,

$$P_j^* = \frac{\partial C}{\partial Q_j}, \quad j = 1, 2, ..., M.$$

Thus, the efficient set of prices $P^* = (P_1^*, P_2^*, ..., P_M^*)$ is characterized by the equality of price and marginal cost in each market.

Now impose the breakeven constraint that

$$\sum_{i=1}^{M} P_i Q_i = C(Q_1, Q_2, ..., Q_m).$$

The Ramsey problem is now to choose prices $P_1, P_2, ..., P_m$ to maximize the following Lagrangian:

$$L = \int_{P}^{\infty}\sum_{i=1}^{m} Q_i \, dP_i + (\lambda+1)\cdot\left[\sum_{i=1}^{m} P_i Q_i - C(\cdot)\right].$$

This yields the first order conditions:

$$\sum_{j=1}^{M}\left(\frac{P_j - \dfrac{\partial C}{\partial Q_j}}{P_j}\right)\epsilon_{ji}\,\frac{P_j Q_j}{P_i Q_i} = \frac{\lambda}{1+\lambda}, \quad i=1, 2, ..., M$$

$$\epsilon_{ji} \equiv -\frac{\partial Q_j}{\partial P_i}\cdot\frac{P_i}{Q_j}$$

$$\sum_{j=1}^{M} P_j Q_j - C(Q_1, Q_2, ..., Q_m) = 0.$$

In the case where demands are independent, these conditions simplify to the IER:

$$\lambda Q_i + (\lambda+1)\cdot\left[P_i - \frac{\partial C}{\partial Q_i}\right]\cdot\frac{\partial Q_i}{\partial P_i} = 0$$

or

$$\left(\frac{P_i - \dfrac{\partial C}{\partial Q_i}}{P_i}\right) = \frac{\lambda}{1+\lambda}\cdot\frac{1}{\epsilon_{ii}}$$

$$\epsilon_{ii} = -\frac{Q_i}{P_i}\cdot\left(\frac{\partial Q_i}{\partial P_i}\right).$$

In the general case we can rewrite these conditions to read:

$$\frac{\lambda}{1+\lambda} = \left[\frac{P_i - \dfrac{\partial C}{\partial Q_i}}{P_i}\right] S_i = \left[\frac{P_k - \dfrac{\partial C}{\partial Q_k}}{p_k}\right] S_k$$

where i and k are any two services and S_i, the superelasticity of Q_i, is given by[1]

$$S_i = \frac{1}{\displaystyle\sum_{j=1}^{M} r_{ji}\,\phi_{ji}} \;,\; r_{ji} \equiv \frac{P_j Q_j}{P_i Q_i}$$

where ϕ_{ji} is the elasticity of the inverse demand function $P_j(Q_1, Q_2, ..., Q_m)$ with respect to Q_i. In other words,

$$\phi_{ji} \equiv \frac{\partial P_j}{\partial Q_i} \cdot \frac{Q_i}{P_j}$$

and ϕ_{ji} is refered to as the flexibility of Q_j with respect to P_i.

Another way to derive the Ramsey pricing rule is to write consumer surplus as follows:

$$\int_P^\infty \sum_{i=1}^M Q_i\, dp = U(Q_1, Q_2, ..., Q_M) - \sum_{i=1}^M P_i Q_i .$$

Total surplus is now written as $U(Q_1, Q_2, ..., Q_M) - C(Q_1, Q_2, ..., Q_M)$, and the Lagrangian is

$$\mathcal{L} = U(Q_1, Q_2, ..., Q_M) - C(Q_1, Q_2, ..., Q_M) + \bar{\lambda} \cdot \left[\sum_{i=1}^M P_i Q_i - C(Q_1, Q_2, ..., Q_M)\right]$$

where $P_i = P_i(Q_1, Q_2, ..., Q_M)$ is the inverse demand function. Maximizing $\mathcal{L}$ w.r.t. Q_i we have

$$\frac{\partial \mathcal{L}}{\partial Q_i} = \frac{\partial U}{\partial Q_i} - \frac{\partial C}{\partial Q_i} + \bar{\lambda} \cdot \left[MR_i - MC_i\right] = 0$$

$$MR_i = \frac{\partial}{\partial Q_i}\left[\sum_{i=1}^M P_i Q_i\right]$$

$$MC_i \equiv \frac{\partial C}{\partial Q_i}.$$

[1] This follows Rohlfs, [1979].

From the utilize maximization of individual consumers, $\partial U/\partial Q_i = P_i$, so

$$P_i - MC_i + \tilde{\lambda} \cdot \left(MR_i - MC_i \right) = 0$$

or, for any two outputs i and j

$$\frac{P_i - MC_i}{MC_i - MR_i} = \frac{P_j - MC_i}{MC_j - MR_i} = \tilde{\lambda}.$$

Noting that $MR_i = P_i \cdot \left(1 + \sum_{j=1}^{M} r_{ji}\phi_{ji} \right)$ we can substitute into this expression to read

$$\left(\frac{P_i - MC_i}{P_i} \right) S_i = \left(\frac{P_j - MC_j}{P_j} \right) S_i$$

where S_i in the superelasticity defined above.

Externalities and efficient pricing

An externality is a consequence of a person's action which is not taken into account by that person. An example is industrial pollution, which does not impose any direct costs on the firms doing the polluting, but hurts communities nearby. Two kinds of externalities have been proposed as being relevant to the pricing of service on a telecommunications network: (1) call externalities and (2) network size externalities.

The call externality arises when a telephone call confers a benefit on the recipient, as well as the originator, who pays for all of the call. If the recipient's benefit from the call is the same as the originator's, then the social benefit from the call is twice the marginal cost of the call. The network externality arises when a new user joins a network and, thereby, increases the communications possibilities open to the pre-existing members of the network. In theory, efficient pricing should take account of these externalities. Call externalities would argue for reductions in the price of a call [see Bailey and Willig, 1977, equation (22)]. Network size externalities would argue for reductions in access prices. See Rohlfs [1979].

The call externality is probably not too important. It only involves two people and can probably be easily "internalized." For example, two frequent callers could arrange to share the cost of calling. Furthermore, not all call externalities are positive externalities; there are certain phone calls that one is annoyed to receive. Since the telephone company cannot be expected to distinguish between positive and negative call externalities, it is probably not useful to incorporate them into pricing formulas. For this reason, and because call externalities can probably be internalized fairly well, they do not provide a strong case for call price reductions.

Size of network externalities may be more important. They have been analyzed by Bailey and Willig [1977], Littlechild [1975], Squire [1973], Rohlfs [1974] and Griffin [1982]. To follow Rohlfs' analysis, make the following definitions:

msv_j = marginal social value if individual j joins the network

$\hat{u}_k$ = individual $k's$ utility if j joins the network

u_k = individual $k's$ utility if j does not join

y_k = $k's$ income

Then

$$msv_j = \sum_k \left(\frac{\hat{u}_k - u_k}{\partial u_k / \partial y_k} \right).$$

Define the externality factor

$$e = \frac{1}{n} \sum_{\substack{\text{marginal} \\ \text{subscribers } j}} \frac{msv_j}{mpv_j}$$

where mpv_j is the marginal private value of j's joining the network. Rohlfs shows that the marginal condition for an unconstrained Pareto optimum is

$$e \cdot P_{\text{access}} = \text{Marginal cost of access} .$$

Clearly, it is difficult to measure e. Rohlfs [1979] and, subsequently, Griffin [1982] take the view that one should proceed by making extreme assumptions which yield bounds on e. Assuming that the value of a communications link is the same to both ends of the line and that the externality cannot be internalized, $e = 2$. If it can be perfectly internalized, then $e = 1$. Hence, Griffin [1982] and Rohlfs [1979] conduct analyses under three alternative assumptions, $e = 1, e = 1\frac{1}{2}, e = 2$, and argue that these cases capture all the interesting possible effects of the access externality.

In maximizing total surplus subject to a breakeven constraint, Rohlfs obtains the following expression for Ramsey prices for access and all other services (indexed by i):

$$\frac{eP_{\text{access}} - mc_{\text{access}}}{mc_{\text{access}} - mr_{\text{access}}} = \frac{P_i - mc_i}{mc_i - mr_i}$$

where mr = marginal revenue and is defined so as to include cross-elastic effects.

In the case of independent demands, Griffin [1982] derives a much simpler expression under the assumption that e is constant. In the two service case of long distance calls and local service he writes

$$\eta_1 \cdot \left[\frac{P_1 - mc_1}{P_1} \right] = \left[\frac{P_2 - mc_{2/e}}{P_2} \right] \cdot \left[\frac{e\eta_2}{\eta_2 \cdot (1-e) + 1} \right]$$

where η_1 is the price elasticity of demand for long distance service and η_2 is the price elasticity for local service.

These results suggest the possibility that cross subsidy would be optimal when prices are chosen to maximize total surplus, since $e > 1$ is likely. Rohlfs investigated this issue in the context of local service pricing and found that only if the externality factor were at its upper bound of $e = 2$, would the then-prevailing access prices be Pareto efficient. For anything short of this, access was priced too low. Griffin [1982] and Rohlfs [1979] both found that access externalities did not justify cross subsidy in Ramsey pricing, when the breakeven constraint is imposed, although its presence lowered the Ramsey access price closer to marginal cost of access than would other wise be the case.

The optimal two part tariff

We begin with the following definitions:

θ_{max} = maximum value of θ for which a density function is defined
$g(\theta)$ = density function of θ
$G(\theta)$ = c.d.f. of θ
v = marginal cost of access
c = marginal cost of consumption
F = fixed cost of the firm
$q(P,\theta)$ = demand of consumer θ at a usage charge of P. This demand results from individual surplus maximization by θ.
$U(Q,\theta)$ = benefit in money terms to consumer θ of consuming Q
θ_0 = marginal consumer type

The individual demands $Q(P,\theta)$ apply only to those consumers who subscribe to the service of the utility. The result from maximizing net benefit:

$$\max_Q [U(Q, \theta) - PQ - E]$$

or

$$\frac{\partial U}{\partial Q} = P \implies Q = q(P, \theta).$$

The marginal consumer θ_0 is defined by

$$U(q(P,\theta_0), \theta_0) - P \cdot q(P,\theta_0) - E = 0$$

which defines an implicit function $\theta_0 = \theta_0(P, E)$ with the following properties:

$$\frac{\partial \theta_0}{\partial P} = \frac{q(P,\theta_0)}{\partial U/\partial \theta} = q(P, \theta_0) \frac{\partial \theta_0}{\partial E}.$$

We assume weak monotonicity, so $\partial U/\partial \theta > 0$ and raising either p or E increases the taste variable of the marginal consumer type.

Aggregate consumer surplus is given by

$$CS = \int_{\theta_0}^{\bar{\theta}} \left\{ U(q(P, \theta), \theta) - p \cdot q(P,\theta) - E \right\} g(\theta) d\theta .$$

Producer surplus, Π, must equal F.

$$\Pi = \int_{\theta_0}^{\bar{\theta}} \left\{ (P - c) \cdot q(P, \theta) + E - v \right\} g(\theta) d\theta = F .$$

The results stated in the text follow from maximizing the following Lagrangian:

$$\mathscr{L} = W + (1+\lambda)\Pi .$$

$$\frac{\partial \mathscr{L}}{\partial P} = -\bar{Q} + (1+\lambda) \cdot \left[Q + (P-C)\bar{Q}_P - g(\theta_0) \cdot ((P-C)q(P, \theta_0) + E - v) \frac{\partial \theta_0}{\partial P} \right] = 0$$

$$\frac{\partial \mathscr{L}}{\partial E} = -(1-G(\theta_0)) + (1+\lambda) \cdot \left[1 - G(\theta_0) - g(\theta_0) \cdot ((P-C)q(P, \theta_0) + E - v) \frac{\partial \theta_0}{\partial P} \right] = 0$$

$$\frac{\partial \mathscr{L}}{\partial \lambda} = \Pi = 0$$

Note: $\bar{Q} \equiv \int_{\theta_0}^{\bar{\theta}} q(P, \theta) g(\theta) d\theta.$

Simplifying, we obtain

$$\frac{P-C}{P} = \frac{\lambda}{1+\lambda} \cdot \left[\frac{q(P, \theta_0)}{\bar{Q}} - 1 \right] \cdot \frac{1}{\xi}, \xi \equiv - \frac{\bar{Q}_P P}{\bar{Q}}$$

$$\frac{(P-C)q(P, \theta_0) + E}{E} = \frac{\lambda}{1+\lambda} \cdot \frac{1}{e}, e \equiv \frac{g(\theta_0) \frac{\partial \bar{Q}}{\partial E} \cdot E}{1 - G(\theta_0)}$$

which are the expressions in the text.

Derivation of optimal nonuniform price schedules

In this appendix we will derive optimal nonuniform pricing rules mathematically. Our aim is to give the technical reader a background so that he can solve for nonuniform pricing rules himself. The presentation is not rigorous; for a careful treatment, see Goldman, Leland and Sibley [1984]. There are several analytical approaches one can take, each having its own features of convenience. We will present three of them.

A. $P(Q)$ the control variable

The procedure is to calculate aggregate consumer surplus and producer surplus within a given dQ market, and then to sum over all dQ markets. The key to the analysis is the marginal consumer group at Q. Let willingness to pay be denoted by $\rho(Q,\theta)$, with

$$\rho_Q < 0, \quad \rho_\theta > 0 \quad \text{(strong monotonicity)} \, .$$

The marginal consumer group at $Q, \hat{\theta}$, is defined by the self-selection condition

$$\rho(Q, \hat{\theta}) = P(Q)$$

so that

$$\frac{\partial \hat{\theta}}{\partial P(\theta)} = \frac{1}{\rho_\theta} > 0.$$

The marginal cost of production is a constant, c. Considering a dQ market located at a particular quantity Q, aggregate consumer surplus is given by

$$\int_{\hat{\theta}}^{\bar{\theta}} (\rho(Q, \theta) - P(Q)) g(\theta) dQ$$

and producer surplus by

$$\int_{\underline{\theta}}^{\bar{\theta}} (P(Q) - c)g(\theta)d\theta = (1 - G(\hat{\theta})) \cdot (P(Q) - c)$$

so that total surplus over all Q is given by

$$TS = \int_0^{\infty} \left\{ \int_{\underline{\theta}}^{\bar{\theta}} (\rho(Q, \theta) - P(Q))g(\theta)d\theta + (1 - G(\hat{\theta})) \cdot (P(Q) - c) \right\} dQ.$$

The breakeven constraint is given by

$$\int_0^{\infty} (1 - G(\hat{\theta})) \cdot (P(Q) - c)dQ = F$$

where F is fixed cost, and c is marginal cost.

Next form the following Lagrangian:

$$\mathcal{L} = \int_0^{\infty} \left\{ \int_{\underline{\theta}}^{\bar{\theta}} (\rho(Q, \theta) - P(Q))g(\theta)d\theta + (1 - G(\hat{\theta})) \cdot (P(Q) - c) \right\} dQ$$

$$+ \lambda \cdot \left\{ \int_0^{\infty} (1 - G(\hat{\theta})) \cdot (P(Q) - c)dQ \right\} - (1 + \lambda)F.$$

The necessary condition for optimality is given by setting the variation $\delta\mathcal{L} = 0$ for any variation δP:

$$\delta\mathcal{L} = \int_0^{\infty} \left\{ (-\rho(Q, \hat{\theta}) + P(Q))g(\hat{\theta})\frac{\partial\hat{\theta}}{\partial p} - (1 - G(\hat{\theta})) \right.$$

$$\left. + 1 - G(\hat{\theta}) - g(\hat{\theta}) \cdot (P(Q) - c)\frac{\partial\hat{\theta}}{\partial p} \right\} \delta P dQ$$

$$+ \lambda \int_0^{\infty} \left[-g(\hat{\theta})\frac{\partial\hat{\theta}}{\partial P} \cdot (P(Q) - c) + 1 - G(\hat{\theta}) \right] \delta P \, dQ = 0.$$

Because $\rho(Q, \hat{\theta}) = P(Q)$, this reduces to the following expression:

$$0 = \int_0^{\infty} \left\{ -(1 + \lambda) \cdot (P(Q) - c)g(\hat{\theta})\frac{\partial\hat{\theta}}{\partial P} + \lambda \cdot (1 - G(\hat{\theta})) \right\} \delta P dQ$$

so that for the variation $\delta\mathscr{L}$ to vanish for any variation δP, the quantity in curly brackets must vanish at each Q:

$$- (1+\lambda) \cdot (P(Q)-c) \cdot \frac{\partial\hat{\theta}}{\partial P} \cdot g(\hat{\theta}) + \lambda \cdot (1-G(\hat{\theta})) = 0$$

or, rewriting

$$\frac{P(Q)-c}{P(Q)} = \frac{\lambda}{1+\lambda} \cdot \frac{(1-G(\hat{\theta}))}{P(Q)g(\hat{\theta})\dfrac{\partial\hat{\theta}}{\partial P}} = \frac{\lambda}{1+\lambda} \cdot \left[\frac{-\partial\ln(1-G(\hat{\theta}))}{\partial\ln P(Q)}\right]$$

$$= \frac{\lambda}{1+\lambda} \cdot \frac{1}{\epsilon(Q, P(Q))}.$$

This formulation of the nonuniform pricing problem is theoretically appealing because it links optimal nonuniform pricing with Ramsey pricing. The quantity $1 - G(\hat{\theta})$ is the demand in a given dQ market and $\epsilon(Q, P(Q))$ is its price elasticity. Thus, we have the IER for optimal nonuniform pricing which is derived intuitively in the text. From a computational standpoint, however, this approach is cumbersome, as is discussed in the Appendix to Chapter 7.

B. $Q^*(\theta)$ as a control variable

Write consumer surplus for an individual consumer as

$$U(Q, \theta) - R(Q), U_Q \equiv \rho(Q, \theta)$$

where $U_\theta > 0$, $U_{Q\theta} = \rho_\theta > 0$ (strong monotonicity) and $R(Q)$ is total outlay; $R'(Q) \equiv P(Q)$ is the marginal price at Q. In this approach, we write the self-selection condition as follows:

$$U_Q(Q^*, \theta) = P(Q^*).$$

Define indirect utility $V(\theta)$ as

$$V(\theta) = \max_Q \left[U(Q, \theta) - R(Q)\right] = U(Q^*, \theta) - R(Q^*).$$

From the self-selection condition we have

$$V'(\theta) = (U_Q - P(Q^*)) \cdot \frac{dQ^*}{d\theta} + U_\theta(Q^*, \theta) = U_\theta(Q^*, \theta).$$

Total surplus is now given by

$$\int_{\theta_0}^{\bar{\theta}} V(\theta)g(\theta)d\theta + \int_{\theta_0}^{\bar{\theta}} (U(Q^*, \theta) - V(\theta) - cQ^*)g(\theta)d\theta$$

where θ_0 is the marginal consumer group at zero consumption, defined by:

$$U_Q(0, \theta_0) = P(0).$$

The relevant Lagrangian is

$$\mathscr{L} = \int_{\theta_0}^{\bar{\theta}} V(\theta)g(\theta)d\theta + (1+\lambda) \cdot \int_{\theta_0}^{\bar{\theta}} \left[U(Q^*, \theta) - V(\theta) - cQ^* \right] g(\theta)d\theta - \lambda F.$$

It will be convenient to integrate by parts:

$$\int_{\theta_0}^{\bar{\theta}} V(\theta)g(\theta)d\theta = V(\theta) \cdot (G(\theta)-1) \Big|_{\theta_0}^{\bar{\theta}} - \int_{\theta_0}^{\bar{\theta}} V'(\theta) \cdot (G(\theta)-1)d\theta$$

$$= \int_{\theta_0}^{\bar{\theta}} U_\theta(Q^*, \theta) \cdot (1-G(\theta))dQ$$

because $G(\bar{\theta}) - 1 = 0$ and $V(\theta_0) = 0$. Substituting back into the Lagrangian

$$\mathscr{L} = \int_{\theta_0}^{\bar{\theta}} \left\{ \lambda \cdot (G(\theta)-1)U_\theta(Q^*, \theta) + (1+\lambda) \cdot (U(Q^*, \theta) - cQ^*)g(\theta) \right\} d\theta.$$

Now take a variation δQ^* in the optimal consumption for each θ; for $\delta \mathscr{L}$ to vanish for any such variation, it must be true that

$$\lambda(G(\theta)-1)U_{\theta Q} + (1+\lambda) \cdot (U_Q - c) \cdot g(\theta) = 0$$

or

$$\frac{U_Q - c}{U_Q} = \frac{\lambda}{1+\lambda} \cdot U_{\theta Q} \cdot \frac{1-G(\theta)}{g(\theta)} .$$

This formulation is usually more convenient numerically than using $P(Q)$ as a control variable and integrating over Q. If we note that

$$U_Q = P(Q^*), \theta = \hat{\theta}(Q^*)$$

and

$$\frac{\partial \hat{\theta}}{\partial P} = \frac{1}{U_{\theta Q}} > 0$$

then we can rewrite this as the Ramsey rule we derived above:

$$\frac{P(Q) - c}{P(Q)} = \frac{\lambda}{1+\lambda} \cdot \frac{1 - G(\hat{\theta})}{g(\hat{\theta}) \frac{\partial \hat{\theta}}{\partial P} \cdot P(Q)} \cdot$$

C. $\hat{\theta}$ as the control variable

From the self-selection condition

$$\rho(Q, \hat{\theta}) = P(Q)$$

we defined above the function $\hat{\theta}(Q, P)$. Equally well, though, we could use $\hat{\theta}$ as a control variable and let P adjust to meet the self-selection condition. In a dQ market aggregate consumer surplus is given by

$$\int_{\underline{\theta}}^{\bar{\theta}} (\rho(Q, \theta) - \rho(Q, \hat{\theta}))\, g(\theta)d\theta$$

and producer surplus is given by

$$\int_{\underline{\theta}}^{\bar{\theta}} (\rho(Q, \hat{\theta}) - c)\, g(\theta)d\theta = (1 - G(\hat{\theta})) \cdot (\rho(Q, \hat{\theta}) - c).$$

Thus, we can form the Lagrangian

$$\mathcal{L} = \int_0^\infty \left\{ \int_{\underline{\theta}}^{\bar{\theta}} (\rho(Q, \theta) - \rho(Q, \hat{\theta}))g(\theta)d\theta + (1 - G(\hat{\theta})) \cdot (\rho(Q, \hat{\theta}) - c) \right\} dQ$$

$$+ \lambda \left\{ \int_0^\infty (1 - G(\hat{\theta})) \cdot (\rho(Q, \hat{\theta}) - c)dQ \right\} - (1+\lambda)F.$$

Now take a variation in $\hat{\theta}(Q)$:

$$\delta\mathcal{L} = \int_0^\infty \left\{ (-\rho(Q, \hat{\theta}) + \rho(Q, \hat{\theta}))g(\hat{\theta}) - \rho_\theta \cdot (1 - G(\hat{\theta})) \right.$$

$$\left. + (1 - G(\hat{\theta})) \cdot \rho_\theta - g(\hat{\theta}) \cdot (\rho(Q, \hat{\theta}) - c) \right\} \delta\hat{\theta}(Q)dQ$$

$$+ \lambda \cdot \int_0^\infty \left\{ -g(\hat{\theta}) \cdot (\rho(Q, \hat{\theta}) - c) + (1 - G(\hat{\theta}))\rho_\theta \right\} \delta\hat{\theta}(Q)dQ.$$

For $\hat{\theta}(Q)$ to be optimal, $\delta\mathcal{L}$ must vanish for any variation $\delta\hat{\theta}(Q)$. Therefore, we have

$$-(1+\lambda) \cdot g(\hat{\theta}) \cdot (\rho(Q, \hat{\theta})-c) + \lambda \cdot (1-G(\hat{\theta})) \cdot \rho_\theta = 0$$

or

$$\frac{\rho(Q, \hat{\theta})-c}{\rho(Q, \hat{\theta})} = \frac{\lambda}{1+\lambda} \cdot \frac{(1-G(\hat{\theta}))\rho_\theta}{\rho(q, \hat{\theta})g(\hat{\theta})}.$$

Using the facts that

$$\rho(Q, \hat{\theta}) = P(Q)$$

$$\frac{\partial\hat{\theta}}{\partial P} = \frac{1}{\rho_\theta}$$

from self-selection, we can write this as the IER for nonuniform pricing:

$$\frac{P(Q)-c}{P(Q)} = \frac{\lambda}{1+\lambda} \cdot \frac{(1-G(\hat{\theta}))}{P(Q)g(\hat{\theta})\dfrac{\partial\hat{\theta}}{\partial P}} = \frac{\lambda}{1+\lambda} \cdot \frac{1}{\epsilon[Q, P(Q)]}.$$

Other solution techniques have been employed in the literature. Suppose that it is optimal for type θ to consume $Q^*(\theta)$ with a total outlay $R(Q^*(\theta))$. This level of consumption could be sustained by a two-part tariff with a usage charge $p(\theta) = R'(Q^*(\theta))$ and an entry fee $E(\theta)$ that will ensure that total outlay is still $R(Q^*(\theta))$. Hence, instead of maximizing welfare with respect to a single outlay function $R(Q)$, one could maximize with respect to $E(\theta)$ and $p(\theta)$. This is the approach taken by Roberts [1979]. Other writers, such as Spence [1980] and Panzar and Postlewaite [1983] assume that the distribution of θ is discrete. For each consumer type i, a consumption Q_i and total outlay R_i are chosen, subject to the self-selection constraint that type i prefers (Q_i, R_i) to (Q_j, R_j), so as to maximize total welfare.

D. An example

Since the published literature is not replete with examples of nonuniform pricing which can be solved in closed form, an example may be useful. Suppose that willingness to pay is given by

$$\rho(Q, \theta) = a - bQ + \theta$$

and that θ is uniformly distributed on the unit interval. For simplicity we will assume that the goal is to maximize profits.

1. $P(Q)$ as control variable The self-selection condition is now

$$a - bQ + \hat{\theta} = P(Q)$$

so that

$$\frac{\partial \hat{\theta}}{\partial P} = 1 .$$

Profit is

$$\Pi = \int_0^\infty \int_\theta^1 (P(Q)-c)d\ dQ$$

where $\hat{\theta} = P(Q) + bQ - a$. To maximize Π we have

$$\delta\Pi = \int_0^\infty \left[-(P(Q)-c) + 1 - \hat{\theta} \right] \delta P dQ = 0$$

or

$$- (P(Q)-c) + 1 - P(Q) - bQ + a = 0$$

$$- 2P(Q) + c + 1 - bQ + a = 0$$

$$P(Q) = \frac{c + 1 + a - bQ}{2} .$$

Not all of this price schedule is relevant, of course, because $\bar{\theta} = 1$. At $\theta = 1$

$$a - bQ + 1 = \frac{c + 1 + a - bQ}{2}$$

$$a - bQ + 1 = c$$

$$Q = \frac{a + 1 - c}{b} = Q^*(1)$$

on this price schedule. At this consumption level

$$P(Q)\Big|_{Q=Q^*(1)} = \frac{c + 1 + a}{2} - \frac{b}{2} \cdot \left[\frac{a + 1-c}{b} \right] = c$$

so that marginal price is equal to marginal cost at the consumption level of the highest user. Beyond the consumption level

$$Q = \frac{a + 1-c}{b}$$

the marginal price function is not relevant because no consumers are buying there.

E. *Jumps and gaps in optimal price schedules*

The development thus far has made a number of strong assumptions about the shapes of optimal nonuniform prices. In particular, we have assumed that consumer self-selection can be characterized by the first order condition $\rho(Q,\hat{\theta}) = P(Q)$, or a variant of it, and that the optimal price schedule is correctly calculated from the requirement that the variation $\delta\mathcal{L}$ vanish. We refer to this as the First Order Approach (FOA). This conforms to the usage of Rogerson [1985] who analyses the limitations of this approach in the closely related principal-agent literature. In this section we will explore situations in which the FOA approach is not correct.

There exist two situations in which this occurs. The first situation is when the relationship between Q and θ is not weakly monotonic. The entire development above as assumed that $Q^*(\theta)$ and $\hat{\theta}(Q)$ are continuous and weakly increasing functions. As we will see, this need not be the case. Second, we have assumed that the second-order conditions for a maximum of profits or welfare are met in all cases where the first-order condition is satisfied. This, too, need not occur. When we take account of these possibilities, we will see that their effects are that optimal price schedules will display upward jumps and gaps — i.e., regions of consumption within which no consumer buys.

For simplicity, we will deal with the case of profit maximization with a zero marginal cost. We will further assume that θ is uniformly distributed on the unit interval. The assumption of uniformity is not important. By redefining the taste variable as $G(\theta)$ we can transform any distribution to the uniform. Total profit may be written

$$\Pi = \int_0^{Q_{max}} (1-\hat{\theta}(Q))\rho(Q,\hat{\theta})dQ$$

where Q_{max} is the largest amount consumed by any individual consumer. Let us denote the integrand by $I(Q,\hat{\theta})$. The pointwise optimization approach is to solve for a path $\hat{\theta}(Q)$ given by the condition:

$$\frac{\partial I}{\partial\hat{\theta}} = (1-\hat{\theta})\rho_\theta - \rho = 0$$

There are two sets of second-order conditions which must hold for this solution technique to be correct. First, individual consumers, facing the marginal price $\rho(Q,\hat{\theta}(Q)) = P(Q)$ must be at global maxima with respect to their own consumer surplus. Second, the second-order condition for profit maximization must hold at each Q; this is the same as requiring $\partial^2 I/\partial\hat{\theta}^2 \leq 0$.

To see when these conditions will fail to be met, differentiate the first order condition for $\hat{\theta}$ with respect to Q:

$$\frac{\partial^2 I}{\partial\hat{\theta}^2} \cdot \frac{d\hat{\theta}}{dQ} + \frac{\partial^2 I}{\partial\hat{\theta}\partial Q} = 0$$

or

$$\frac{\partial \hat{\theta}}{dQ} = - \frac{\partial^2 I / \partial \hat{\theta} \partial Q}{\partial^2 I / \partial \hat{\theta}^2} .$$

If we were to characterize consumer choice by the first-order condition $\rho(Q, \hat{\theta}) = P(Q)$ and then observe that if $d\hat{\theta}/dQ < 0$ locally, this would mean that at Q the marginal price curve $P(Q)$ cuts willingness to pay $\rho(Q, \hat{\theta}(Q))$ from *above*. Hence consumers of type $\hat{\theta}$ are at a local *minimum* of their consumer surplus, not a maximum and the FOA technique fails. On the other hand, it could be that $\partial^2 I / \partial \hat{\theta} \partial Q < 0$ and $\partial^2 I / \partial \hat{\theta}^2 > 0$; in such a case $d\hat{\theta}/dQ > 0$, so that monotonicity between Q and θ is maintained for self-selection, but $\hat{\theta}(Q)$ represents a local minimum of profit.

There are, in all, four cases of interest:

Case   I   : $\partial^2 I / \partial Q \partial \theta > 0$, $\partial^2 I / \partial \hat{\theta}^2 < 0$

Case   II : $\partial^2 I / \partial Q \partial \theta < 0$, $\partial^2 I / \partial \hat{\theta}^2 < 0$

Case III   : $\partial^2 I / \partial Q \partial \theta > 0$, $\partial^2 I \partial \hat{\theta}^2 > 0$

Case   IV : $\partial^2 I / \partial Q \partial \theta < 0$, $\partial^2 I / \partial \hat{\theta}^2 > 0$

In Case I $\hat{\theta}$ and Q are monotonic and profit is maximized; the FOA technique is correct in this case. In Case II profit is locally maximized but $d\hat{\theta}/dQ < 0$; this is the case considered by Goldman, Leland and Sibley [1984] and leads to "gaps" in price schedule. Case III violates second-order conditions for profit maximization and also the monotonicity condition. Case IV meets the monotonicity condition, but violates profit maximization. Cases III and IV give rise to "bunching" as analyzed by Roberts [1979] and Mirrlees [1976].

Because Case I is covered by the discussion above, we will analyze Cases II-IV.

Case II

The maximization problem of interest is

$$\max_{\hat{\theta}(Q)} \int_0^{Q_{max}} (1-\hat{\theta}) \cdot \rho(Q, \hat{\theta}) dQ$$

$$s.t. \quad \frac{d\hat{\theta}}{dQ} \geq 0$$

The correct solution is best obtained by use of the maximum principle.

Let $\hat{\theta}(Q)$ be a state variable and $u \equiv d\hat{\theta}/dQ$ the control variable.[1] Write H, the Hamiltonian, as

$$H = (1-\hat{\theta})\, \rho(Q, \hat{\theta}) + \psi(Q)u$$

where $\psi(Q)$ is the costate variable. We will assume u to be piecewise continuous. Along the optimal path

$$\frac{\partial H}{\partial u} = \psi(Q) \leq 0$$

$$-\psi'(Q) = (1-\hat{\theta})\rho_\theta - \rho .$$

Second-order conditions on the variational problem are met if and only if

$$\frac{\partial^2 H}{\partial \hat{\theta}^2} = (1-\hat{\theta})\, \rho_{\theta\theta} - {}^2\rho_\theta \leq 0.$$

The transversality condition at $Q = 0$ is that either $\hat{\theta}(0) = 0$ or $\psi(0) = 0$. Generally, $\psi(0) = 0$ implies that some consumers are excluded from the market. The marginal consumer at $Q = 0$ is then given by

$$(1 - \hat{\theta}(0))\, \rho_\theta \left.\right|_{\substack{\theta = \hat{\theta}(0) \\ Q = 0}} = \rho(0, \hat{\theta}(0)) .$$

At the upper range of consumption, the monotonicity constraint, obviously, cannot be violated at the level of consumption of $\theta = 1$; if it were, the $\theta = 1$ group would simply reduce consumption. Hence, the largest individual level of consumption is $Q^*(1)$. The transversality condition governing $Q^*(1)$ is that $\rho(Q^*(1), 1) = 0$. To see why, imagine that this condition is not met so that $\theta = 1$ consumes an amount $\bar{Q}(1)$ for which $\rho(\bar{Q}(1), 1) > 0$. We can adapt the outlay schedule $\bar{R}(Q)$ in the following way:

$$\tilde{R}(Q) = \bar{R}(Q) + \int_{\bar{Q}(1)}^{Q^*(1)} \rho(Q, 1)dQ - \epsilon$$

where ϵ is any positive number such that $\tilde{R}(Q) \geq \bar{R}(Q)$. Clearly, the $\theta = 1$ group gains by buying under $\tilde{R}(Q)$ and will buy up to the point $Q^*(1)$ where $\rho(Q^*(1), 1) = 0$ and, in addition, the firm makes at least as much profit. Therefore, $\rho(\bar{Q}(1), 1) > 0$ cannot be optimal.

Collecting these conditions we have:

---

[1] See Pontriagin, *et al* [1962].

(i) $\psi\ (0) \leqq 0$ $\psi(0) < 0 \Rightarrow \theta*(0) = 0$

(ii) $\psi\ (Q) \leqq 0$ $\psi(Q) < 0 \Rightarrow \dfrac{d\hat{\theta}}{dQ} = 0$

(iii) $\psi\ (Q*(1)) = 0$

(iv) $-\psi'(Q) = (1 - \hat{\theta}) \cdot \rho_\theta - \rho$

(v)   where the constraint $u \geqq 0$ is not binding, $\psi(Q) \equiv 0$ and $(1 - \hat{\theta}) \cdot \rho_\theta - \rho = 0$.

In a range of Q wherein $d\hat{\theta}/dQ = 0$ (equivalently, $\psi(Q) < 0$) there is a "gap" in consumption in the sense that no consumer group but $\hat{\theta}$ buys in this range. Because the single type $\hat{\theta}$ has only an infinitesimal effect on total profit, we may as well assume that $\hat{\theta}$ buys at the upper end of the range. Hence, if $\psi < 0$ for $Q \in [Q_A, Q_B]$, then $[Q_A, Q_B)$ is a gap in which nobody consumes.

We now analyze an extended numerical example due to Hayne E. Leland which illustrates some of the problems posed by the FOA approach to nonuniform pricing and their correct solution. Suppose that θ is uniformly distributed over $[0, 1]$ and that willingness to pay is given by

$$\rho(Q, \theta) = \theta + \theta^2 + 2 \cdot (1-Q), \, Q \in [0, 1)$$

$$= \theta + (2-Q)\theta^2, \, Q \in [1, 2)$$

$$= \theta + (2-Q), \, Q \in [2, 3].$$

These willingness pay curves are continuous with $\rho_Q < 0, \rho_\theta > 0$. Cost is zero. The profit integral is written so as to perform the maximization using $\hat{\theta}$

$$\text{profit} = \Pi = \int_0^1 (1-\hat{\theta}) \cdot (\hat{\theta} + \hat{\theta}^2 + 2 \cdot (1-Q))dQ$$

$$+ \int_1^2 (1-\hat{\theta}) (\hat{\theta} + (2-Q) \cdot \hat{\theta}^2)dQ$$

$$+ \int_2^3 (1-\hat{\theta}) \cdot (\hat{\theta} + 2-Q))dQ.$$

Suppose that we were to ignore the constraint $d\hat{\theta}/dQ \geqq 0$ and maximize Π pointwise, as we did above. In the interval $[0, 1]$ this would lead to the first-order condition

$$- (\hat{\theta} + \hat{\theta}^2 + 2 \cdot (1-Q)) + (1-\hat{\theta}) \cdot (1 + 2\hat{\theta}) = 0.$$

Because this expression is identically zero, we can differentiate totally with respect to Q. Doing so,

$$-\frac{d\hat{\theta}}{dQ} = \frac{2 - (1-\hat{\theta})}{6\hat{\theta}} > 0$$

so that $d\hat{\theta}/dQ < 0$ and the monotonicity constraint is violated.
Leland's solution to this problem is the following:

$$\theta^*(Q) = 0, \; Q\epsilon[0, .5)$$

$$= \sqrt{\frac{2Q-1}{3}}, \; Q\epsilon[.5, .95)$$

$$= .548, \; Q\epsilon[.95, 2.096)$$

$$= \frac{Q-1}{2}, \; Q\epsilon[2.096, 3].$$

(The reader can verify that the unconstrained solution holds true in the regions $Q\epsilon[.5, .95)$ and $Q\epsilon[2.096, 3)$.) We can verify that Leland's solution meets the optimality conditions:
(i') $\quad \psi(0) = -\frac{1}{4} < 0, \hat{\theta}(0) = 0$

(ii') $\quad \psi(.5) = -\frac{1}{4} + \int_0^{.5}(1-2Q)dQ = 0$

(iii') $\quad \psi(Q) \equiv 0, \; Q\epsilon[.5, .95)$

(iv') $\quad \int_{.95}^{2.096} [(1-\hat{\theta})\rho_\theta - \rho]dQ = 0$ when $\hat{\theta} = $ constant $= .548$

(v') $\quad \psi(Q) \equiv 0, \; Q\epsilon[2.096, 3]$

(vi') $\quad \psi(3) = 0$.

The marginal price schedule which supports this function $\hat{\theta}(Q)$ is:

$$P(Q) = 2 - 2Q, \; Q \epsilon[0, .5)$$

$$= \sqrt{\left[\frac{2Q-1}{3}\right]} + \frac{2Q-1}{3} + 2 \cdot (1-Q), \; Q \epsilon[.5, .95)$$

$$= .8483 + 2 \cdot (1-Q), \; Q \epsilon[.95, 1)$$

$$= .548 + .3003 \cdot (2-Q), \; Q \epsilon[1, 2.096]$$

$$= 1.5 - .5Q, \; Q \epsilon[2.096, 3].$$

To check the second-order conditions on the Hamiltonian,

$$\frac{\partial^2 H}{\partial \hat{\theta}^2} = -6\hat{\theta} < 0 \quad Q\epsilon[0,1)$$

$$= 2 \cdot (1-6\hat{\theta} + 3\hat{\theta}Q - Q) < 0, Q\epsilon[1,2)$$

$$= -2 < 0, Q\epsilon[2,3].$$

Since the left and right limits of $\partial^2 H/\partial\hat{\theta}^2$ are the same at $Q = 1$ and $Q = 2$, $\partial^2 H/\partial\hat{\theta}^2$ is continuous and everywhere negative. Hence, H is strictly concave and the solution represents a global maximum. This solution has the "gap" feature referred to above. No consumer buys in the range [0, .5] or in the range [.95, 2.090].

Case III

In this case the monotonicity constraint is violated and second-order conditions for a profit maximum are not met. These second-order conditions are

$$\frac{\partial^2 I}{\partial\hat{\theta}^2} = (1-\hat{\theta})\rho_{\theta\theta} - 2\rho_\theta \leqq 0.$$

It is clearly true that at $\hat{\theta} = 1$, the second-order condition holds, so we are not concerned with a global failure. We will assume that the set of θ wherein the violation occurs is connected, so that there are, at most, two local maxima to compare.

The optimal $\hat{\theta}(Q)$ is discontinuous at such a point, taking an upward jump. No explicit constraint of the form $d\hat{\theta}/dQ \geqq 0$ is necessary here. The jump in $\hat{\theta}(Q)$ can only be supported by a vertical jump in the marginal price schedule, at which point $d\hat{\theta}/dQ$ is infinite.

Case IV

This case is of some interest because it shows that jumps in the optimal price schedule can occur even if the monotonicity constraint is not violated. Thus, where $\partial^2 I/\partial\hat{\theta}^2$ is positive, an upward jump in $\hat{\theta}(Q)$ is called for even though $\partial^2 I/\partial\hat{\theta}\partial Q$ could be negative, which would lead to $d\hat{\theta}/dQ > 0$. Once again, jumps in $\hat{\theta}$ can only be supported by upward jumps in $P(Q)$. In Cases III and IV, the monotonicity constraint is not what leads to bunching, and it is always met by a price function $P(Q) = \rho(Q, \hat{\theta})$ which obeys the second-order conditions for a maximum.

Cases II-IV illustrate the variety of shapes which may occur in optimal price schedules. In Case II, the optimal price schedule leads to consumption gaps. In Cases III and IV the optimal price schedule has an upward discontinuity, so that a number of consumer types will consume the same amount; Roberts [1979] has referred to such an effect as "bunching". Case IV shows, though, that bunching can occur even when the monotonicity constraint is *not* violated if the second-order condition on profit maximization is violated in the F.O.A.

As this discussion shows, there are two kinds of second-order conditions which can go awry and invalidate the FOA technique. If the second-order condition for the individual consumer is violated, but that for profit maximization is not, the optimal solution is a price schedule which leads to gaps. If profits are at a local minimum, the result is a jump in the price schedule — whether or not the monotonicity constraint is violated for self-selection.

Efficient prices with flowthrough

A. Conjectural variation model

1. Computation of dP/dP_{Bk}

The two equations characterizing downstream market equilibrium are

$$qvP' + P - C_q = 0 \tag{A1}$$

$$q \cdot P(nq) - C(q, P_{B1}, P_{B2}, ..., P_{BN}, \omega) - H = 0 . \tag{A2}$$

In (A1), $v \equiv dQ/dq$ is the conjectural variation defined in Chapters 2 and 6 in the text. We wish to compute dP/dP_{Bk}. Differentiating this system totally we obtain the following system of equations:

$$\begin{bmatrix} z & q \cdot (v \cdot q \cdot P'' + P') \\ (n-v)qP' & q^2 P' \end{bmatrix} \begin{bmatrix} dq \\ dn \end{bmatrix} = \begin{bmatrix} \dfrac{\partial \chi_{Bk}}{\partial q} \\ \chi_B \end{bmatrix} dP_{Bk} \tag{A3}$$

$$z \equiv nvqP'' + (n+v) \cdot P' - C_{qq}, \, \chi_{Bk} \equiv X_{Bk}/n_k .$$

Equation (A3) uses the fact that $\partial C/\partial P_{Bk} = \chi_{Bk}$ from Shepherd's Lemma. The Jacobian determinant of this system is

$$J = q^2 \cdot P' \cdot \left[qv^2 P'' + 2vP' - C_{qq} \right] > 0 . \tag{A4}$$

Solving this system we have:

$$\frac{dq}{dP_{Bk}} = \frac{(\chi_{Bk} qe \, P' - q\chi_{Bk}t)}{J}, \, t \equiv vq \, P'' + P' \tag{A5}$$

$$\frac{dn}{dP_{Bk}} = \frac{\chi_{Bk} \cdot z - e \cdot \chi_{Bk} \cdot (n-v) \cdot P'}{J} . \tag{A6}$$

where $e \equiv \dfrac{\partial \chi_{Bk}}{\partial q} \cdot \dfrac{q}{\chi_{Bk}}$, the scale elasticity of demand. From $Q = nq$,

$$\frac{dP}{dP_{Bk}} = P' \cdot \frac{dQ}{dP_{Bk}} - \left[n \frac{\partial q}{\partial P_{Bk}} + q \frac{\partial n}{\partial P_{Bk}} \right] \cdot P'$$

$$= \frac{X_{Bk}}{J} \cdot (e \cdot q \cdot P' \cdot v + q \cdot a) \cdot P' \tag{A7}$$

where

$$a \equiv vP' - Cqq < 0.$$

Thus, if $nP' - Cqq < 0$, we know that $dP/dP_{Bk} > 0$. In the special case $v = 1$, this is the necessary condition for stability in a Cournot market derived by Seade [1980] for the case where n is fixed. Simplifying, we obtain

$$\frac{dP}{dP_{Bk}} = \chi_{Bk} \cdot \left[\frac{vP' \cdot (e+1) - Cqq}{q \cdot (2v \, P' + v^2 q \, P'' - Cqq)} \right]. \tag{A8}$$

where χ_B is average consumption of the utility's business service

$$\chi_{Bk} \equiv \frac{X_{Bk}}{n}$$

With $e=1$ and $Cqq = 0$ we get equation (7) in the text.

2. Computation of dP/dX_R

The inverse demand function $P(Q, X_R)$ is potentially cross-elastic between Q and X_R. To determine dP/dX_R we compute dq/dX_R; since price is equal to average cost, which demands only on q, this is sufficient. We must solve the following system of equations:

$$\begin{bmatrix} z & q \cdot (v \cdot q \cdot P'' + P') \\ (n-v)qP' & q^2 \cdot P' \end{bmatrix} \begin{bmatrix} dq \\ dn \end{bmatrix} = \begin{bmatrix} -q \cdot v \cdot \dfrac{\partial P'}{\partial X_R} - \dfrac{\partial P}{\partial X_R} \\ -q \dfrac{\partial P}{\partial X_R} \end{bmatrix} dX_R \tag{A9}$$

where $\dfrac{\partial P'}{\partial X_R} \equiv \dfrac{\partial^2 P}{\partial Q \partial X_R}$. Solving this system we obtain

$$\frac{dq}{dX_R} = \frac{vq^3}{J} \cdot \left[-P' \frac{\partial P'}{\partial X_R} + P'' \cdot \frac{\partial P}{\partial X_R} \right]. \tag{A10}$$

Clearly if $v=0$, P is linear in Q and X_R, or both,

$$\frac{dq}{dX_R} = 0. \tag{A11}$$

From the market equilibrium condition that

$$P = P(Q, X_R) = \frac{C(q; P_{B1}, P_{B2}, ..., B_{BN}, \omega) + H}{q}$$

we see that $dP/dX_R = 0$, since changing X_R leaves average cost unchanged.

3. *Derivation of* $\partial P_j / \partial P_{Bk}$ *with J downstream markets*

At quantities $(X_R, Q_1, Q_2, ..., Q_J)$ price in downstream industry j is given by

$$P_j(Q_j, X_R, Q_{-j}) = \frac{C_j(q_j, P_{B1}, P_{B2}, ..., P_{BN}, \omega) + H_j}{q_j} \tag{A12}$$

where firms in each downstream industry act according to the conjectural variation model with free entry. That is,

$$q_j\, v_j\, \frac{\partial P_j}{\partial Q_j} + P_j - \frac{\partial C_j}{\partial Q_j} = 0$$

$$q_j\, P(n_j q_j, n_{-j} q_{-j}) - C_j - H_j = 0.$$

Differentiation of P_j w.r.t. P_{Bk} (and using $dP/dX_R = 0$) yields

$$\frac{\partial P_j}{\partial P_{Bk}} = \frac{\partial P_j}{\partial P_{Bk}}\bigg|_{Q_{-j} = \text{const.}} + \sum_{\ell \neq j} \frac{\partial P_j}{\partial Q_\ell} \cdot \frac{\partial Q_\ell}{\partial P_{Bk}}. \tag{A13}$$

Our proof that $\partial P/\partial X_R = 0$ extends to this case. Consider any $Q_\ell \in Q_{-j}$ and the same calculations show that $\partial P_j/\partial Q_\ell = 0$ if $v_j = 0$, Q_j is linear, or both. Under such conditions

$$\frac{\partial P_j}{\partial P_{Bk}} = \frac{\partial P_j}{\partial P_{Bk}}\bigg|_{Q_{-j} = \text{const.}} = \frac{x_j^k}{q_j} \tag{A14}$$

B. *Optimal nonuniform pricing with flowthrough*

Let there be N downstream industries, within each of which firms are identical and perfectly competitive. Furthermore, assume the following:

Assumptions

1. Tariffs consist of usage charges $\{w_1, w_2, ..., w_N\}$ and rate steps $\{\epsilon_1, \epsilon_2, ..., \epsilon_N\}$ which are continuous from the right. $\{w_i\}$ and $\{\epsilon_i\}$ are assumed to be "fully separating", meaning that in rate step k only firms in industry k are in equilibrium.

2. Industry supply curves are flat.

3. Firms produce at minimum average cost.

4. Let $X_i(w)$ and $X_j(w)$ be the equilibrium demand curves for X by typical firms in industries i and j. If $X_i(w) > X_j(w)$, then $X_i(w') > X_j(w')$ for all $w' \neq w$.

5. Let $\epsilon_k^* \equiv X_k^*(w_k) - \hat{X}_k$. For $i \leq k$

$$\frac{\partial[\epsilon_k^* g_k]}{\partial w_i} < 0,$$

where g_k is the equilibrium number of firms in industry k.

6. Let $\Delta \equiv \sup_{\{i,w\}} |X_i^*(w) - X_j^*(w)|$. Δ exists and is finite.

Discussion

One might ask if Assumption 1 is unduly restrictive, since it appears to rule out tariffs in which more than one type of firm equilibrate on the same rate step. However, this is no real restriction, because if it is optimal for firms in industry i to be paying the same marginal price as those in $i+1$, the optimal values of w_i and w_{i+1} will be the same. Assumptions 2 and 3 are very strong and rule out most market structures which display imperfect competition. Clearly, if downstream markets are all perfectly competitive and factors are in perfectly elastic supply then Assumptions 2 and 3 are met. One is tempted to ask whether or not perfectly contestable markets meet these assumptions. The answer depends on the cost structure downstream. In the case where downstream average cost functions follow the usual U-shape but firms are large relative to market demand, Sharkey [1982, pp. 170-179] has shown that when firms compete with prices as pure strategies, there do not exist Bertrand-Nash equilibria in which (a) profits are zero (b) firms produce at minimum average cost and (c) market demand is satisfied at a price equal to minimum average cost. Baumol, Panzar and Willig [1982, pp. 32-40] show that these conditions can be met when average cost curves are flat over ranges of output going from $q_j^{\min}$ to $q_j^{\max}$ as long as output per firm falls in the interval $[q_j^{\min}, q_j^{\max}]$. The fact that we are dealing with nonuniform price schedules, however, makes it questionable that a downstream firm's average costs could be flat over a finite and, possibly, large interval. There are two possible resolutions to this dilemma. First, one could assume that by the time firm output reaches $q_j^{\min}$, the scale elasticity of demand is zero. Second, one could simply assume that input costs $R(x)$ are a sufficiently small fraction of total cost that a downstream firm's average cost curve is approximately flat regardless of any quantity discounts or premia displayed by $R(x)$. We leave it to the reader to decide if either one of these rationales is appealing. If so, then the following analysis applies to contestable markets with flat-bottomed average cost curves, as well as to perfectly competitive markets. Assumption 4 is the key noncrossing assumption on individual demand curves for X. In the present context, however, it is stronger than usual because $X_i(w_i, q_i^*)$ is to be understood as the equilibrium demand for X by a firm in industry i. Hence the noncrossing assumption is much more than simply a strong statement about the technologies in industries i and $i+1$. Assumption 5 is also a statement about multimarket equilibrium relationships. $\epsilon_k^* g_k$ represents total demand in rate step k by the industry whose firms equilibrate in that rate step. When w_i rises, average cost in industry k rises, and with it the equilibrium output price P_k. Ignoring other industries, this induces $\epsilon_k^* g_k$ to fall. Prices in other industries $j \geqq i$, $j \neq k$ go up, too, and offset this direct effect and work to change g_k through cross-elastic effects on the output demand curve in industry k. To the extent that industries k and j are substitutes for each other, this effect, *cetris paribus,* would be to *raise* g_k, working against the "own" effect of P_k on $\epsilon_k^* g_k$. Assumption 5 amounts to saying that when costs to downstream firms rise because of an increased marginal price, the net effect on demand in each rate step by the industries which equilibrate in those rate steps is negative. Assumption 6 is technical and requires no special explanation. We should note however that the assumption of full separation implies the following inequalities.

$$2\Delta \geqq \epsilon \geqq \epsilon_i , \epsilon \equiv \max_{\{i\}} \epsilon_i .$$

Thus, for Δ sufficiently small $\epsilon = o(\Delta)$.

The maximization problem

We wish to choose $\{w_i\}$ and $\{\epsilon_i\}$ to maximize total surplus subject to the constraint that producer surplus be nonnegative:

$$\underset{\substack{\{w_1, w_2 ..., w_k\} \\ \{\epsilon_1, \epsilon_2 ..., \epsilon_N\}}}{\text{maximize}} [CS + PS] \quad s.t. \quad PS - \phi \geqq 0 \tag{1}$$

and subject to Assumptions 1 to 6. We obtain CS and PS by computing consumer surplus and producer surplus in each rate step k and then summing over all k, $k = 1, 2, ..., N$.

$$CS = \sum_{k=1}^{N} \left\{ g_k \cdot \left[\int_{\hat{X}_k}^{X_k^*(w_k)} P_k F_x^k dx - w_k \epsilon_k^* \right] + \sum_{j \geq k+1} g_j \left[\int_{\hat{X}_k}^{\hat{X}_{k+1}} P_j F_x^j dx - w_k \epsilon_k \right] \right\}$$

$$PS = \sum_{k=1}^{N} (w_k - c) \cdot \left[\epsilon_k^* g_k + \epsilon_k \cdot \sum_{j \geq k+1} g_j \right].$$

where ϕ represents the fixed costs of the regulated firm and c its marginal cost, assumed constant. The quantities being summed from $k = 1$ to $k = N$ are the consumer surplus and producer surplus generated in each rate step by consumers who are buying in that rate step; this includes, for rate step k, the industry k which is in equilibrium on that rate step as well as those with indices $k+1, k+2, ..., N$. As defined in the text (and suppressing other inputs B)

$$\epsilon_k^* \equiv X_k^*(w_k) - \hat{X}_k \tag{B1}$$

$$\epsilon_k = \hat{X}_{k+1} - \hat{X}_k \tag{B2}$$

$$g_k \equiv \frac{Q_k(P_k, P^k)}{q_k^*}, \quad P^k \equiv (P_1, P_2, ..., P_{k-1}, P_{k+1}, ..., P_N) \tag{B3}$$

$$X_k^*(w_k) = \arg \max_X \left[P_k q_k - \hat{R}_k - w_k \cdot (X - \hat{X}_k) \right] \tag{B4}$$

$$q_k^* = F^k \left[X_k^*(w_k) \right]. \tag{B5}$$

With these assumptions and notation in hand we can state a theorem which links efficient nonuniform pricing with flowthrough to standard nonuniform pricing. The theorem asserts that as $\Delta \to 0$, marginal prices may be chosen by maximizing welfare pointwise, as we did in Chapter 5 when we maximized welfare in independent increment markets.

Theorem. Under assumptions (A1)-(A5), as $\Delta \to 0$ the necessary conditions for a solution to (I) include the following equations (up to second-order effects):

$$\lambda \cdot \left[\epsilon_i^* g_i + \epsilon_i \cdot \sum_{j \geq i+1} g_j \right] + (1 + \lambda) g_i (w_i - c) \cdot \frac{\partial \epsilon_i^*}{\partial w_i} = 0 \tag{B6}$$

$i = 1, 2, ..., N$

$$\sum_{i=1}^{N} (w_i - c) \cdot \left[\epsilon_i^* g_i + \epsilon_i \sum_{j \geq i+1} g_j \right] - \phi = 0, \, i=1, 2, ..., N. \tag{B7}$$

Proof:

1. The first-order conditions to (I) are given by:

$$\mathcal{L} = CS + (1 + \lambda)PS \tag{B8}$$

$$\frac{\partial \mathcal{L}}{\partial w_i} = \frac{\partial CS}{\partial w_i} + (1 + \lambda)\frac{\partial PS}{\partial w_i} = 0, \, i=1, 2, ..., N \tag{B9}$$

$$\frac{\partial \mathcal{L}}{\partial \epsilon_i} = \frac{\partial CS}{\partial \epsilon_i} + (1 + \lambda)\frac{\partial PS}{\partial \epsilon_i} = 0 \tag{B10}$$

$$\frac{\partial \mathcal{L}}{\partial \lambda} = PS - \phi \geq 0, \, \lambda(PS - \phi) = 0 \tag{B11}$$

where

$$\frac{\partial CS}{\partial w_i} = \sum_{k=1}^{N} \frac{\partial CS_k}{\partial w_i}, \quad \frac{\partial PS}{\partial w_i} = \sum_{k=1}^{N} \frac{\partial PS_k}{\partial w_i}.$$

We will not discuss (B10) explicitly, but will concentrate on interpreting (B9). This is done for brevity; (B10) adds nothing to the discussion below. We will calculate each of these derivatives, show whether they are of order Δ or Δ^2, and then examine the case of small Δ.

2. $\dfrac{\partial CS_k}{\partial w_i}$ when $k < i$ is given by the following expression:

$$\frac{\partial CS_k}{\partial w_i} = \left(\int_{\hat{X}_k}^{X_k^*(w_k)} \left(P_k F_x^k - w_k \epsilon_k^* \right) \cdot \left[\frac{\partial g_k}{\partial P_i} \cdot \frac{\epsilon_i^*}{q_i^*} + \sum_{\ell \geq i+1} \frac{\partial g_k}{\partial P_\ell} \cdot \frac{\epsilon_i}{q_\ell^*} \right] \right.$$

$$\tag{B12}$$

$$\left. + \sum_{j=k+1}^{N} \int_{\hat{X}_k}^{\hat{X}_{kH}} \left(P_k F_x^j - w_k \right) \cdot \left[\frac{\partial g_j}{\partial P_i} \cdot \frac{\epsilon_i^*}{q_i^*} + \sum_{\ell \geq i+1} \frac{\partial g_j}{\partial P_\ell} \cdot \frac{\epsilon_i}{q_\ell^*} \right] \right)$$

$$+ \sum_{j \geq i} g_j \int_{\hat{X}_k}^{\hat{X}_{kH}} \frac{\partial P_j}{\partial w_i} F_x^j \, dx \,.$$

This expression makes extensive use of the facts that

$$\frac{\partial P_i}{\partial w_i} = \frac{\epsilon_i^*}{q_i^*} \text{ and } \frac{\partial P_\ell}{\partial w_i} = \frac{\epsilon_i}{q_\ell^*} \quad \text{for } \ell > i \,.$$

The logic of this expression is simple, although the number of multimarket effects is large. In rate step k the industry whose firms are in equilibrium on that rate step earns consumer surplus equal to

$$\left\{ \int_{\hat{X}_k}^{X_k^*(w_k)} P_k F_x^k dx - w_k \, \epsilon_k^* \right\} g_k \,.$$

A change in the marginal price w_i for a higher rate step (recall $k > i$) does not affect marginal or average cost in industry k, but it does affect g_k, the equilibrium number of firms in industry k. It does so because output prices rise in $P_i, P_{i+1}, ..., P_N$. These output price effects change g_k through cross-elasticities of demand between P_k and P_i, P_{i+1}, etc., given by terms such as $\partial g_k/\partial P_i$ and $\partial g_k/\partial P_{i+1}$. The sum of all such effects g_k is

$$\frac{\partial g_k}{\partial P_i} \cdot \frac{\epsilon_i^*}{q_i^*} + \sum_{j=i+1}^{N} \epsilon_i \frac{\partial g_k}{\partial P_j} \cdot \frac{1}{q_j^*} \,.$$

The second set of terms takes the consumer surplus earned in rate step k by all firms with indices $k + 1$ or higher; by definition, such firms consume ϵ_k, the entire rate step. The analysis is similar; for each rate step $j \geq k + 1$ we must calculate the effects on g_j of changes in P_j induced by the change in w_i as well as all cross-elasticity effects between the industry j in equilibrium on rate step j, industry i and other industries ℓ where $\ell \geq i+1$ and $\ell \neq j$.

We can now use the Mean Value Theorem to rewrite the surplus integrals in rate step k as functions which are proportional to either ϵ_k^* or ϵ_k. Doing so, we obtain the following expressions:

$$\int_{\hat{X}_k}^{X_k^*(w_k)} P_k F_x^k dx = P_k F_x^k(\overline{X}_{kk}) \cdot \epsilon_k^* \,, \hat{X}_k < \overline{X}_{kk} < X_k^*(w_k) \qquad \text{(B13)}$$

$$\int_{\hat{X}_k}^{\hat{X}_{k+1}} P_k F_x^k dx = P_k F_x^k(\overline{X}_{kj}) \cdot \epsilon_k \,, \hat{X}_k < \overline{X}_{kj} < \hat{X}_{k+1}. \qquad \text{(B14)}$$

$$\int_{\hat{X}_k}^{\hat{X}_{k+1}} F_x^j dx = F_x^j\left[\overline{X}_{kj}\right]\epsilon_k$$

If we substitute (B13) and (B14) into (B12) we obtain

$$\frac{\partial CS_k}{\partial w_i} = \left(P_k F_x^k(\overline{X}_{kk}) - w_k\right) \cdot \left[\frac{\partial g_k}{\partial P_i} \cdot \frac{\epsilon_i^* \epsilon_k^*}{q_i^*} + \sum_{j=i+1} \frac{\epsilon_k^* \epsilon_i}{q_j^*} \cdot \frac{\partial g_k}{\partial P_j}\right]$$

$$\qquad \qquad \text{(B15)}$$

$$+ \sum_{j=k+1}^{N} \left(P_k F_x^k(\overline{X}_{kj}) - w_k\right) \cdot \left[\frac{\partial g_j}{\partial P_i} \cdot \frac{\epsilon_i^* \epsilon_k}{q_i^*} + \sum_{\substack{\ell \geq i+1 \\ \ell \neq j}} \frac{\epsilon_k \epsilon_i}{q_\ell^*} \cdot \frac{\partial g_j}{\partial P_\ell}\right]$$

$$+ \frac{g_i \epsilon_i^* F_x^j(\overline{X}_{kj}) \epsilon_i^*}{q_i^*} + \sum_{\ell \geq i+1} \frac{\epsilon_i \epsilon_k g_\ell F_x^\ell(\overline{X}_{k\ell})}{q_\ell^*}$$

Now let $\Delta \to 0$. For Δ sufficiently small, $\epsilon = o(\Delta)$ where $\epsilon = \max_k \epsilon_k$. Thus as $\Delta \to 0$

$$\frac{\partial CS_k}{\partial w_i} \to \Delta^2 \cdot \left\{ \left(P_k F_x^k(\overline{X}_{kk}) - w_k\right) \cdot \sum_{j=k}^{N} \frac{\partial g_k}{\partial P_j} \cdot \frac{1}{q_j^*} \right.$$

$$+ \sum_{j=k+1}^{N} \left(P_k F_x^j(\overline{X}_{kj}) - w_k\right) \sum_{\substack{\ell \geq i \\ \ell \neq j}} \frac{\partial g_j}{\partial P_\ell} \cdot \frac{1}{q_\ell^*}$$

$$+ \frac{g_i F_x^j(\overline{X}_{kj})}{q_i^*} + \sum_{\ell \geq i+1} \frac{g_\ell \times F_x^\ell(\overline{X}_{k\ell})}{q_\ell^*} \right\}.$$

Inspecting the terms in the curly brackets (multiplying Δ^2) it is not hard to see that they depend on total outlay and marginal price. From the equilibrium price condition

$$P_k = \psi(R_k^*)$$

$$R_k^* = \hat{X}_1 w_j + (\hat{X}_2 - \hat{X}_1)w_2 + \cdots + (X_k^* - \hat{X}_k) \cdot w_k$$

so that as $\Delta \rightarrow 0$ R_k becomes an integral of the marginal prices over rate steps:

$$R_k \rightarrow \int_0^{x_k^*} w(X)\,dX.$$

P_k is a function of q_k and R_k. Given this, since the other terms

$$\frac{\partial g_k}{\partial P_j}, q_j^*, \frac{\partial g_j}{\partial P_\ell}, q_\ell^*$$

are defined in terms of output prices, they are also functions of the integrals of marginal prices up to different consumption levels $X_k^*(w)$. Terms such as

$$P_k F_x^k(\hat{X}_{kk}) - w_k$$

depend on R_k and w_k.

We will assume that $\hat{R}_k$ remains bounded above as $\epsilon \rightarrow 0$. To do otherwise would lead to downstream industries going bankrupt. From the condition for individual firms profit maximization in each downstream industry we have

$$F_x^k = \frac{w_k}{P_k}$$

so that if P_k is bounded from above, q_k is bounded away from zero. Hence, the terms in curly brackets are bounded above and

$$\frac{\partial CS_k}{\partial w_i} = o(\Delta^2). \tag{B16}$$

3. Now consider $\partial CS_k / \partial w_i$ where $k > i$. From our implicit assumption that the derivatives of Q_i are bounded for all i, so are the derivatives of g_i, $\forall_i$. Hence for small Δ, $\partial CS_k / \partial w_i$ is proportional to Δ^2. Using the same procedure as that used in Step 2, it can be shown that

$$\frac{\partial CS_k}{\partial w_i} = o(\Delta^2) \quad \text{for} \quad k > i. \tag{B17}$$

4. The only remaining term to examine is $\dfrac{\partial CS_i}{\partial w_i}$. Straightforward calculation leads to the following expression:

$$\frac{\partial CS_i}{\partial w_i} = - \epsilon_i^* g_i + \int_{\hat{x}_i}^{x_i^{*(w_i)}} F_x^i dx \cdot \frac{\epsilon_i^*}{q_i^*} \cdot g_i + \int_{\hat{x}_i}^{x_i^{*(w_i)}} \left(P_i F_x^i dx - w_i \epsilon_i^* \right) \cdot \sum_{k=i+1}^{N} \frac{\partial g_i}{\partial P_k} \cdot \frac{\epsilon_k}{q_k^*}$$

$$+ \sum_{j=i+1}^{N} \int_{\hat{x}_i}^{\hat{x}_{i+1}} \left(P_j F_x^j dx - w_i \epsilon_i \right) \cdot \left\{ \frac{\partial g_j}{\partial P_j} \cdot \frac{\epsilon_i}{q_j^*} + \sum_{\substack{\ell \geq i+1 \\ \ell \neq j}} \frac{\partial g_j}{\partial P_\ell} \cdot \frac{\epsilon_i}{q_\ell^*} \right\} \tag{B18}$$

$$+ \sum_{j \geq i+1} \left\{ \int_{\hat{x}_i}^{\hat{x}_{i+1}} F_x^j dx \cdot \frac{\epsilon_i}{q_j^*} - \epsilon_i \right\} g_j.$$

Using the Mean Value Theorem as in Step 2 we can rewrite this expression and ignore terms which are $o(\Delta^2)$, so that from Steps 2 and 3, for small Δ

$$\frac{\partial CS}{\partial w_i} \cong - \left[\epsilon_i^* g_i + \epsilon_i \sum_{j \geq i+1} g_i \right]. \tag{B19}$$

5. We now turn to $\dfrac{\partial PS}{\partial w_i}$. Straightforward calculation of the sort used in Step 2 yields the following expressions for $k < i$:

$$\frac{\partial PS_k}{\partial w_i} \cong (w_k - c) \left\{ \frac{\epsilon_k^* \epsilon_k^*}{q_i^*} \frac{\partial g_k}{\partial P_i} + \sum_{j \geq i+1} \frac{\epsilon_k \epsilon_i}{q_j^*} \frac{\partial g_k}{\partial P_j} \right\}. \tag{B20}$$

For sufficiently small Δ the term is $o(\Delta^2)$ and can be ignored.

6. Now let $k > i$. We can write producer surplus and its derivative in the following way:

$$PS_k = (w_k - c) \cdot \left[\epsilon_k^* g_k + \epsilon_k \sum_{j \geq k+1} g_j \right] \tag{B21}$$

$$\frac{\partial PS_k}{\partial w_i} = (w_k - c) \cdot \left\{ \frac{\partial [\epsilon_k^* g_k]}{\partial w_i} + \epsilon_k \cdot \sum_{j \geq k+1} \left[\frac{\partial g_j}{\partial P_i} \cdot \frac{\epsilon_i}{q_i^*} + \sum_{\substack{\ell \geq i+1 \\ \ell \neq j}} \frac{\partial g_j}{\partial P_\ell} \cdot \frac{\epsilon_i}{q_\ell^*} \right] \right\}$$

The second group of terms in brackets is $o(\Delta^2)$ and may be ignored for small Δ. From Assumption 5 we have that

$$\frac{\partial [\epsilon_k^* g_k]}{\partial w_i} < 0. \tag{B22}$$

Performing the indicated differentiation

$$\frac{\partial [\epsilon_k^* g_k]}{\partial w_i} = \epsilon_k^* \frac{\partial g_k}{\partial P_k} \cdot \frac{\epsilon_i}{q_k^*} + g_k \frac{\partial X_k^*}{\partial q_k^*} \cdot \frac{\partial q_k^*}{\partial P_k} \cdot \frac{\epsilon_i}{q_k^*} + \frac{\partial g_k}{\partial P_i} \cdot \frac{\epsilon_k^* \epsilon_i^*}{q_i^*}$$

$$+ \sum_{\substack{\ell \geq i+1 \\ \ell \neq k}} \frac{\partial g_k}{\partial P_\ell} \cdot \epsilon_k^* \cdot \frac{\epsilon_i}{q_\ell^*}$$

The first term on the RHS is negative and the second is positive. The third and fourth terms could be either positive or negative, depending on whether goods Q_j are substitutes or complements for good Q_k. Whatever the case, by Assumption 5, the negative term(s) must dominate; they are all $o(\epsilon^2)$ and, for small Δ, $o(\Delta^2)$. Because the second term on the RHS is positive we can take absolute value and obtain

$$\left| \frac{\partial [\epsilon_k^* g_k]}{\partial w_i} \right| \leq | \text{ negative terms } | = o(\Delta^2). \tag{B23}$$

As $\Delta \to 0$, we may ignore the effects of w_i on $\epsilon_k^* g_k$.

7. Let $k = i$. The derivative of producer surplus in this case is given by

$$\frac{\partial PS_i}{\partial w_i} = (w_i - c) \cdot \left[\frac{\partial}{\partial w_i} \left[\epsilon_i^* g_i + \epsilon_i \sum_{j \geq i+1} g_j \right] \right] \tag{B24}$$

$$+ \epsilon_i^* g_i + \epsilon_i \sum_{j \geq i+1} g_j$$

$$= (w_i - c) \cdot \left[g_i \frac{\partial X_i^*}{\partial w_i} + \epsilon_i^* \cdot \sum_{j \geq i+1} \frac{\partial g_j}{\partial P_i} \cdot \frac{\epsilon_i}{q_j^*} + \epsilon_i^* \frac{\partial g_i}{\partial P_i} \cdot \frac{\epsilon_i^*}{q_i} \right.$$

$$\left. + \epsilon_i \sum_{j \geq i+1} \left[\sum_{\substack{\ell \geq i+1 \\ \ell \neq j}} \frac{\partial g_j}{\partial P_\ell} \cdot \frac{\epsilon_i}{q_\ell^*} \right] \right] + \epsilon_i^* g_i + \epsilon_i \sum_{j \geq i+1} g_j .$$

Therefore, for small Δ

$$\frac{\partial PS_i}{\partial w_i} \cong \left[(w_i - c) g_i \frac{\partial \epsilon_i^*}{\partial w_i} + \epsilon_i^* g_i + \sum_{j \geq i+1} g_j \epsilon_i \right] .$$

8. Going back to equation (B9) which defines the first order condition for the optimal marginal price schedule, for $\Delta \to 0$ we can ignore all terms which are $o(\Delta^2)$. Therefore, to a first approximation,

$$\frac{\partial \mathcal{L}}{\partial w_i} \cong \frac{\partial CS}{\partial w_i} + \frac{\partial PS}{\partial w_i} (1 + \lambda) = 0 \qquad \text{(B25)}$$

or

$$\lambda \cdot \left[\epsilon_i^* g_i + \epsilon_i \sum_{k \geq i+1}^{N} g_k \right] + (1 + \lambda)(w_i - c) g_i \frac{\partial \epsilon_i^*}{\partial w_i} \cong 0 \qquad \text{(B26)}$$

which is equation (61a) in the text.

Q.E.D

Computation and evaluation of optimal price schedules

A. Introduction

The optimal nonuniform price schedule $P^*(Q)$ generates more consumer surplus for a given revenue requirement than any other self-selecting tariff. In operational terms however, it is important to know just how much better it does over arguably simpler Ramsey and Fully Distributed Cost pricing rules. To answer this question, we need to be able to compute these alternative pricing rules and evaluate the consumer surplus and revenues generated for a variety of assumptions about demand and cost conditions.

These computations represent a potentially difficult numerical problem where the willingness to pay reflects differences in tastes across a population of individuals. The consumer surplus and revenue integrals have themselves to be integrated over consumer types. In the case of the optimal nonuniform pricing rule, there are functions to be twice integrated that involve an optimal price schedule $P^*(Q)$ that is only implicitly defined.

This implicit definition of the price schedule $P^*(Q)$ arises from the fact that the optimal price is derived from the first order conditions specific to a given customer type θ. The optimal price schedule is then defined in terms of the maximum quantity consumer type θ will purchase. In other words, given a willingness to pay function $p(Q,\theta)$ decreasing in Q and increasing in consumer type θ, the maximum type θ will consume is given as the Q for which $P = p(Q,\theta)$. Thus, provided the self-selection constraint is satisfied it is possible to define (implicitly) the unique function $P = P^*(Q)$ for all consumer types θ.

While the optimal price schedule is stated in terms of $P^*(Q)$, the implicit definition of this function presents severe numerical difficulties in the computation of consumer and producer surplus associated with the schedule. It is more straightforward to compute these quantities in

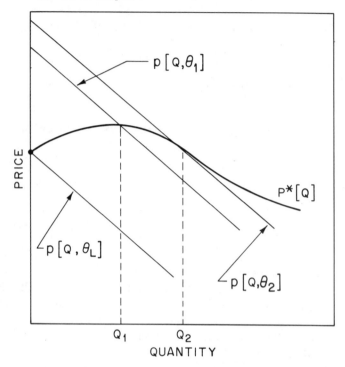

PRICE

$p[Q,\theta_1]$

$P^*[Q]$

$p[Q,\theta_L]$

$p[Q,\theta_2]$

Q_1 Q_2

QUANTITY

Figure A7.1

terms of $P^+(\theta)$. In Figure A7.1 we see depicted an arbitrary nonuniform price schedule where the price can be expressed as a function of the quantity demanded. Consumer type θ_i has a willingness to pay function $p(Q, \theta_i)$. On the price schedule θ_L will consume zero,[1] in which case $P^+(\theta_L) = P^*(Q=0)$. Consumer type θ_1 consumes Q_1, in which case $P^+(\theta_1) = P^*(Q = Q_1)$. Similarly $P^+(\theta_2) = P^*(Q = Q_2)$. With a continuum of consumer types θ, it is immaterial whether we compute consumer surplus and revenues using $P^*(Q)$ or $P^+(\theta)$. The advantages of $P^+(\theta)$ over $P^*(Q)$ are twofold. Not only does $P^+(\theta)$ facilitate the numerical computation of revenue and surplus but also, in the case of the optimal nonuniform price schedule, $P^+(\theta)$ can be written as an analytic function of certain well defined probability integrals.

In this appendix, we shall demonstrate how to compute total revenue and surplus for an arbitrary price schedule $P^+(\theta)$ and then show how to

[1]
  In the case where the willingness to pay is linear in the logarithms of Q and θ, the horizontal axis can be thought of as scaled as the logarithm of Q, in which case "zero" corresponding to $Q = 1$ can be thought of as the minimal unit of consumption.

evaluate $P^+(\theta)$ for Optimal Nonuniform Pricing, Optimal Two-Part Tariff, Ramsey Pricing, and Fully Distributed Cost pricing rules.

B. Evaluating revenue and consumer surplus

Consider individual θ_0 who consumes Q_0 at price $P^*(Q_0) = P^+(\theta_0)$. The total utility of such an individual can be computed

$$U(\theta_0) = \int_{Q_L}^{Q_0} p(Q, \theta_0)\, dQ$$

where Q_L represents the minimal unit of consumption. For linear and loglinear demand cases, the willingness to pay $P(Q, \theta_0)$ is linear and loglinear respectively so that $U(\theta_0)$ is easily determined.[2] However, total surplus represents the difference between utility and revenue, where revenue is computed as

$$R(\theta_0) = \int_{Q_L}^{Q_0} P^*(Q)\, dQ + Q_L \cdot P^*(Q_L)$$

$$= \int_{\theta_L}^{\theta_0} P^+(\theta)\, \frac{dQ}{d\theta}\, d\theta + Q_L \cdot P^+(\theta_L)$$

where $\dfrac{dQ}{d\theta} > 0$ represents the Jacobian of the transformation from Q to θ along the optimal price path

$$\frac{dQ}{d\theta} = \frac{\partial Q}{\partial P}\, \frac{dP^+(\theta)}{d\theta} + \frac{\partial Q}{\partial \theta}$$

for $\partial Q / \partial P$ and $\partial Q / \partial \theta$ the partial derivatives of the demand function $Q = Q(P, \theta)$. Given the demand functions and the definition of $P^+(\theta)$, this total derivative is readily computed.

Once utility and revenue are computed, the consumer surplus of θ_0 is given as

$$CS(\theta_0) = U(\theta_0) - R(\theta_0)$$

---

[2] There is one problem in the loglinear case, which is that surplus integrals do not exist where the price elasticity is less than unity. Therefore, we assume that willingness to pay is constant between zero and Q_L; for $Q \geqq Q_L$, willingness to pay declines with increased consumption. This is a behavioral assumption about demand which is not implausible in the telecommunication context because most interstate messages take a minute or more to complete.

The contribution to producer surplus by individual θ_0 is

$$PS(\theta_0) = R(\theta_0) - \int_0^{Q_0} c(Q)dQ$$

$$= R(\theta_0) - c \cdot Q_0$$

for constant marginal cost c.

The only computational difficulty at this point involves $R(\theta_0)$. For most price schedules considered in this book, $P^+(\theta) = P^+$ for $\theta \geqslant \theta_L$, so that $R(\theta_0)$ is a trivial computation. However for the optimal nonuniform pricing case, most of the variability in $P^+(\theta)$ occurs for small θ, so that it is necessary to use numerical quadrature in terms of the logarithm of θ to obtain an accurate measure of $R(\theta_0)$.

To obtain measures of the aggregate consumer and producer surplus, $CS(\theta_0)$ and $PS(\theta_0)$ are integrated across consumer types

$$CS = \int_{\theta_L}^{\bar{\theta}} CS(\theta)g(\theta)d\theta$$

and

$$PS = \int_{\theta_L}^{\bar{\theta}} PS(\theta)g(\theta)d\theta$$

where $g(\theta)$ is a measure of the number of consumers of type θ and $\bar{\theta}$ is the maximal consumer type index. CS and PS are computed by by constructing a grid of θ values [note that $R(\theta_i) = R(\theta_{i-1}) + \int_{\theta_{i-1}}^{\theta_i} P^+(\theta) \frac{dQ}{d\theta} d\theta$ for $\theta_{i-1} < \theta_i$]. Fitting a spline to the quadrature estimates of $CS(\theta)$ and $PS(\theta)$, and integrating the spline provides an estimate of CS and PS. Again, it is useful to perform this second integral in units of the logarithm of θ.

In the case of more than one market, the resulting consumer surplus and net revenue contributions are simply summed across markets.

This procedure was used to evaluate all consumer surplus and net revenue contribution integrals reported in the text.

C. The computation of optimal nonuniform prices

1. The single market case

It should be recalled that the necessary conditions for an optimal nonuniform price $P^*(Q)$ define

$$P^*(Q) = c + \frac{\lambda}{1+\lambda} \frac{1-G(\hat{\theta})}{g(\hat{\theta}) \cdot \hat{\theta}_P} \tag{1}$$

where $g(\theta)$ represents the distribution of consumer types and $\hat{\theta}$ is the consumer type who chooses to consume at the quantity price pair Q, $P^*(Q)$; $\hat{\theta} = \hat{\theta}(P^*(Q), Q)$, $\hat{\theta}_P = \partial\hat{\theta}(P, Q)/\partial P$, and λ is the Lagrange multiplier. This formulation of the necessary conditions is particularly convenient from an analytic point of view and as noted in the text, gives rise to an interesting Ramsey interpretation of the optimal price schedule. However, it is evident that it is not particularly convenient from a computational point of view, as $P^*(Q)$ is only implicitly defined.

Fortunately there exists a computationally tractable method of defining the optimal price schedule that permits graphical methods to be used to solve for the optimal price schedule.

Take a linear demand function

$$Q = a + bP + \gamma\theta \tag{2}$$

or, expressed in a slightly more convenient form

$$Q^* = a^* + b^*(P - c) + \theta$$

where $Q^* = Q/\gamma$, $b^* = b/\gamma$ and $a^* = (a + bc)/\gamma$. This demand function is depicted in the upper right quadrant of Figure A7.2, for various values of θ. In this figure, note that when $(P - c) = 0$, $Q^* - a^* = \theta$. This allows us to plot the inverse of the hazard rate $(1 - G(\theta))/g(\theta)$ in the lower right quadrant. Recall that this hazard rate has the interpretation of being the percentage of consumers in the marginal consumer group. The lower left quadrant has a line with slope $\hat{\theta}_P = -1/b^*$.

This construction is particularly convenient. Suppose we have some optimal price P associated with a small ΔQ market. This market is indexed by the marginal consumer group θ which chooses to consume at that price. The value of θ is readily determined by the intersection of the willingness to pay and optimal price schedules in the upper right quadrant. By construction, the left axis gives

$$-\frac{1}{b^*} \cdot \frac{1 - G[\theta]}{g[\theta]} = \frac{P[Q]}{\epsilon(Q, P[Q])}$$

(as shown in Chapter 5). From the Ramsey interpretation of the optimal nonuniform price, this quantity times a constant gives the optimal price for that ΔQ market over marginal cost. In other words

$$P[Q] - c = m\, P[Q]/\epsilon(Q, P[Q]).$$

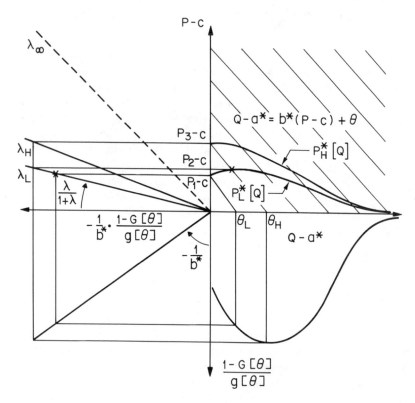

Figure A7.2

The value of m is given as the slope of the line in the upper left quadrant. Note that if we let the constant m be given as

$$m = \lambda/(1 + \lambda)$$

such a price satisfies the necessary conditions (1) for the optimal nonuniform price.

With this figure it is a simple matter to construct the family of optimal price schedules by graphical means alone. Suppose that consumer group θ_L consumes the minimal consumption of a^* units and would be priced out of the market altogether if the price were any higher. From the figure, such a price must be P_1. For what Lagrange multiplier would the pair $P = P_1$ and $Q = a^*$ be on the optimal price schedule? This value, λ_L, is readily calculated from the slope of the line that passes through the intersection marked by the asterisk in the upper left quadrant. Once λ_L is determined it is a trivial matter to trace out the remainder of the optimal price schedule. For consumer group θ_H

the optimal price is P_2 which can be determined from the intersection marked by the asterisk in the upper right quadrant. Thus we have constructed the optimal price schedule $P_L^*[Q]$ indexed by marginal consumer group θ_L.

Suppose consumer group θ_H consumes a^* on the optimal price schedule. The Lagrange multiplier λ_H that implies that such a price is optimal is again determined by an intersection in the upper left quadrant. Given λ_H, one can then easily determine the optimal price schedule $P_H^*[Q]$ indexed by the marginal consumer group θ_H. It is clear that the family of optimal price schedules is uniquely indexed by the marginal consumer group which consumes the minimal consumption level on each schedule.

For any *particular* consumer group θ, the contribution to producer surplus is given by the area under the optimal price schedule up to the consumption of θ. Thus the contribution of θ_H given $P_L^*[Q]$ is the area under $P_L^*[Q]$ up to the asterisk. The consumer surplus of θ_H is the area between $P_L^*[Q]$ and the willingness to pay function indexed by θ_H. The total producer and consumer surplus is found by multiplying the individual measures by the number of consumers of type θ_H, $g(\theta_H)$ and integrating over θ.

For the Lagrange multiplier $\lambda = 0$, it is evident from the figure that the optimal price schedule lies along the horizontal axis of the upper right quadrant: price equals marginal cost and producer surplus equals zero. In the figure λ and thus the producer surplus is increasing in the index of the marginal consumer group that characterizes each member of the family of optimal price schedules. This suggests the following simple algorithm for determining an optimal price schedule:

1. Choose a θ_λ close to zero.
2. Solve for λ such that consumption on the optimal price schedule is zero (or some small positive quantity) given λ and θ_λ.
3. If net revenue equals the revenue requirement stop; otherwise
4. Increase θ_λ.
5. If θ_λ is less than the maximum θ such that $d\lambda(\theta)/d\theta > 0$ go to 2; otherwise
6. Revenue requirement cannot be met by nonuniform price schedule.

Step 2 is elementary for the linear and log-linear demand functions. In the linear case the demand function is

$$Q = a + bP + \gamma\theta$$

Willingness to pay for quantity q by consumer type θ is thus

$$P = (Q - \gamma\theta - a)/b$$

and consumer type θ who is willing to pay P for quantity Q is

$$\theta = (Q - bP - a)/\gamma$$

where the partial with respect to P given Q is given by

$$\hat{\theta}_P = -b/\gamma$$

Hence

$$\lambda = \alpha/(\beta - \alpha)$$

where

$$\begin{cases} \alpha = -(\gamma\theta_\lambda + a)/b - c \\ \beta = \dfrac{1 - G[\theta_\lambda]}{g[\theta_\lambda]} \end{cases}$$

The optimal price schedule can thus be determined

$$P[\theta] = c - \frac{\lambda}{1 + \lambda} \left[\frac{1 - G[\theta]}{g[\theta]} \frac{\gamma}{b} \right] \doteq \theta > \theta_\lambda \qquad (3)$$

In the log linear case:

$$Q = a P^b \theta^\gamma.$$

Willingness to pay for quantity Q by consumer type θ is

$$P = (Q/a\theta^\gamma)^{1/b}$$

and consumer type θ who is willing to pay P for quantity Q is

$$\theta = (Q/aP^b)^{1/\gamma}$$

where the partial with respect to P given Q is given by

$$\hat{\theta}_P = \frac{b}{\gamma} (Q/a)^{1/\gamma} P^{-\frac{b}{\gamma} - 1}.$$

Hence

$$\lambda = \alpha/(\beta - \alpha)$$

where, for a minimal consumption unit Q_L,

$$\begin{cases} \alpha = (Q_L/a\theta_\lambda^\gamma)^{1/b} - c \\ \beta = -\dfrac{1 - G[\theta_\lambda]}{\theta_\lambda g[\theta_\lambda]} \dfrac{\gamma}{b} - (Q_L/a\theta_\lambda^\gamma)\dfrac{1}{b}. \end{cases}$$

The optimal price schedule can then be determined using

$$\frac{P[\theta]-c}{P[\theta]} = -\frac{\lambda}{1+\lambda}\left[\frac{1-G(\theta)}{\theta g(\theta)}\frac{\gamma}{b}\right] \doteq \theta > \theta_\lambda. \tag{4}$$

2. Application to multiple markets

In many important applications optimal nonlinear prices have to be computed for several different markets simultaneously, as for example where there are day, evening and night tariffs offered.[3] This problem would appear intrinsically difficult as not only would demand and cost structures differ across markets, but also demands in different markets would be interdependent. Fortunately, results of Mirman and Sibley [1980] referred to in the text reduce this potentially difficult problem to the simpler problem of independent demands. In this section we shall suggest how the algorithm may be modified to compute optimal nonuniform prices for multiple markets with independent demands.

In the multiple markets case the objective will be to maximize the sum of producer and consumer surplus over the markets subject to a breakeven constraint

$$\max_{\{P_j[\theta]\}} \sum_{j=1}^{M} [CS_j + PS_j]$$

such that

$$\sum_{j=1}^{M} PS_j = F$$

which yields the Lagrangian

$$\max_{\{P_j[\theta]\}} L = \sum_{j=1}^{M} [CS_j + PS_j] + \lambda\left[\sum_{j=1}^{M} PS_j - F\right]. \tag{5}$$

Since demands are independent, for given λ the necessary conditions for a maximum will be identical to the necessary conditions for each market taken by itself. Hence the optimal nonlinear price schedule in each market will satisfy the necessary conditions for a maximum in (5), where λ is varied across all markets in such a way that the net revenue requirement F is satisfied.

---

[3] By allowing for different marginal costs in different markets, it should be obvious that this approach allows the computation of optimal nonlinear prices in a peak load pricing context.

As in section 4 it is still possible to index the family of optimal nonlinear prices by θ_λ. For each market it is possible to determine a λ_j such that consumption on the optimal price schedule indexed by λ_j is zero for $\theta = \theta_\lambda$. If we choose $\lambda = \min_j \lambda_j$ then consumption on the optimal nonlinear price schedule is greater than or equal to zero.[4] Then determine a $\theta_j^* \leqslant \theta_\lambda$ such that $Q_j(P_j[\theta_j^*], \theta_j^*) = 0$, and thus define the optimal price schedule for market j where θ_j^* replaces θ_λ. This procedure ensures that the implied λ will be feasible in each market.

The nonlinear price schedules can be evaluated as before, and θ_λ varied until the net revenue constraint is met.

3. Optimal Ramsey prices

The optimal Ramsey prices are given as the solution to

$$\frac{P_i - c_i}{P_i} = \frac{\lambda}{1+\lambda} \cdot \frac{1}{\epsilon_i} \qquad i = 1, ..., M \tag{6}$$

where ϵ_i is the elasticity of demand in market i

$$\epsilon_i = \frac{dQ_i(P)}{dP} \cdot \frac{P}{Q_i(P)}$$

and where Q_i is the total demand in that market given a price P_i that, unlike the price schedules described in the previous sections does not vary with the quantity demanded

$$Q_i(P) = \int_{\theta_L}^{\bar{\theta}} q(P, \theta)\, g(\theta)d\theta$$

where as before θ_L is defined as the consumer type who on the optimal price schedule $P^+(\theta) = P_i$ would consume the minimal consumption Q_L.

In the case of log linear demand, the total demand in market i is given as

$$Q_i(P) = \int_{\theta_L}^{\bar{\theta}} a_i P^{b_i}\theta^{\gamma_i} g(\theta)d\theta$$

and the elasticity of demand ϵ_i is

4
Let $\Delta = \lambda/(1+\lambda)$. Then since $d\Delta/d\lambda > 0$,

$$\frac{dQ_j}{d\lambda} = \frac{dQ_j}{dP} \cdot \frac{dP_j[\theta]}{d\lambda} \leqslant 0.$$

$$\epsilon_i = \frac{dQ_i(P)}{dP} \cdot \frac{P}{Q_i(P)} = b_i.$$

Then use (6) to compute the price given the Lagrange multiplier λ. Producer surplus is increasing in λ, so that the optimal price is found where λ is increased to the point where producer surplus just equals the revenue requirement F.

Another algorithm which is analogous to the optimal price algorithm of the previous section, varies not the Lagrange multiplier but the consumer group θ_L who consume Q_L at the optimal price. Given the marginal consumer group θ we can solve for the implied Lagrange multiplier λ

$$\lambda_i = \alpha/(\beta - \alpha)$$

$$\begin{cases} \alpha = \left[Q_L/a_i\theta_L^{\gamma_i} \right]^{1/b_i} \\ \beta = \left[Q_L/a_i\theta_L^{\gamma_i} \right]^{1/b_i} \cdot \frac{1}{b_i} \end{cases}$$

Choose $\lambda = \max_i\{\lambda_i\}$ and increase θ_L until the revenue requirement is net.

With linear demands the situation is a little more difficult. In this case

$$Q_i(P) = [a_i + b_iP + \gamma\bar{\theta}]\Delta$$

where $\bar{\theta}$ is the truncated mean consumer type

$$\bar{\theta} = \int_{\theta_L}^{\bar{\theta}} \theta \frac{g(\theta)}{\Delta} \, d\theta$$

for $\Delta = G[\bar{\theta}] - G[\theta_L]$.

$$\frac{dQ}{dp} = a \cdot \frac{d\theta_L}{dp} \cdot \frac{d\Delta}{d\theta_L} + b \cdot \Delta + b.p. \frac{d\theta_L}{dp} \cdot \frac{d\Delta}{d\theta_L}$$

$$+ \gamma \cdot \frac{d\theta_L}{dp} \cdot \frac{d\bar{\theta}\Delta}{d\theta_L}$$

where

$$\frac{d\theta_L}{dp} = -\frac{b}{\gamma}, \frac{d\Delta}{d\theta_L} = -g(\theta_L)$$

and, in the case of a lognormal distribution of customer types θ

$$\frac{d\bar{\theta}\Delta}{d\theta_L} = -\mu \cdot A \cdot g(A)$$

where $A = \exp[\ln(\theta) - \sigma^2]$.

In this case, the optimal price is given as the solution of the nonlinear equation (8) for given θ_L, and the analysis proceeds exactly as before.

4. Fully distributed cost pricing (FDC)

In the relative output method of fully distributed cost pricing, prices are set so that the revenue R does not exceed the fully distributed cost:

$$R_i = AC_i + f_i F \qquad i=1, ..., M$$

where $R_i \, AC_i$ is the attributable cost and

$$f_i = \frac{Q_i}{\sum_{\ell=1}^{M} Q_\ell}.$$

For constant marginal cost this yields

$$P_i Q_i = c_i Q_i + f_i F$$

which implies a pricing rule

$$P_i^{FDC} = c_i + k$$

so that prices represent a constant markup on marginal cost where the markup

$$k = F / \sum_{i=1}^{M} Q_i$$

is constant across the M markets.

In application, test period quantities are used to determine the markup which applied to current prices will in general affect demands Q_i. A *demand compatible* FDC pricing rule is one for which

$$k = F / \sum_{i=1}^{M} Q_i(P_i^{FDC}).$$

Expressed another way, this is

$$k \sum_{i=1}^{M} Q_i(c_i + k) - F = 0$$

which may be solved for the markup, k.

D. Data used for simulations

1. Prices and Quantities by Service, 1978

From the TELPOL study we begin with an aggregation of all message services into Day MTS, Non-Day MTS, MT WATS and FBD WATS. Their prices and quantities in 1978 were as follows:

Table A-7-1

Service	Quantity	Price (Average Revenue)
Day MTS	11.81×10^9 minutes	$.363/min
Non-Day MTS	21.59×10^9 minutes	$.203/min
MT WATS	$.055 \times 10^6$ lines	$7.03 \times 10_3$/line
FBD WATS	$.185 \times 10^6$ lines	17.05×10^3/line

Source: Table 2.3,   Marfisi *et al.* 1981.

From *WATS — A Statistical Overview* for 1978 we get average usage per line (averaged over inward line and outward lines) of 31.62 hours per line per month for MT WATS and 125 hours per line per month for FBD WATS. Therefore, the average revenue per minute for MT and FBD WAB is calculated as follows:

MT WATS: $\dfrac{\text{Revenue}}{\text{Minutes}} = \dfrac{\$586}{31.62 \times 60} = \$.308/min$

FBD WATS: $\dfrac{\text{Revenue}}{\text{Minutes}} = \dfrac{1421}{125 \times 60} = \$.189/min.$

Collecting these results, we have prices on a per minute basis:

Table A-7-2

Service	Price ($/min)
Day MTS	.363
Non-Day MTS	.203
MT WATS	.308
FBD WATS	.189

2. Price and Quantity for Business Users

Marfisi *et al.* [1981, p. 16, footnote 1] state that 67 percent of Day MTS and 8 percent of Non-Day MTS traffic is generated by business users. Thus prices and quantities of business service are:

Table A-7-3

Service	Quantity (10^9 mins)	Price ($/min)
Day MTS	7.91	.363
Non-Day MTS	1.74	.203
MT WATS	4.21	.308
FBD WATS	4.924	.189

This yields an average price for 1978 of $.289/min.

In order to get average monthly minutes per business customer, we start with the 1977 figure of $39.31 from the AT&T report, *The Dilemma of Telecommunications Policy,* Exhibit 8, Table 4. The inflation rate of interstate revenue per message generally was 2.1 percent between 1977 and 1978.[5] We will assume that minutes per message did not change between 1977 and 1978, which is not unreasonable, given that there were no major tariff changes during that period. The implied business price per minute for 1977, then, is $.283. Dividing this into $39.31 yields monthly usage per business customer of 139 minutes. We assume that this figure holds good for 1978, too.

3. Day and Non-Day Prices, 1978

Based on conversations with AT&T personnel, we assume that about 20 percent of WATS usage took place in the Non-Day period in 1978. This leads to monthly usage figures of 111 Day minutes and 28 Non-Day minutes per customer. To construct Day and Non-Day prices we use the 80/20 split between Day/Non-Day WATS usage to construct the following table:

---

[5] See *General Long Lines and Selected Interstate Statistics, 1963-1982,* AT&T Long Lines, Business Research, May 28, 1982.

Table A-7-4

a. Day

Service	Quantity (10^9 minutes)	Price ($/min)
MTS	7.91	.363
MT WATS	3.37	.308
FBD WATS	3.94	.189
	15.22	

Average Price = .32

b. Non-Day

Service	Quantity (10^9 minutes)	Price ($/min)
MTS	1.724	.203
MT WATS	.840	.308
FBD WATS	.984	.189
	3.548	

Average Price = .22

4. Estimating the Distribution of Tastes

We base our estimation on Table A-7-4, which gives the distribution of monthly billing for business customers. First, we divide the entries in this table by the average business price of $.283 to obtain a distribution of monthly minutes of interstate usage. We assume that the customer has a linear demand curve:

$$Q_B = a - bP_B + \theta = \alpha + \theta, \alpha \equiv a - bP_B.$$

Following Mitchell [1978] we assume that $\ln\theta$ is normally distributed with mean μ and variance σ^2. Indeed, the lognormal distribution is commonly used within the Bell system to describe traffic patterns. From this assumption it follows that Q follows a three-parameter lognormal distribution with parameters (α, μ, σ^2). Maximum likelihood estimates of these parameters are as follows:

Table A-7-5

Parameter	Estimated Value	Standard Error
α	−1.02537	.1199702
μ	2.520551	.1686388
σ	2.322309	.5468682

It is straightforward to compute the truncated mean $\bar{\bar{\theta}}$:

$$\bar{\bar{\theta}} = \int_{\theta_0}^{\infty} \theta \cdot g(\theta) \cdot d\theta \left(\frac{1}{1-G(\theta_0)} \right) = 215.813$$

where

$$g(\theta) = \text{lognormal density}$$

$$\theta_0 = \text{marginal consumer at zero consumption}$$

$$1 - G(\theta_0) = .141, \text{ from Table A-7-4.}$$

Therefore

$$\int_{\theta_0}^{\infty} \theta \cdot g(\theta) d\theta = \bar{\bar{\theta}} \cdot \left[1 - G(\theta_0) \right] = 185.448.$$

5. Parameters of Isoelastic Demand Functions

For convenience, most of our simulations will assume that individuals' demand functions are isoelastic, not linear, and take the form:

$$Q_D = \lambda_D \cdot \theta \cdot P_D^{-\epsilon_D}$$

$$Q_N = \lambda_N \cdot \theta \cdot P_N^{-\epsilon_N}$$

where $\epsilon_D = .534$ and $\epsilon_N = .77$ in the base case. Using our estimates of prices and quantities:

$$\bar{Q}_D = 111 \quad P_D = \$.32$$

$$\bar{Q}_N = 28 \quad P_N = \$.22$$

we compute λ_D and λ_N to be

$\lambda_D = .325725$

$\lambda_N = .0470545.$

When we use these demand functions it will be with the same distribution of θ whose parameter estimates were derived under the assumption that demand curves are linear. Hence, it is necessary to check that the isoelastic demand system is at least roughly consistent with the distribution of Table A-7-4 and our price and quantity data. To do so we simulated the effects of prices $P_D = \$.32$ and $P_N = \$.22$ on the isoelastic demand system:

$$Q_D = .325725 \cdot \theta \cdot P_D^{-.534}$$

$$Q_N = .0470545 \cdot \theta \cdot P_N^{-.77}$$

$$\mu = 2.53$$

$$\sigma = 2.32$$

The results were quite similar to the observed data (and, obviously, the results of a linear system):

	Day	Non-Day	Total Business
Average Usage	105.77	26.57	132.34
$1 - G(\theta_0)$	.19	.39	.19

The average total usage result of 132.34 is fairly close to our estimate of 139 minutes and the percentage of customers priced out of the market, 19 percent, is reasonably close to the 14.1 percent in Table 7.4.

6. Parameters of Linear Demand Functions

We wish to calibrate demand functions of the form

$$Q_D = a_D - b_D P_D + \gamma_D \theta$$

$$Q_N = a_N - b_N P_N + \gamma_N \theta$$

where

$$Q_D + Q_N = Q_B = \alpha + \theta, \quad \alpha = a_D + a_N - b_D P_D - b_N P_N$$

and our estimate of α, from above, is -1.025327. This leads to average consumption of $185.448 - 1.025327 = 184.423$, considerably above the 139 minute figure given above. (This strongly suggests that the distribution of monthly billing given in Table A-7-4 is a very coarse summary of a much larger data base which produced the monthly usage figure of $39.31.) Using the 80/20 split between Day and Non-Day that we advocate above,

$$Q_D = .8 \times (\alpha + \theta) = -1.0026 + .8\theta$$

$$Q_N = .2 \times (\alpha + \theta) = -.0227 + .2\theta$$

and average usage in the two periods is estimated at 147.54 minutes for Day and 36.88 minutes for Non-Day. In conventional fashion we can calculate the various parameters:

$$b_D = \frac{.534 \times 147.54}{.32} = 246.21$$

$$a_D = -1.0026 + 78.78 = 77.78$$

$$b_N = \frac{.77 \times 36.88}{.22} = 128.8$$

$$a_N = -.0227 + 28.336 = 28.3133.$$

References

American Telephone and Telegraph Company. 1978. *The Dilemma of Telecommunications Policy: Report of the Industry Task Force.*

Anderson, J. E. 1976. "The Social Cost of Input Distortions: A Comment and a Generalization," *American Economic Review,* 66(1): 235-38.

Atkinson, A. B. and Stiglitz, J. E. 1980. *Lectures on Public Economics* McGraw-Hill, New York.

Baumol, W. J. and Bradford, D. F. 1970. "Optimal Departures from Marginal Cost Pricing," *American Economic Review* 60: 265-83.

Baumol, W. J., Panzar, J. C. and Willig, R. D. 1982. *Contestable Markets and the Theory of Industry Structure,* Harcourt, Brace, Jovanovich, New York.

Boiteux, M. 1949. "La Tarification des demandes en point," *Revue Genérale de l'Electricité,* 58: 321-40.

Boiteux, M. 1951. "La tarification au coût marginal et les demandes aléatories," *Cahiers du séminaire d'econometric* 1: 56-69.

Boiteux, M. 1960. "Peak Load Pricing," *Journal of Business* 33: 157-79.

Brander, J. and Spencer, B. 1983. "Second Best Pricing of Publicly Produced Inputs: The Case of Downstream Imperfect Competition," *Journal of Public Economics* 20: 113-119.

Braeutigam, R. R. 1979. "Optimal Pricing with Intermodal Competition," *American Economic Review* 69(1), 38-49.

Braeutigam, R. R. 1980. "An Analysis of Fully Distributed Cost Pricing in Regulated Industries," *Bell Journal of Economics,* 11(1), 182-196.

Brown, G. M. and Johnson, M. B. 1969. "Public Utility Pricing and Output Under Risk," *American Economic Review* 59: 119-28.

Brown, D. J. and Heal, G. M. 1980. "Two Part Tariffs, Marginal Cost Pricing and Increasing Returns in a General Equilibrium Framework" *Journal of Public Economics* 13: 25-49.

Brown, D. J. and Heal, G. M. 1983. "The Optimality of Regulated Pricing: A General Equilibrium Analysis," in Aliprantis, Burkinshaw and Rothman (ed.) Lecture Notes in Economics and Mathematical Systems, Vol. 244, *Advances in Equilibrium Theory,* Springer-Verlag, Berlin, Heidelberg, 1985.

Carlton, D. W. 1977. "Pricing with Stochastic Demand," *American Economic Review* 67: 1006-10.

Coase, R. H. 1946. "The Marginal Cost Controversy" *Economica* 13: 169-189.

Crew, M. A. and Kleindorfer, P. H. 1976. "Peak Load Pricing with a Diverge Technology," *Bell Journal of Economics* 7(1), 207-231.

Daly, G. and Mayor, T. 1980. "Estimating the Value of a Missing Market: The Economics of Directory Assistance," *Journal of Law and Economics* 23: 147-166.

Ebrill, L. P. and Slutsky, S. M., "Pricing Rules for Intermediate and Final Good Regulated Industries," mimeo, 1984(a).

Ebrill, L. P. and Slutsky, S. M., "The Ramsey Rule, Production Efficiency and Intermediate Goods," mimeo, 1984(b).

Faulhaber, G. R. 1975. "Cross Subsidization: Pricing in Public Enterprises," *American Economic Review* 65: 966-77.

Faulhaber, G. R. and Panzar, J. L. 1977. "Optimal Two Part Tariffs with Self-Selection," Bell Laboratories Economic Discussion Paper No. 74.

Federal Communications Commission 1977. 66 FCC 2nd (1977) (*Notice*)

Federal Communications Communication 1979. Docket 20003, 70 FCC (2nd) (*Notice*).

Federal Communications Commission 78 FCC, Docket 20003, 2nd (*Order*).

Federal Communications Commission 1981. 83 FCC, Docket 20003, (2nd) (*Order*).

Feldstein, M. 1972. "Equity and Efficiency in Public Sector Pricing: The Optimal Two Part Tariff," *Quarterly Journal of Economics* 86: 175-87.

Gabor, A. 1955. "A Note of Block Tariffs," *Review of Economic Studies* 23: 32-41.

Goldman, M. B., Leland, H. E. and Sibley, D. S. 1984. "Optimal Nonuniform Pricing," *Review of Economic Studies*, April, 1984.

Griffin, J. 1982. "The Welfare Implication of Externalities and Price Elasticities for Telecommunication Pricing," *Review of Economics and Statistics*, LXIV (1): 59-66.

Hirshleiffer, J. 1958. "Peak Loads and Efficient Pricing: A Comment," *Quarterly Journal of Economics* 72: 451-462.

Houthakker, H. S. 1951. "Electricity Tariffs in Theory and Practice," *Economic Journal* 61: 1-25.

Interstate Commerce Commission Docket 347 (Sub 1), *Decision and Order*.

Kahn, A. E. 1970. *The Economics of Regulation*, John Wiley, New York.

Katz, M. L. 1983. "Nonuniform Pricing, Output and Welfare under Monopoly," *Review of Economic Studies* (50): 37-56.

Leland, H. E. and Meyer, R. A. 1976. "Monopoly Pricing Structures with Imperfect Information," *Bell Journal of Economics*.

Katz, M. L. 1984. "Price Discrimination and Monopolistic Competition," *Econometrica*.

Littlechild, S. C., "Two Part Tariffs and Consumption Externalities," *Bell Journal of Economics* 6: 661-70.

MacKensie, G. 1979. "Consumer's Surplus Without Apology: A Comment" *American Economic Review* 69(3), 465-68.

Marfisi, E. P., Murphy, M. M., Rohlfs, J. H. and Silverstein, D. 1981. *Evaluating Changes in Telecommunication Policy: Whose Ox Will Be Gared?* American Telephone and Telegraph Company, December, 1981.

Mirrlees, J. M. 1971. "An Exploration in the Theory of Optimal Taxation," *Review of Economic Studies* 38: 175-208.

Mirrlees, J. M. 1976. "Optimal Tax Theory: A Synthesis," *Journal of Public Economics*.

Mirman, L. J. and Sibley, D. S. 1980. "Optimal Nonlinear Prices for Multiproduct Monopolies," *Bell Journal of Economics*, (11): 659-70.

Mirman, L. J. and Tauman, Y. 1982. "Demand Compatible, Equitable, Cost Sharing Prices," *Mathematics of Operations Research*. 40-66.

Mirman, L. J., Samet D. and Tauman, Y. 1983. "Axiomatic Approach to the Allocation of a Fixed Cost Through Prices," *Bell Journal of Economics* 14(1): 139-151.

Mitchell, B. M. 1978 "Optimal Pricing of Local Telephone Service," *American Economic Review* 68: 517-37.

Mitchell, B. M., Manning, W. G. and Acton, J. P. 1978. *Peak Lood Pricing: European Lesson for U. S. Energy Policy* Ballinger, Cambridge, Mass.

Mussa, R. and Rosen, S. 1978. "Monopoly and Product Quality," *Journal of Economic Theory* 18: 301-17.

Ng, Y-K and Weissner, M. 1974. "Optimal Pricing with a Budget Constraint the Case of the Two-Part Tariff" *Review of Economic Studies* XLI.

Oi, W. Y. 1971. "A Disneyland Dilemma: Two Part Tariffs for a Mickey Mouse Monopoly," *Quarterly Journal of Economics* 85: 77-90.

Ordover, J. A. and Panzar, J. C. 1980. "On the Nonexistence of Pareto Superior Outlay Schedules," *Bell Journal of Economics* 11: 351-54.

Ordover, J. O. and Panzar, J. C. 1982. "On the Nonlinear Pricing of Inputs," *International Economic Review* 23 (3): 659-676.

Oren, S. S., Smith, S. A. and Wilson, R. B. 1982. "Nonlinear Tariffs in Markets with Interdependent Demand," Report No. 37, Program in Information Policy, Stanford University.

Oren, S. S., Smith, S. A. and Wilson, R. B. 1982 "Competitive Nonlinear Tariffs," *Journal of Economic Theory*.

Owen, B. M. and Braeutigam, R. R. 1978. *The Regulation Game: Strategic Use of the Administrative Process* Ballinger, Cambridge, Mass.

Panzar, J. C. and Sibley, D. S. 1978. "Public Utility Under Risk: the Case of Self-Rationing," *American Economic Review* 68: 888-95.

Panzar, J. C. and Postlewaite, A. W. 1983. "Sustainable Outlay Schedules," mimeo.

Panzar, J. C. 1979. "The Pareto Domination of Usage Insensitive Pricing," in Dordick (ed.), *Proceedings of the Sixth Annual Telecommunications Policy Research Conference,* D. C. Heath/Lexington.

Pavarini, C. 1979. "The Effect of Flat-to-Measured Rate Conversions on Local Telephone Usage" in Wenders (ed.) *Pricing in Regulated Industries: Theory and Application*, Mountain States Telephone Company, Denver, Colo., pp. 52-75.

Perry, M. K. 1982. "Oligopoly and Consistent Conjectural Variations," *Bell Journal of Economics* 13(1): 197-205.

Pontriagin, L. S., Boltyanskii, V. G., Gamkrelidze, R. V. and Mischenko, E. F., *Mathematical Theory of Optimal Processes*, Interscience — Wiley, New York, 1962.

Ramsey, F. P. 1927. "A Contribution to the Theory of Taxation" *Economic Journal* 37: 47-61.

Roberts, K. W. S. 1979. "Welfare Considerations of Nonlinear Pricing," *Economic Journal* 89: 66-83.

Rogerson, W. P. 1985. "The First-Order Approach to the Principle-Agent Problem," forthcoming in *Econometrica*.

Rohlfs, J. H. 1974. "A Theory of Interdependent Demands for a Communication Service," *Bell Journal of Economics and Management Service* 5(1): 16-37.

Rohlfs, J. H. 1976. "Evaluation of Changes in a Sub-optimal Economy" *Review of Economic Studies* XLIII (2): 359-62.

Rohlfs, J. H. 1979. "Economically-Efficient Bell System Pricing," Bell Laboratories Economics Discussion Paper No. 138.

Sadka, E. 1976. "On Income Distribution, Incentive Effects and Optimal Income Taxation," *Review of Economic Studies* 43: 261-267.

Samet, D. and Tauman, Y. 1982. "A Characterization of Price Mechanisms and the Determination of Marginal Cost Prices Under a Set of Axions," *Econometrica* (1982): 895-910.

Schmallensee, R. 1976. "Another Look at the Social Valuation of Input Price Changes," *American Economic Review* 66(1): 239-43.

Schmitz, A., Just, R. E. and Hueth, D. L. 1982. *Applied Welfare Economics and Public Policy*, Prentice Hall, Englewood Cliffs, N.J.

Seade, J. K. 1976. "On Income Distribution, Incentive Effects and Optimal Income Taxation," *Review of Economic Studies"* 43: 261-67.

Seade, J. K. 1977. "On the Shape of Optimal Tax Schedules," *Journal of Public Economics*, 7(2): 203-236.

Seade, J. K. 1980. "On the Effects of Entry," *Econometrica* 48: 479-89.

Sharkey, W. W. 1982. "Suggestions for a Game Theoretic Approach to Public Utility Pricing and Cost Allocation," *Bell Journal of Economics* 13: 57-68.

Sharkey, W. W. 1982. *The Theory of Natural Monopoly*, Cambridge University Press.

Sherman, R. and Visscher, M. 1978. "Second Best Pricing with Stochastic Demand," *American Economic Review*, 68: 41-53.

Spence, A. M. 1980. "Multiproduct Quantity-Dependent Prices and Profitability Constraints," *Review of Economic Studies*, 47: 821-41.

Spence, A. M. 1976. "Nonlinear Prices and Welfare," *Journal of Public Economics* 8: 1-18.

Steiner, P. O. 1971. "Peak Loads and Efficient Pricing," *Quarterly Journal of Economics*, 71: 585-610.

Stiglitz, J. E. 1977. "Monopoly, Nonlinear Pricing and Imperfect Information. The Insurance Market," *Review of Economic Studies* 44: 407-30.

US Congress, Communications Act of 1934. 47 USC.

US Congress, 1978, Public Utility Regulatory Policy Act, Public Law 95-117, 95th Congress.

Visscher, M. 1973. "Welfare-Maximizing Price and Output with Stochastic Demand," *American Economic Review* 63: 224-9.

Williamson, O. E. 1966. "Peak-Load Pricing and Optimal Capacity under Indivisibility Constraints," *American Economic Review* 56: 810-27.

Williamson, O. E. 1974. "Peak Lood Pricing: Some Further Remarks" *Bell Journal of Economics* 5: 223-8.

Willig, R. D. 1976. "Consumer's Surplus Without Apology," *American Economic Review* 66: 589-97.

Willig, R. D. 1978. "Pareto-Superior Nonlinear Outlay Schedule," *Bell Journal of Economics* 9: 56-69.

Willig, R. D. and Klein, R. W. "Network Externalities and Optimal Telecommunications Policy: A Preliminary Sketch," *Proceedings of the Fifth Annual Telecommunications Policy Research Conference.* (Available from National Telecommunications Information Service, Washington, D.C.)

Willig, R. D. 1983, "Sector-Differentiated Capital Taxation with Imperfect Competition and Interindustry Flows," *Journal of Public Economics* 21: 295-316.

Zajac, E. E. 1974. "Note on an Extension of the Ramsey Inverse Elasticity of Demand Pricing or Taxation Formula," *Journal of Public Economics* 3: 181-184.

Zajac, E. E. 1979. *Fairness or Efficiency: an Introduction to Public Utility Pricing*, Ballinger, Cambridge, Mass.

Index